THE COMMONWEALTH AND INTERNATIONAL LIBRARY

*Joint Chairmen of the Honorary Editorial Advisory Board*

SIR ROBERT ROBINSON, O.M., F.R.S., LONDON

DEAN ATHELSTAN SPILHAUS, MINNESOTA

*Publisher:* ROBERT MAXWELL, M.C., M.P.

PERGAMON OXFORD FRENCH SERIES

*General Editors:* C. V. JAMES, I. C. THIMANN

# A SHORT HISTORY OF FRANCE

# A SHORT
# HISTORY OF FRANCE

*by*

D. J. PETERS, M.A.

*Chief History Master, Nottingham High School*

## PERGAMON PRESS

OXFORD · LONDON · EDINBURGH · NEW YORK

TORONTO · SYDNEY · PARIS · BRAUNSCHWEIG

Pergamon Press Ltd., Headington Hill Hall, Oxford
4 & 5 Fitzroy Square, London W.1

Pergamon Press (Scotland) Ltd., 2 & 3 Teviot Place, Edinburgh 1

Pergamon Press Inc., 44–01 21st Street, Long Island City, New York 11101

Pergamon of Canada, Ltd., 6 Adelaide Street East, Toronto, Ontario

Pergamon Press (Aust.) Pty. Ltd., 20–22 Margaret Street,
Sydney, New South Wales

Pergamon Press S.A.R.L., 24 rue des Écoles, Paris 5e

Vieweg & Sohn GmbH, Burgplatz 1, Braunschweig

Copyright © 1966 Pergamon Press Ltd.
First edition 1966
Library of Congress Catalog Card No. 66–26872

*Printed in Great Britain by A. Wheaton & Co. Ltd., Exeter*

# Contents

# *Illustrations*

# Preface

EARLY in 1963 it was suggested to me that a short History of France would be of considerable value to students of the French language and of French literature who were not necessarily specialist historians. I have attempted, therefore, to write a brief account of the more significant events in the history of France, and to mention, in each chapter, some of the more important men of letters so that they may be seen, as it were, against the background of the chief occurrences of their times.

I hope that the book may be of some little value not only to those students of modern languages to whom French is so important, but to those who visit France and would like to know something of the background of the country. This book is not intended to be a work of scholarship, and it owes much to writers like Professor Brogan and Professor Cobban. The lists of suggested further reading will help those who wish to discover more about specific periods from the writings of men whose knowledge of French history is greater by far than mine could ever hope to be. I owe much to them, and a list of them all in this preface would be tedious and inappropriate.

However, to them and to Dr. I. C. Thimann, who first suggested the work, I wish to offer my grateful thanks. I should also like to express my gratitude to some of my friends on the Council of the Historical Association, and to Miss Barbara Powlett, whose suggestions have helped me to make the book more accurate and, in places, more readable. I wish to say how much I owe to the encouragement of my parents and my wife, and last, but by no means least, I wish to say how much of my enthusiasm for France and for French history was awakened by the late Alan Richards, with whom I spent several holidays in France, and who knew

vii

Paris especially well. His love for everything French earned him many friends across the Channel, and did much to inspire his friends in England with a love of the country of Voltaire, Victor Hugo and Maupassant.

D. J. P.

*Burton Joyce,*
*Nottinghamshire,*
*Easter Day, 1966*

# CHAPTER 1

## *The Origins of France*

ALTHOUGH comparatively little is known concerning the history
and people of France before the Roman period, and although the
making of France in the period before Charlemagne is a subject
for the specialist in early medieval history, there are some few
events in the ancient past which can provide us with a starting
point for this brief survey. A knowledge of French history is
essential to any understanding of the unique and vastly important
contribution of France to the literature and culture, both of
western Europe in general and to England, her closest neighbour,
in particular.

Without going into the fields of archaeology and prehistory,
which can scarcely be dealt with on a national basis, a French
history may be said to begin when, in about 600 B.C., Greek
colonists founded what was to become the city of Marseilles. It
was one of many Greek city-states founded on the coasts of the
Mediterranean; but its existence points to the possibilities of the
creation in southern France of a very primitive trading or barter-
ing society. Only two centuries later we find men described as
Gauls living in the Alpine regions, attacking the new Italian state
of Rome, and even taking the capital. However, that future world
power recovered sufficiently to make nothing of this setback, and,
by 123 B.C., a Roman province in Gallic territory had been
founded.

In the sixth decade B.C., Caesar conquered the whole of Gaul,
and this area remained part of the Roman Empire until the
barbarian invasions of the fifth century A.D. In fact, the period
of Roman occupation, from 50 B.C. to A.D. 481, had important

1

consequences for the future state of France. The population, a mixture of Mediterranean, Alpine and Germanic peoples, was combined with Latin-speaking peoples from all over the Roman Empire. Previously, there had probably been a Celtic language, spoken in various forms by the tribes of Aquitaine, and by others inhabiting the lands as far north as those of the Belgae. Now, the Latin language, or simplified forms of it, gave France some unity with the other countries which came under the rule of Rome. The provinces of Gaul, Gallia Narbonensis, Aquitania, Gallia Belgica and Gallia Celtica began to be ruled in the Roman way, with magistrates, a provincial government with military officials and a slave-owning economy.

The Roman domination had the consequence of bringing to Gaul not only a system of government, but also techniques of constructing houses, public buildings and roads; writing; the calendar; and even the cultivation of vines and olives, to say nothing of new religious beliefs. The ruling classes, in a way, absorbed such forms of Greek civilization which the Latin culture provided. Roman architecture—aqueducts, temples and theatres for example—was introduced; and excellent examples survive in Provence, as at Nîmes, Arles and at the Pont du Gard. Roman law was introduced, and parts of it have survived to the present day, especially in the code of French civil law.

The growth of a civilized French state was only possible because Gaul was protected from the barbarians to the north and east by the Roman legions on the Rhine; but in the third century A.D., as the unity of Rome began to crumble, such barbarians as the Franks and Alemanni began to invade the settled territories, looting and destroying. Order was restored, but only temporarily, and on a military basis, with commanders (*duces* and *comites*) ruling over seventeen Gallic provinces. The Roman economy was becoming stagnant. Towns and trade dwindled, and society became a primitive yet hereditary affair, just at the time when a new religion, Christianity, was spreading through the Roman Empire. When Christianity became the official state religion under the Emperor Constantine and his successors, bishops were

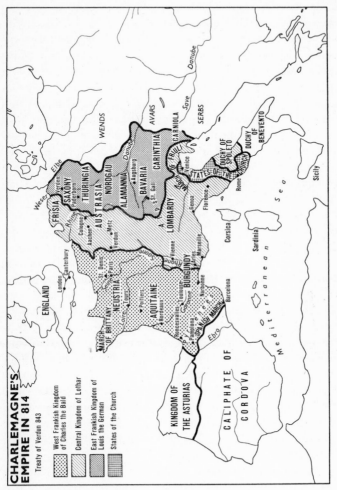

MAP 1

**CHARLEMAGNE'S EMPIRE IN 814**

Treaty of Verdun 843

West Frankish Kingdom of Charles the Bald

Central Kingdom of Lothar

East Frankish Kingdom of Louis the German

States of the Church

appointed as rulers and pastors over districts based upon the old territorial districts and provinces of the Roman administration. Christianity was imposed on the people of Gaul as the last obedience to the civilization of Rome.

This obedience was to end soon; for in the fourth century some Germans began to come into the Gallic provinces. Some came, as individuals, to join the Roman armies. Some came in groups for the same purpose. Others came as bands of settlers, envious of the Roman civilization which they were so soon to destroy, not deliberately but by sheer weight of numbers. These entered with or without the agreement of the Roman government, bringing with them their own laws and customs and way of life. Gradually the Roman army became barbarian and mercenary, and thus unreliable when faced by the emergency of wholesale barbarian invasion.

These barbarians, who began the destruction of the Empire, were of several races. In Gaul there were the Burgundians, the Visigoths and the Franks; of these, the Visigoths were, at first, the most important. The invaders came from eastern Europe and from Asia, and the Visigoths soon founded an independent state based on Toulouse; while the Franks took the lands east of the Somme. All the barbarians settled alongside the native Gallo-Romans, introducing their languages, laws, customs, farming methods and warlike habits. Little evidence remains of the Visigothic occupation of France, but in north-eastern France more Germanic place-names and customs survive. There are various reasons for this, but the chief may be religious. The Visigoths and Burgundians were converted to the Arian version of Christianity, unacceptable to the orthodox; whereas the Franks remained pagan longer and were then converted to the official Roman version of the faith.

By the beginning of the sixth century the Frankish chieftain Clovis had been baptized into the orthodox faith, and had managed to unite the Frankish territories and to defeat a second wave of invaders, the Alemanni. In his reign (482–511) he also pushed back the Visigoths and conquered the Burgundians, and

set up a sort of primitive capital in the old Gallic town of Lutetia
Parisii (Paris), which was on the island in the Seine now called the
Île-de-la-Cité. Clovis was the ancestor of the Merovingian kings,
a dynasty which ruled in France until 751. This was a very
primitive period, when the amount and strength of government
depended upon the character and ability of the ruler. It was also
a time when each king, in accordance with the custom of the
Frankish people, divided his inheritance equally among his sons.
On several occasions, the realm had three or four rulers; generally
they ruled with the aid of officials called counts, as in late Roman
times.

Merovingian customs and laws were very different from
Roman ones; in fact, they were often similar to those to be found
in Saxon England. So far as language was concerned, the
Teutonic survived in what are now the Flemish-speaking areas;
but the other Franks adopted the corrupted Latin language, and
so began the development of what is now French. But the other
gifts of the Roman civilization, or what was left of them, decayed
rapidly. Towns and trade became of negligible importance. So
did education. However, a new warrior aristocracy emerged, and
began to grow in importance just as the Merovingian kings
declined. By the seventh century, Gaul had split into Aquitania,
Austrasia (in the east), Neustria (in the west) and Burgundy.

Gradually the real power of the state was taken from the kings,
and these became little more than puppets, obeying a chief
official called the Mayor of the Palace (Latin, *Major domus*). The
most important Frankish state to emerge from this primitive
time was Austrasia—possibly because there was a greater
Frankish population in that area. From these Austrasians came
the dynasty of the Carolingians, so named after Charlemagne
(Carolus Magnus, Charles the Great). These Carolingians were
to succeed in setting up a united Frankish state once more. This
was the achievement of Charles Martel and his son Pepin. They
also made war on the Moslem invaders from Spain, thus preventing the spread of Islam beyond the Pyrenees. The battle of
Tours was the turning point. It was decisive militarily and vital

politically, as it prevented the Moslem conquest of Latin Europe.

Pepin crowned himself as king, having negotiated an agreement to this effect with the Pope as a result of an alliance to attack the Lombards who had set up a barbarian (and Arian) state in northern Italy. The Papal alliance proved to be a most important factor in the establishment of a united France; and was continued by Pepin's son, Charlemagne, who spent most of his life at war, fighting Saxons, Lombards, Moslems and Slavs.

The state he ruled, centred on Aix-la-Chapelle, consisted of France, western Germany and northern Italy. One can hardly call Aix his capital, however, as he was continually on the move, either on campaigns or in the mere routine of governing his kingdom. He ruled his state in person, so far as possible; for there was little permanent machinery of government. This, despite the fact that Charlemagne was crowned Roman Emperor in Rome in 800. The title meant little to the Franks, but was a useful status symbol in western Europe. It became important in later medieval Germany, but even then "the Empire" was never "Holy, nor Roman, nor an Empire". He had four officials, the seneschal, the constable, the butler and the chamberlain, to assist him in government. There was also a chancellor and a few other advisors. This was the period of the birth of feudalism and of the manorial system, which meant a kind of primitive self-sufficiency in administration. Charlemagne introduced *missi dominici*—royal envoys—to travel around the Empire to see that his authority was observed.

Charlemagne's reign had some considerable cultural importance. There occurred the Carolingian Renaissance, which was basically a revival in the study and use of Latin. Copies of the works of ancient writers were made for libraries, in the new "Carolingian" minuscule script; schools were set up where classical philosophers, such as Boethius, were studied. But it was a minor Renaissance with few real achievements to its credit except the mere survival of learning. Later generations were to make much of Charlemagne's paladins—but the legend was to be over-glamourized. Charlemagne's death would have seen the immediate partition of his empire; but as only one son, Louis, survived him, the collapse of Carolingian unity did not come until 843, when Louis's kingdom was divided between his three surviving sons. It is interesting that, in the previous year, after the battle of Fontenoy, the oath of Strasbourg was made in two languages—Romance and Germanic. The former version is the first surviving example of what was to become the French language.

In the partition treaty of Verdun—the "birthday of modern nationalities", as it has been called—the Empire was split into eastern Francia, under Louis the German; Lotharingia, under Lothar, stretching from Rome to Frisia; and western Francia, under Charles the Bald. The latter state was to become the modern France. In fact, Lothar was the true Emperor, ruler of the richest and most important of the three states. But Lotharingia, without geographical, economic or national unity, was to dwindle away. The same fate did not meet the other two kingdoms, but their unity was only maintained with considerable difficulty by a series of weak kings in a period of growing feudalism.

Feudal government, the organization of disorder, was strengthened in the ninth century when Viking invaders began to sail up the rivers of France into the interior. Gradually, their plundering raids gave way to settlement, until, in 911, the Vikings living in northern France made the treaty of St. Clair-sur-Epte with Charles the Simple, gaining official recognition as owners of the territory which was henceforth known as Normandy. The Vikings also accepted Christianity, and rapidly took and developed whatever they thought was good in the civilization and culture of the Franks. Normandy, together with other duchies such as Aquitaine and Gascony, made up the French state which, under weaker and weaker Carolingians, awaited the accession of Hugh Capet in 987.

In the period so briefly reviewed in this introductory chapter, the main interest in literary matters must be the development of the French language by barbarians who adopted the corrupt Latin of the late Roman Empire. Such writers who were at work, like Gregory of Tours, who wrote a History of the Franks and died in 594; and Eginhard, Charlemagne's secretary and author of the *Vita Caroli*, wrote in Latin. However, as may be seen in the oath of Strasbourg, a French language was developing, and, with the accession of the first Capetian in 987, we may say that the true history of France had begun.

## RECOMMENDED READING

*Medieval France*. Ed. ARTHUR TILLEY. Cambridge, 1922. (Chapters 7 and 8.)
*A History of Early Medieval Europe, 476–911*. MARGARET DEANESLY. Methuen, 1956. (Chapters 4, 6, 15–19, 22, 23, 26–9.)
*The Barbarian West*. J. M. WALLACE-HADRILL. Hutchinson, 1947.

## CHAPTER 2

# The Capetians to St. Louis

HUGH CAPET, 987–96
(descendant of Robert the Strong, Duke of Francia)
|
ROBERT II (the Pious), 996–1031
|
HENRY I, 1031–60
|
PHILIP I, 1060–1108
|
LOUIS VI (le Gros), 1108–37
|
LOUIS VII (le Jeune), 1137–80
|
PHILIP II (Augustus), 1180–1223
|
LOUIS VIII, 1223–6
|
ST. LOUIS IX, 1226–70

FRANCE, from the tenth to the twelfth centuries, was a collection of small feudal states, with a monarchy which was, at first, weak, ruling only over a small domain, claiming suzerainty over other rulers in a half-hearted way, but gradually growing in strength and prestige. From the time of the Treaty of Verdun in 843, there had been Carolingian kings, mostly feeble, ruling over a France which degenerated into anarchy. These monarchs had failed to preserve or to establish any effective lordship. Real power was variously in the hands of the Viking invaders or of such lords who were wise enough to build castles for self-defence. Eventually, the Carolingians came to depend on one of these lords, the "Duke of France", ruling a small area which happened

9

to include Paris and Orleans. When, in 987, Louis V, the last of the Carolingians, died, Hugh Capet, Duke of France, was elected King and was recognized as such by the Emperor Otto III.

The Carolingians had been reverenced as anointed kings, if not obeyed as such. Hugh Capet, now king, was merely a magnate elected to office by his equals. His only asset was his domain, the compact area of the Île de France. He could rule effectively only over his own barons; his rule over the feudal lords of France, some of whom were stronger than he, was only nominal. He could not, for example, command the obedience of the Vikings in Normandy; and Philip I, at a later date, saw their duke, William, become King of England in his own right, and more powerful than his suzerain.

The Normans, in fact, rapidly assimilated the language and institutions of France, and went on to use and develop them in the colonization of England, Sicily and southern Italy. Normandy was also the only feudal state, until 1066, where the ruler commanded by right of conquest, unencumbered by hereditary officials, custom and church privilege. The Norman conquest of England in 1066 had important results for France, owing to the shifting of Norman power across the Channel, besides the fact that William became an anointed king as well as a supposed Capetian vassal. Even more significant was when an historical accident made the King of England, Henry II, ruler also of the so-called Angevin Empire—this when Louis VII divorced his wife, Eleanor of Aquitaine, in 1152, and she promptly married Henry of Anjou, the Plantagenet who came to the English throne in 1154.

The other great duchies of France in the early Capetian period were Anjou and Touraine, the dukes of which ruled Poitou, Saintonge, La Marche, Limousin, Périgord, Angoumois and Auvergne; Toulouse (which ruled Rouerge, Albigeois, Quercy and several other districts); and Flanders, Champagne and Burgundy. All were of some importance; but Toulouse was the centre of a district of remarkable cultural interest. Whereas northern France was the Languedoil—so called from the *langue*

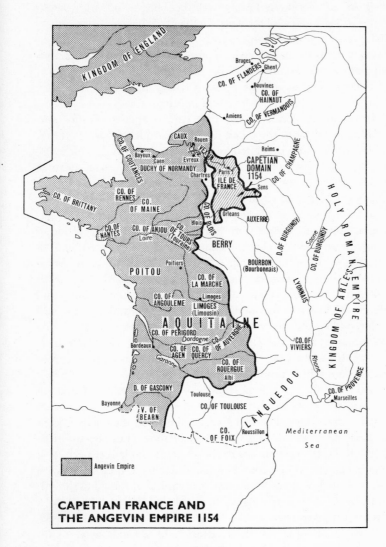

**CAPETIAN FRANCE AND
THE ANGEVIN EMPIRE 1154**

MAP 2

*d'oïl,* or *oui*—southern France was the Languedoc (from *langue d'oc,* a different form of the word for "yes"). This area of Provence, then, had its own language, with other differences accentuated by the courtly civilization which produced songs in the vernacular tongue by troubadours, men like Bertrand de Born and Bernard de Ventadour, as well as Richard I, the famous *Cœur de Lion,* who sang passionately of love and fighting.

It would be unfair to say that early Capetian France was divided merely into these half-dozen great duchies and counties. There were many other feudal territories, each only nominally subordinate to an overlord. Their activities, however, were of little concern to the Capetian kings, who devoted themselves to making a reality of royal power in the Île de France alone, at least until the end of the reign of Louis VI. Therefore the dukes, counts and their vassals were left undisturbed. The condition of France was one of chronic anarchy, of private wars and of quarrels over land ownership and allegiance. What made it possible for the Capetian monarchy to grow in strength was, primarily, the accident of survival. Supported by the bishops and clergy, who saw in the monarchy a slight guarantee of law and order, and by the townsmen, who were always, in a sense, outside the feudal system, the Capetians had the great advantage that, until 1316, when Louis X died without a son, there were eleven generations which produced a male heir.

This was of supreme importance, for the persistence of Capetian survival meant the growth of an hereditary, rather than of an elective monarchy. The first six Capetians had their sons elected as kings-designate during their own lifetimes, but, by the time of Philip II, the custom was dropped. It was no longer necessary. Hugh Capet, Robert the Pious and Henry I quarrelled with various neighbouring lords, and made allies of the Church and, until 1049, of the Normans; but little prospect of building a strong monarchy was visible. Philip I was a weak monarch too, but he did begin to add territories, in a small way, to his domain. Gâtinais, Corbie, part of the Vexin were taken, and he bought the town of Bourges from its lord, who wanted money to go on crusade. But, in these years of crusading enthusiasm in Europe, the king of France was an insignificant ruler with an insignificant role. Yet from Philip I's time onwards, the Capetians did have a practical interest in lands beyond the River Loire; and Philip himself even quarrelled with the Pope over church appointments which might concern the internal power and security of the crown.

Louis VI was a more able ruler, but he, too, devoted his chief activity to strengthening his power in his own lands. He came to an agreement with the French bishops and thereafter posed as a protector of the Church. He then carried on a long war with the Normans and Flemings, and with brigands in his domain like Thomas de Marle. The war with the Normans was a dangerous venture. His opponent, Henry I, was so strong that Louis was completely unsuccessful. On one occasion he was nearly captured in battle. Only Henry's death in 1135 saved the Capetian king from utter defeat. However, one successful aspect of his policy was his determination to be rid of Etienne de Garlande and his family, who monopolized many of the chief offices of state and church. He achieved this in 1127; and thereafter he was well served by Suger, the abbot of Saint-Denis, who eventually became his biographer and the chief minister of Louis VII. Suger was an intelligent and hard-working servant of the monarchy, who set up a staff to administer Louis's realm in a business-like way.

Louis VII was a courageous man who inherited a realm which Suger and Louis le Gros had done their best to strengthen. The new king was 16, and newly married to the dominating Eleanor of Aquitaine. They were not ideally suited; she said that she thought she had married a king, but had found that she had married a monk. The marriage, made in 1137, lasted until 1152, when it was annulled. Even then, Eleanor was only about 30 years old. Louis was no "monk", but he always remained loyal to the Church, even when he was put under an interdict for his views on investiture. Eventually, however, this ban was lifted on the intercession of St. Bernard, who became Louis's friend and adviser. It was St. Bernard, from Dijon, who encouraged Louis to take the cross in 1146. Louis needed no spur for this, however. He had an adventurous spirit and was very much concerned at the news of the fall of Edessa, besides wanting to do penance for the burning of a church full of people at Vitri, in the course of a campaign against Champagne.

In 1147 the forces of Louis and of the German emperor, Conrad III, met at Ratisbon. But this second crusade was an utter failure. Louis reached the Holy Sepulchre but without an army. Most of his troops had died of disease and starvation at Attalia, on the coast of Asia Minor. This dismal lack of success was made worse by the estrangement of Louis from Eleanor, who had accompanied her husband; and, on their return in 1149, steps were taken which ended in an annulment for consanguinity in 1152. Eleanor promptly married Henry Plantagenet, of Anjou, and heir to the English throne. By 1154 her new husband was King of England and ruler of Aquitaine, Normandy and Anjou. It seemed that Louis had helped to create his most dangerous enemy. However, Louis's luck held. Henry had five sons by Eleanor, who had provided only daughters for Louis; but Henry's sons quarrelled bitterly with their father and amongst themselves, whereas Louis's only son, born in 1165 to Adela of Champagne, became Philip Augustus, the creator of a strong French monarchy.

Louis's other good fortune was that in Suger he had a pious, simple, moderate and statesmanlike minister, until the abbot's death in 1151. Suger was the model of a medieval administrator, and Louis recognized his value. Even after Suger's death, Louis was wise enough to know the value of the support of the Church, and, during the Papal schism which began in 1159, he supported the orthodox Pope, Alexander III. In fact, from 1163, Alexander, the supporter of Thomas Becket against Henry II, lived in the Capetian town of Sens. Louis also supported Becket, whose eventual murder at Canterbury in 1170 caused Henry almost as much difficulty as did the unexpected birth of Prince Philip to Adela and Louis in 1165. Louis's divorce of Eleanor was, despite the criticism of Suger and of later historians, a wise move.

By his third marriage, to Adela, Louis saved the line of Capetian kings; he made the right choice in his moves with the Church, and in 1179 he had his son Philip crowned. By then, Louis was old and paralysed. When he died in 1180 he left a domain which was still small, and a military reputation which was not great. But he had strenthened his kingdom in many ways, by an alliance with the Church, by judicial reforms, and by wise administration. He had been on crusade and on pilgrimage; he had befriended the monastic orders; and he had established new towns, encouraged trade, and given charters freely. Philip II inherited a kingdom where, as his father had said, "We have only bread, wine and gaiety." Philip was a feudal suzerain, still, rather than a king. England was better governed, with a more complex machinery of government. But Henry II's empire was too great to be ruled easily, and was to be the victim of the family quarrels, for among his sons plainly there could be no agreement on inheritance. Eleanor, too, encouraged her sons to rebel against their father, and Louis VII had helped them when they had appealed to him as their feudal suzerain.

If Philip's administration was somewhat primitive, by comparison with Henry II's it was sound and honest. And with Philip's accession, at the age of 15, there began a new growth in French royal power, accompanied by the steady annexation of lands which was to give to Philip his title of "Augustus", because he "augmented" the kingdom. It was the time, as we shall see, when the romantic lengends of Charlemagne were to be a favourite theme of poets. If, as is said, the French kings were *petits bourgeois* before they were *grands seigneurs*, then Philip was born a *petit bourgeois*. But by determination, ability and good fortune, he began the destruction of the Angevin Empire. It may even be that the events of the third Crusade, when Philip accompanied Richard Cœur de Lion to the Holy Land, in 1191, gave the French king the ambition and desire to destroy his rival's continental power.

Philip certainly extended his domain whenever he could. Early in his reign he declared the lands of Isabella of Vermandois forfeit, when she died, despite the fact that her husband was Philip of Flanders, Philip II's own uncle and godfather. By the Treaty of Aumâle, the young King obtained the Vermandois and a promise of the reversion of Artois. He went on to demand from Henry II of England the Vexin, a district on the Norman frontier which had been the dowry for Philip's half-sister, Margaret, when she had married Henry II's eldest son, who had since died. However, he did agree that Henry might retain the Vexin as a dowry for another half-sister, Alice, who was betrothed to the young Richard. Even when plans were being made for the third crusade, by Philip and Henry II, the former was helping Richard in a rebellion against the latter. Henry died in July 1189, in Chinon; and Richard did then inherit the whole empire, thus becoming Philip's greatest enemy, with no possibility of an alliance ever being made between the two again.

However, a crusading vow was a serious matter, and so the two kings set off on crusade in the same year. On the journey Richard repudiated his betrothal to Alice, and married Berengaria of Navarre. This insult to Philip, coupled with his eclipse in all military affairs by the English king, probably caused him to return to Paris in 1191, leaving Richard behind as the sole leader of the venture. On his own journey home, Richard was imprisoned, first by Leopold of Austria, and then by the Emperor Henry VI, on the grounds that he was an ally of the Welf leader, Henry the Lion; and during Richard's captivity, Philip allied himself with John, and received a part of Normandy and Touraine for his support of this treacherous younger brother. Richard, however, was eventually ransomed, and returned to defend his lands in France. It was while campaigning there that he died at Châlus in the Limousin, and John became the ruler of the Angevin inheritance.

Had Richard lived, and had he built more castles like his famous Château-Gaillard at Les Andelys, Philip might have succumbed. But the accession of John gave Philip his great opportunity. First, he seized Evreux, and then listened to the complaints of various Poitevin barons against John. Chief complainant was Hugh of Lusignan, Count of La Marche, whose betrothed, the 12-year-old Isabella of Angoulême, had been taken to wife by John. When the English king refused to appear to answer the charges against him, Philip sentenced him to be deprived of all his French fiefs. When, in the campaign which followed, John took prisoner his own nephew and rival, Arthur of Brittany, and had him murdered, Philip found that he had feudal law and general opinion on his side, against the unprincipled and unscrupulous (if unlucky) King of England.

In 1204 Philip took the Château-Gaillard, and soon he had taken all Normandy. John's ablest advisor, his mother Eleanor, died in the same year. Within a matter of weeks, Philip had taken Maine, Anjou and part of Poitou. Gascony, of course, was still in John's hands; but the northern territories of France were firmly in Philip's keeping. There had been little loyalty to John north of the River Loire, and the ancient rights of the Dukes of Normandy passed to the Capetian Kings. Philip had become the greatest ruler in France, and this was confirmed in 1214, at Bouvines, near Tournai, where he defeated Otto IV of Germany and his ally, John. The consequences were far reaching. The English barons went on to extort Magna Carta from their disreputable and defeated king; the links between Normandy and England were cut, and the English nobles ceased to hold lands across the Channel. The rulers of England began to be English, rather than Norman-French.

Philip had some failures, of course, to mar his career. For example, on the death of his first wife, Isabella, he married Ingeborg of Denmark; but, when he tried to get this marriage annulled, in order to marry Agnes of Meran, Pope Celestine III and his successor, Innocent III, would not co-operate. Innocent, indeed, placed France under an interdict in 1200—a ban which was not lifted until Agnes was dead and Philip agreed to reinstate the imprisoned Ingeborg in 1213. But even tragic events seemed to produce useful results for Philip. It was in his reign that the Albigensian heresy grew in the Languedoc. Against this peculiar Catharist belief, Innocent III eventually preached a "crusade", which was aimed particularly against the county of Toulouse. Although Philip took no part in this war of extermination of heretics, which was led by Simon de Montfort, when the heresy and the whole civilization of the south of France were being wiped out, he did allow his son Louis to take part, and invested Simon with Béziers and Carcassonne. Within ten years Simon's son, Amaury, feeling himself incapable of ruling the area, resigned his claims to the new King, Louis VIII, whose brief reign was spent in making those rights a reality. By the Peace of Meaux, in 1229, Capetian rule reached the Mediterranean for the first time.

Philip Augustus had not lived to see it, but the credit for the extension of the domain was entirely his. To his other achievements must be added the policy whereby sub-tenants were made to take an oath of fealty direct to the sovereign, his encouragement of towns and industry, and even the creation of Paris as a true capital for his newly enlarged kingdom. For example, the cathedral of Notre Dame was completed around 1230, and he gave considerable privileges to the University of Paris, as well as building walls for the city. His new *baillis*, royal administrators, began to do valuable work in the whole enlarged state.

Louis IX (1226–70) was perhaps not only the ideal of a medieval king, but also an ideal ruler to follow Philip II and Louis VIII. He was a pious and religious man, concerned with the spread of royal justice and sound administration. Far from being as unscrupulous as Philip, he was a moral ruler, who, by trying to be a good king within the framework of feudalism, did much to destroy that system. He made laws on such various subjects as currency, private warfare and prostitution. He valued peace so highly that he made treaties with James I of Aragon (the Peace of Corbeil, 1258) and Henry III of England (Peace of Paris, 1259), giving up his claims to Toussillon and Catalonia, and to lands in Quercy and Périgord. His respect for justice meant that many, and even the English barons, called upon him as an arbiter. But his greatest achievements were in administration— in his use of the Parlement of Paris as a court of appeal, in his use of church patronage, the development of the Chambre des Comptes (Exchequer), and the control of his officials, like English sheriffs and judges, and known as *baillis, sénéchaux, prévôts, viguiers* and *enquêteurs*. The royal income from fines and fees grew enormously. Towns came under royal control. All the rights of a feudal monarch were exploited.

Many serfs were freed from personal bondage. A true monument to this religious king is the exquisite Sainte-Chapelle in Paris, built in what was then a new (and to us, Gothic) style as a reliquary for Christ's crown of thorns, which Louis purchased from Baldwin II of Constantinople. The building, much restored, is now crammed behind the Palais de Justice on the Île-de-la-Cité. One criticism of St. Louis which may be made is in the matter of his crusades. The seventh crusade, which he led, sailed from Aigues-Mortes (still a surprisingly impressive example of a medieval town) in 1248, to Damietta, in Egypt. But the crusade was badly led, and Louis was captured near Cairo, and had to be ransomed. His next crusade was even more disastrous. He allowed his brother, Charles of Anjou, the ruler of Sicily, to persuade him to attack the infidel in Tunis; and there he died of fever in 1270, having accomplished nothing as a crusader. This, in a sense, may not have been his fault. By 1270 the old crusading zeal was dead, but Louis was a conservative who still thought it the chief duty of a Christian king to seek out the infidel and to destroy him. On his death, the people of France mourned a great king, and this in itself may help to show how France had become, by this time, a nation united, or nearly so, under the Capetian kings.

Literary interest in this early medieval period must be centred on the way in which the *langue d'oïl* of the north became standard French, largely because of the growing political dominance of the Capetians in their capital of Paris, and the destruction of the Provençal *langue d'oc* by land-hungry freebooters from the north in the Albigensian "crusade". French literature, as distinct from a local Latin literature, began in the twelfth century, with verse romances, the *chansons de geste*, and the Mystery plays. There were some Lives of the Saints, in various forms of French, but largely based upon Latin originals. The *chansons*, recited by *jongleurs*, were mostly long narrative chronicles set to music—usually epics. Of these, the most famous is the Song of Roland, the famous Paladin, friend of Charlemagne, which was probably written in the reign of Louis VII (1137–80), although such a song may have existed a century earlier. However, the early crusading spirit certainly expressed itself in many *chansons*, despite their themes of Charlemagne, and war in Spain by Guillaume d'Orange; and, later, of Alexander the Great in the *romans d'antiquité*, like the mid-twelfth-century *Roman de Troie*.

In 1155 Geoffrey of Monmouth's stories of King Arthur appeared in French verse as the *Roman de Brut*; Chrétien de Troyes, in the later years of the twelfth century, produced poems like *Perceval* and *Lancelot*, about the legends of Arthur. At the same time, the legend of *Tristan et Iseut* became part of the Arthurian collection, and a basic theme of literature—originally a prose work and then in the poetry of Béroul. The German *Tristan* appeared in the early thirteenth century, and has become, eventually, inseparable from Wagner's music. Also in the thirteenth century are to be found the earliest *romans d'aventure*, like *Le Roman de la Violette*, and the *chantefable*, *Aucassin et Nicolette*. With them is the popular *Roman de la Rose*, by de Lorris and de Meung, written from 1230 onwards on the theme of courtly love, with some allegory and satire, some criticism of the social problems of the day, and some display of learning. Its antithesis was the *Roman de Renart*, written by several authors in about 1200, concerning Renart the fox, Chantecler and other animals, satirizing the Church, as did many other *fabliaux*. They are among the earliest examples of popular literature. The most interesting historical work is *The Life of St. Louis*, by de Joinville (1225–1317). This incidentally describes the crusade of 1248 in autobiographical detail.

For lyric poetry for the aristocratic classes, one turns to troubadours like Guillaume de Poitou, Duke of Aquitaine, and Richard, Cœur de Lion. But the culture of Provence did not survive the Albigensian holocaust, even though *trouvères* from the north took over the southern verse forms and the various kinds of courtly love poem. The whole period to the thirteenth century saw the foundations laid, not only of French literature, but also of the French state which was now to grow to be the greatest in Europe.

## RECOMMENDED READING

*A History of Europe from 911 to 1198.* Z. N. BROOKE. Methuen, 1947. (Chapters 4, 10, 14, 21.)

*A History of Europe from 1198 to 1378.* C. W. PREVITÉ-ORTON. Methuen, 1937. (Chapter 5.)

*A History of Medieval Europe.* R. H. C. DAVIS. Longmans, 1957.

*Chronicles of the Crusades.* JOINVILLE and VILLEHARDOUIN (translated by M. R. B. SHAW). Penguin Classics, 1963.

*Europe in the Central Middle Ages,* 962–1154. C. BROOKE. Longmans, 1964.

*Medieval Europe.* MARTIN SCOTT. Longmans, 1964.

*The Capetian Kings of France, 987–1328.* ROBERT FAWTIER (translated by L. BUTLER and R. J. ADAM). Macmillan, 1960.

*The Devil's Brood.* ALFRED DUGGAN. Faber, 1957.

*The Loss of Normandy.* Sir MAURICE POWICKE. Manchester University Press, 2nd edition, 1961.

## CHAPTER 3

# The Last Capetians and the Early Valois Kings

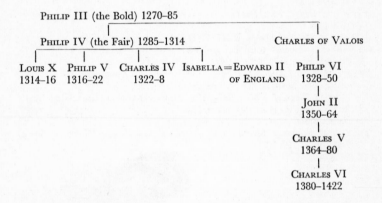

PHILIP III (the Bold) 1270–85

PHILIP IV (the Fair) 1285–1314      CHARLES OF VALOIS

LOUIS X   PHILIP V   CHARLES IV   ISABELLA = EDWARD II   PHILIP VI
1314–16   1316–22   1322–8       OF ENGLAND   1328–50

JOHN II
1350–64

CHARLES V
1364–80

CHARLES VI
1380–1422

ON THE death of St. Louis, the weak monarch Philip the Bold
came to the throne. He had few of his father's virtues, and was
ruled at various times by the favourite, de la Broce, his mother,
Margaret, and his wife, Mary. He took Foix in 1272, so that all
the Languedoc came under Capetian control, but also, rather
foolishly, allowed the Comtât Venaissin around Avignon to go
to the Papacy, which afterwards made its home there. He also
permitted England to take Abbeville, Ponthieu and the Agenais;
but took stronger action when he attacked Aragon on behalf of
Pope Martin IV and Charles of Anjou. This war, however,
ended disastrously in plague and in Philip's own death at
Perpignan.

Philip IV, "the Fair", an enigmatic figure, then became King
at the age of 25. Historians still debate whether he was a monster,

a great king, or a mere puppet. It was said of him, "ce n'est ni un homme ni un bête—c'est un statue". Certainly his ministers, Pierre Flôte, Enguerrand de Marigni and Nogaret, were powerful figures, unscrupulous lawyers, who built up a strong and absolute despotism, taxed France harshly, levied feudal aids, exacted "benevolences" and *maltôtes* (sales taxes), expelled the Jews and took their property, and even went so far as to destroy the powerful Order of the Knights Templar for its wealth. The destruction of the latter was a dramatically tortuous and cruel affair, which contemporaries found to be completely shocking. The crown, in order to gain the Templars' wealth, resorted to sinister methods, which have a modern echo. Some Templars were kept in prison for over two years before facing a "rigged" trial; others were tortured to provide "evidence" of their crimes, and many, including the Master, Jacques de Molai, were burned alive. It was commonly held that de Molai's dying curse was the cause of the rapid end of the direct Capetian line of kings. There were other interesting developments in the reign, such as consultation with the representatives of the nation, and the specialization of the legal and financial departments of state, such as the *étroit conseil*, the *chambre aux deniers* and the *chambre des comptes*. The *Parlement* of Paris developed courts of pleas, requests and inquests.

The summoning of vassals and of representatives of the towns came first in 1302—it was the first meeting of the States General— the nearest to a Parliament that was seen in France before the 1789 Revolution. The 1302 assembly and other assemblies in 1308 and 1314 were called to give support to the crown in such matters as the quarrel with Boniface VIII, and the struggles with Flanders and the Knights Templar. Of course, royal councils were not new, but it was an innovation to summon indirect vassals and representatives of the communes. However, too much must not be made of it, for, although the States General met occasionally until 1614, thereafter there was no meeting until 1789. By contrast, England developed a parliamentary system of government, while France, perhaps because the roots of her governmental system were put down under Philip II and Louis

IX, became a despotism with no strong traditions of representative assembly.

What is interesting in the late thirteenth century is how the new strong French monarchy rose to a supremacy in Europe, which ended, inevitably perhaps, in a struggle with the supra-national power of Rome. The strengthening of governmental institutions, and the coming to power of Philip IV's unscrupulous ministers, produced a situation where there was no respect for the authority of the Church and the Pope. The new men, like Nogaret, were concerned with developing the financial re-sources of the state at any cost; with territorial expansion at the expense of Gascony, Flanders and Burgundy; and with insisting that the clergy should not be immune from royal taxation. It was this which inevitably caused the struggle between Philip and Boniface VIII.

Philip began by trying to gain control of the surviving great fiefs, especially Flanders and Gascony. The former was wealthy because of its cloth industries, the latter was a menace to the crown because it was ruled by Edward I. Flanders, naturally, tended to sympathize with England because of the important connexion through the wool trade. Guy de Dampierre, Count of Flanders, allied himself with England in 1294, but Philip in-tervened and imprisoned the count until 1296. On his release, Guy again made an alliance with England, but as Edward could not bring help, the Flemings were defeated at Furnes. With their count again in French hands, the people of Flanders rose in rebellion, and many Frenchmen were massacred in the Matins of Bruges on 17–18 May 1302. Philip, determined to subdue the Flemings, sent an army under Robert of Artois. The army was routed by the Flemish infantry at Courtrai in July. Pikemen had defeated cavalry, and the supremacy of infantrymen was to be demonstrated again, at a later date, at Poitiers and Agincourt. Meantime, the *clauwaerts*, the nationalists, led by Peter de Coningk, a weaver, had defeated the *leliaerts* and their French allies. Although Philip gained a revenge at Mons en Pevèle in 1304, he was sensible enough to make the Treaty of Athis in

1305, which restored liberty to Flanders, and to Count Robert, son of Guy. But real peace was not made, for Philip found it difficult to accept that it would cost far more to subdue and hold Flanders than France could gain from taking the country. Naturally, the desire to rule Flanders was based on Philip's ambition to be sole ruler in France.

It was this ambition which caused Philip's struggle with the Papacy. After a series of popes who had been insignificant, or Frenchmen, or both, Boniface VIII had been elected Pope in 1294. This great lawyer and diplomat, an ambitious pontiff, was the head of what had become a political institution as well as the Church of Christ. He regarded himself as the heir of the former popes who had proclaimed the doctrine of the plenitude of power. This is seen in his famous bull, *Unam Sanctam*, which uncompromisingly stated that the spiritual power was greater than any secular authority. The popes had won their struggle with the German Hohenstaufen family on this very issue; and now the rise of the sovereign power of France provoked it again. During the crusades, the popes had allowed the use of force in the service of Christianity, clerical property to be taxed, and the weapon of excommunication to be blunted through over-use; now they refused clerical taxation for temporal purposes. Boniface had involved the Papacy in great expense in fighting Frederick of Aragon in Sicily, and in subsidizing Charles of Anjou and Charles of Valois. The French clergy had provided 173,000 florins in tithes, and Boniface claimed that, having paid this, they could not afford to pay royal taxes as well. Philip refused to accept this argument from a pope who was crusading against his rivals, the Colonna family, in Italy; and all whose enemies, as Dante said, were Christians.

The struggle between Philip and Boniface began in 1296 with the bull, *Clericis laicos*, but did not become bitter until Philip tried the Bishop of Pamiers for treason. This was the occasion of the bull, *Ausculta fili*, in 1301, soon to be followed by *Unam Sanctam* and Philip's excommunication. For Nogaret, this was too much. Leading 1600 men, he went to the Papal palace at

B

Anagni and abused the Pope, ill-treating him and accusing him of heresy and tyranny. Only an uprising of the local people saved the Pope from Philip's emissaries, who had imprisoned him; but after a few weeks he died in Rome, broken in spirit after his ill-treatment. Philip's reputation was low indeed, but the insult to the Pope went unpunished. The next Pope, Benedict XI, accepted the Capetian dominance, and his successor, Clement V, eventually absolved Nogaret, allowed the Templars to be dissolved, and even moved the Papacy to Avignon in 1309. Clement had been a French cardinal, and preferred to remain near France rather than to expose himself to the trials of life in the turbulent city of Rome. The Papacy remained in Avignon until 1377.

It was the urgent need for money which caused the attack on the Templars. The crusades were over, and the Templars had become bankers, using their privileges and immunities to become powerful and wealthy. Their existence was an insult to a despotic king; he was jealous of their riches. In 1307 the trial of the Templars began. Royal agents seized their property, and, by judgement of the French bishops and inquisitors, many were sentenced to public burning. The Order was dissolved by the Pope in 1312. But the French monarchy, which had been enabled to prosper and grow with Papal support, now freed itself from the domination of the Church. The Capetians were now independent despots, untrammelled by any religious or spiritual vassalage. At the death of Philip IV, France was unchallenged in power. The centralization of royal power seemed complete. France was populous and prosperous, although Brittany, Burgundy, Flanders and Guienne were not yet annexed to the crown. Feudalism had been replaced by a despotism with great legal and financial powers—even to the extent of debasing the currency, which Philip IV had begun in 1295—and taxes were being collected regularly from laymen and churchmen. Even so, the revenues rarely appeared to suffice for the growing costs of government.

Philip was succeeded by his three sons, Louis X, Philip V and Charles IV; and, with them, the direct Capetian line came to an end, for none produced legitimate sons, but only daughters.

They were therefore followed by their cousin, Philip VI (1328–50), the first Valois king. The last three Capetians were of little importance. Louis X granted charters to Leagues of nobles who were demanding a return to the old customs and protesting against the harsh taxation; but he soon died, and Philip V seized the crown on the death of Louis's posthumously born son, in 1316, despite claims which were made for Louis's daughter, Jeanne. The failure of her claim helped to strengthen the belief in what became known as the Salic law, that a woman could not rule in France, nor even transmit the right to rule. This so-called law was to cause trouble in the future. Charles IV, the last "direct" Capetian, ruled for six years; but the sole interest in his reign was the summoning of States General which were never truly national and always divided by internal rivalry. When Charles died, Philip of Valois was appointed Regent until the birth of Charles's posthumous child; when this proved to be a girl, Philip took the throne and was crowned at Reims in 1328. Philip was a chivalrous knight, but lacked any sense of statesmanship or administrative responsibility. He made a poor king.

The end of the direct Capetian line also gave Edward III of England a claim to France through his mother Isabella, youngest daughter of Philip IV. To this dynastic crisis was added the problem of Flanders. Jacques van Artevelde of Ghent led a rebellion, offering Flemish neutrality to the English in return for the free export of wool to the Netherlands; and, not long after, in 1340 Edward III's claim to France was accepted by the Flemings, to give them legal grounds for rebellion against Philip VI. Philip had, in fact, defeated the Flemings at Mont Cassel, in a battle in support of his vassal Louis, Count of Flanders; but the English could not allow, for economic reasons, the French to dominate the Netherlands completely, and were thus inclined to support van Artevelde.

War was inevitable. Edward made an alliance with the Emperor, Louis IV. Philip made a treaty with John of Bohemia and another with the Scots. The Papacy was already settled in Avignon and unlikely to oppose the French in any way. The

Hundred Years' War therefore began in 1337, with the siege of Guienne by France; but no serious battle took place until June 1340, when an Anglo–Flemish fleet destroyed French ships at anchor off Sluys, at the mouth of the Zwyn. What had made war inevitable was not only the Flemish troubles, exacerbated by the economic necessities of the cloth trade, but also Philip's quarrel with his brother-in-law, Robert of Artois, who had settled in England and become Edward's ally, and also, French intervention on behalf of David Bruce in Scotland, and Philip's natural ambition to conquer and rule Gascony.

When the war began, neither side was in a great hurry. But nor did they realize that fighting would go on, intermittently, until 1451. The English plans in Flanders soon came to an end, for, in 1345, van Artevelde was murdered by a mob, and the war might have ended had it not been for a quarrel over Brittany. Its duke, John, died in 1341 and a dispute over the succession began between Philip's nephew, Charles of Blois, and John's half-brother, John de Montfort, whom Edward supported. War therefore began in earnest, but the period to 1360 was one of long and indeterminate campaigns. Generally, it was one of French defeats, as at Crécy, near Abbeville, in 1346; at Calais, which surrendered in 1347 and remained in English hands until 1558; and at Poitiers, in 1356, where the Black Prince, plundering Poitou, met, defeated and captured King John (1350–4). The Prince, the "flower of chivalry", waited on his captive as a servant; yet the same man was responsible for the ghoulish sack of Limoges. Medieval chivalry did not normally extend to the lower classes.

Possibly more important than these defeats and the significance of the superiority of disciplined longbowmen over forces of too heavily armoured cavalry supported by Genoese arbalestiers, were the activities of the "free companies" of mercenaries, looting many districts of France. Much more important than any of these was the coming of the Black Death, the bubonic plague, which caused the death of one-third of the population of western Europe in 1347, 1348 and 1349. This was to have enormous results, economically and politically, but the plague was only one of the problems which caused serious troubles in France. Defeats by the English, maladministration and the plague meant that Philip VI's few achievements paled into insignificance. He added to his domain Viennois, of which John became Dauphin (the title remaining that of the heir to the throne for centuries), and Montpellier. But in Paris trouble culminated when Etienne Marcel, Provost of the Paris Merchants, became virtual dictator, attempting to make the States General a legislative assembly which would press for constitutional reform. In the countryside there was the revolt of the peasants, the Jacquerie, which spread from Beauvais to Champagne and the Île de France. Nothing like it was to be known again until the Revolution of 1789. For example, the Dauphin's advisers were killed in his presence, and he was forced to wear the tricolour of Paris.

However, in July 1358, Marcel was murdered; the nobles suppressed the peasants and the Dauphin, Charles, acting as Regent for King John, a captive in England, returned to rule in Paris. He refused to accept the terms of release which John was negotiating; but, in 1360, after another English campaign in a countryside desolated by war, Charles agreed to the peace terms of the Treaty of Brétigny. By these, England received Aquitaine, Poitou, Ponthieu and Calais; but the treaty was a mere truce, even though Edward had surrendered his claim to the throne of France. It was almost unbelievable that Philip IV's France should have sunk so low. There had even been the development of a system of *apanages*, by which members of the Valois family were allowed to rule districts like Evreux, Clermont, Bourbon and many others. The consequences were to be disastrous. None was more so than when John gave Burgundy, which escheated to him in 1361, to his son Philip, thus creating a Valois line of dukes there. The situation was made worse when Charles V arranged a marriage for Philip with Margaret, the heiress of Flanders, which meant the growth of a very powerful Flemish–Burgundian state on the eastern frontiers of France. This state was often to rival the power and authority of France itself.

Charles V (1364–80), on the death of his father in England, faced almost insoluble difficulties. France was in ruins. But Charles had real ability, especially in financial and administrative matters. His *élus*, assessors, collected a *fouage*, hearth tax, and the *gabelle*, a tax on salt. Thus he had a regular income, even if the system of collecting it was arbitrary, and too many districts and individuals gained unfair exemptions. Order was maintained, and a military recovery began under du Guesclin, an able soldier who organized a professional army. This was used to defeat Charles the Bad, of Navarre, the leader of an anti-Valois party since 1354, and du Guesclin also began to solve the problem of the free companies, which were still ravaging France, by leading them into Spain to put Don Henry on the throne of Castile instead of Peter the Cruel, who had been deposed in a popular revolt.

This campaign in Spain caused the Black Prince to cross the Pyrenees in 1367 to support Peter, who proved to be an inadequate and dishonest ally. Also, the Black Prince fell ill there, and eventually died of the disease. Peter lost his throne to Henry again, shortly after the English force had returned to Gascony, and was killed by the forces of du Guesclin and Henry of Trastamara. The campaign was certainly no triumph for the English, and Charles V's plans, to create an efficient mercenary army, to refortify Paris, to revive French sea power and to extend the authority of the crown, resulted in the gradual strengthening of a French state which could forget the Treaty of Brétigny and begin the war with England again.

This happened in 1368, and France was now more successful. The Black Prince was seriously ill, French national feeling was growing, and although the English had an able commander in Knollys to replace the great Chandos, they were defeated at Pontvallain in 1370. The new French tactics were, normally, to refuse battle and to remain safely in their strongholds; but despite the Black Prince's massacre of the people of Limoges in 1370, the French forces were now strong enough to oust the English from Poitou and to take control of Brittany. By 1375 the tables were turned; only Calais and Bayonne remained in

English hands. A truce was made. But before long Edward III was dead, Richard II was King in England, and, in 1380, Charles V and du Guesclin died too. The fortunes of France had been restored, and, if only Bayonne and Bordeaux had been taken, the English defeat would have been final. As it was, the English power was to revive in the reign of Charles VI, who came to the French throne as a boy of 12 and then, in 1392, went insane.

The first problem of the new reign was that of Charles VI's "wicked uncles", Louis of Anjou, John of Berry and Philip of Burgundy, besides the powerful Duke of Bourbon. These "princes of the lilies" misused their power so much that, in 1382, the *Maillotins* of Paris, so called from the iron mallets they seized from government stores, rose in rebellion, while the men of Ghent, led by Philip van Artevelde, also rose against their count. Philip of Burgundy sent an army which destroyed the Flemish rebels at Roosebeke and then returned to suppress the *Maillotins* in Paris. However, in 1388, Charles dismissed his uncles, as he was now of age, and restored the government to his father's old servants, the *Marmousets*. These were so called because they were "little monkeys", men of low birth. But the renewal of royal authority did not last. In 1392 Charles, while leading an army against Brittany, went mad, and never completely recovered. For the rest of his life he was the puppet of various advisers. First, Burgundy took control, much to the fury of Louis of Orleans, Charles's younger brother. This eventually caused the struggle between the Burgundian party and the Orleanists, otherwise called the Armagnacs. Louis attempted to gain control of the King's person, even to the extent of becoming the lover of Charles VI's queen, Isabella of Bavaria. It was Philip of Burgundy's son, John the Fearless, who was responsible for the murder of Louis of Orleans in 1407. This was the real cause of the civil war; and as Louis's sons were too young to lead their party in war, it was led on their behalf by Bernard of Armagnac. Gradually this struggle amalgamated all the various local and party conflicts in France. Generally, the Armagnacs were strongest in the south and west, while Burgundian strength was seated in the north and east.

Paris was held in the Burgundian interest by the mob, led by a butcher, Caboche, but eventually the Armagnacs took the city and made a temporary peace in 1415. John of Burgundy had made an alliance with the English, however, and Henry V invaded France to claim the throne. This was the occasion of the battle of Agincourt—a defeat for the Armagnacs rather than for France as a whole. Even in the face of this English triumph, France remained divided. John of Burgundy and Queen Isabella set up a court at Amiens, in opposition to the official government of Charles VI; while the Dauphin, Charles, after a Parisian rebellion in favour of the Burgundians, escaped to set up a court in Poitiers. Only a renewed English invasion caused the rival parties to think of co-operation, but here again the bitterness of the quarrel was shown when, at a meeting on the bridge of Montereau in 1419, John was murdered by the Dauphin's supporters. The feeling of contemporaries was exacerbated by the popular belief that the sinister Isabella was oversexed and also practised black magic.

John's murder was fatal to any hopes of reconciliation. Henry V had already taken Normandy. John's successor, Philip the Good, vowed that the Dauphin should not inherit the crown, and a treaty was made between Henry V and the government of the insane Charles VI (now in the hands of the Burgundians again). This treaty of Troyes decided that the French throne should be inherited by the descendants of Henry V and his new wife, Katharine, Charles's daughter. From the French point of view, all that had been gained since the time of Philip Augustus had been lost. Through unnecessary civil war and the insanity of Charles VI, France had reached the depths of degradation. The struggle to regain national pride was only to begin in the reign of the next king, who was, at that moment, only the shamed *soi-disant* Dauphin. Many held that this odd young man could not be his father's son. In her lighter moments, Isabella even alleged it herself.

The period of triumph and disaster which has been reviewed was not one of great literary developments, save for the writing of the *rondeau* and the *ballade* by such lyric poets as de Machaut and Froissart (1377–1405). The latter, of course, is more famous for his Chronicles, a history of the events of the Hundred Years' War. It was still the age of the *roman*—prose romances of the adventures of knights errant. It was also the age of the Mystery play—a form of primitive drama produced, often, against the west wall of a church, as at Nantes, Rouen and Paris, from about 1400 onwards. There was also the Miracle play—much shorter, and not on a Biblical theme. But it was not until the fifteenth century that literature was to have its triumphant development, in the century which was to give birth to the Renaissance.

### RECOMMENDED READING

*A History of Europe from 1198 to 1378.* C. W. PREVITÉ ORTON. Methuen, 1937 (Chapters 11, 13, 14 and 20.)

*A History of Europe from 1378 to 1494.* W. T. WAUGH. Methuen, 1949. (Chapters 1 and 2.)

*Later Medieval Europe.* D. WALEY. Longmans, 1964.

*The Capetian Kings of France.* R. FAWTIER (translated by L. BUTLER and R. J. ADAM). Macmillan, 1960.

## CHAPTER 4

# *Joan of Arc and the Restoration of France at the End of the Middle Ages*

HENRY V OF ENGLAND = KATHARINE, sister of CHARLES VII

| | |
|---|---|
| HENRY VI | 1422–61 |
| 1422–61, | LOUIS XI |
| murdered | 1461–83 |
| 1471 | |

THE Treaty of Troyes (1420) was the high-water mark of English power in the Hundred Years' War. The treaty was made with a party, however, and, to make it worth having, the Armagnacs had to be either conciliated or defeated. The former proved to be impossible, and so the war went on. An English defeat at Bougé was followed by an English victory at Meaux; but in the late summer of 1422 the situation was put in the melting pot again by the deaths of Henry V and Charles VI. Henry's baby son, the new Henry VI, had been heir of England and, by treaty, of France; but the latter could only mean anything if the Anglo–Burgundian alliance survived. The Duke of Bedford, Henry V's brother, became Regent, and married Burgundy's sister, Anne, to strengthen the family links in the alliance. Bedford ruled in Paris, while Charles, "the Dauphin", was reigning in Bourges. Yet, despite all the advantages held by the Anglo–Burgundians, and Charles's apparent incapacity, all the permanent advantages were on the side of the Armagnacs. After all, from a nationalist viewpoint, the Burgundians were traitors and the English were foreign enemies.

34

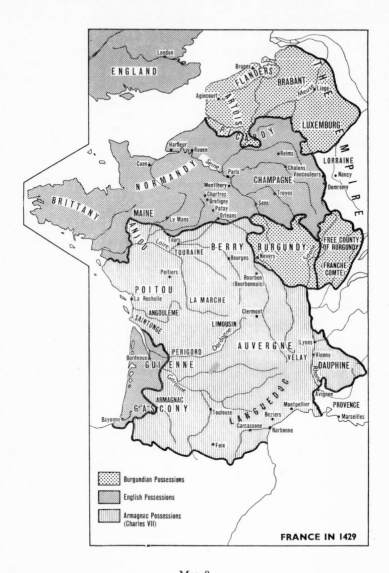

**FRANCE IN 1429**

Legend:
- Burgundian Possessions
- English Possessions
- Armagnac Possessions (Charles VII)

MAP 3

Yet, for the moment, Bedford, an able soldier and born organizer, kept order and tried to win support by governing through French officials and institutions. Charles, still uncrowned, ruling less than half his kingdom, and helped only by the adventurers who had murdered John of Burgundy at Montereau, was depressed and weak. No one could foresee a successful future for him, especially when de la Tremouille began to be so powerful in the court at Bourges, and to conduct yet another civil war, this time against de Richemont, his rival, the Constable of France. The English won a victory at Verneuil in 1424, and took Maine; but the war was conducted only half-heartedly still, possibly because of difficulties for the English at home. Anjou could not be taken by the Anglo–Burgundians until Orléans fell, and this town was being besieged in 1428 and 1429, the Armagnacs losing a counter-attack in 1429, on a supply train, in what was called the Battle of the Herrings. It was at this moment that Joan of Arc arrived at Chinon from Lorraine, and proclaimed her mission to save Orléans and to see Charles crowned at Reims.

She had come at an auspicious moment, for, despite their successes, the English forces in France were smaller than they had been; and Burgundy was furious over Humphrey of Gloucester's so-called marriage with the Countess Josephine of Hainault, who had left her husband, the Duke of Brabant, Burgundy's vassal. There was almost a breach between the Burgundians and the English—and it was only the firmness of this alliance which stood between the Armagnacs and victory in France. Joan, a 19-year-old peasant girl from Domrémy, near Nancy, arrived with stories of the voices of St. Michael, St. Margaret and St. Catherine. A group of theologians examined her and found her good, humble and honest. She was made *Chef de Guerre*, given armour and an army; and her men took her to Orléans. A strange enthusiasm swept over its garrison, and in a little over a week the siege was raised. Many Frenchmen believed she was a saint. The Loire valley was cleared of the Anglo–Burgundians, who were defeated at Patay.

Charles was crowned at Reims in July 1429, and his advisers suggested that an attack should be made on Paris. The King, however, hated war, and he did little to forward these plans or to assist Joan. Not surprisingly, therefore, she was eventually taken prisoner by the Burgundians at Compiègne, when leading an attack from this besieged town. Her captors sold her to the English, who wished to see her proved guilty of witchcraft and heresy, partly to excuse their own defeats, and partly to undermine her prestige in France. She was taken to Cauchon, Bishop of Beauvais, and tried for witchcraft at Rouen. During her trial, Joan showed shrewdness and courage; but her claim to personal inspiration by God was heresy to the Church, especially when she refused to accept its authority. Eventually, she confessed her guilt, partly because she was worn down by deliberate indignities and partly because of a fear of being burned. She was sentenced to life imprisonment, but then relapsed into her former beliefs and was duly burned in Rouen market-place on 30 May 1431. She decided to endure death by fire rather than to serve a sentence of life imprisonment; to burn rather than give up her true beliefs. The reversed verdict of rehabilitation came only twenty-five years later. She was to be canonized in 1919. Despite this late canonization, she was the inspiration of French soldiers from the time of her death onwards.

Certainly, at the time, Charles VII did nothing to save *La Pucelle*, who had so miraculously revived the national spirit of the French. For the moment, he remained the lackey of la Tremouille, who had always been jealous of the Maid of Orléans, and his government remained impotent. Nevertheless, negotiations went on with Burgundy's agents, for Philip was becoming tired of the unpopular English alliance, which became even more unpopular when Henry VI was crowned King of France in Paris. Also, when in 1432 Philip's sister, Anne, married to Bedford, died, the Burgundian alliance weakened perceptibly. Philip was worried, too, about the hostility of the Emperor, Sigismund. So it was not surprising that when la Tremouille fell, negotiations culminated in the Congress of Arras (1435). The

English refused to accept Guienne and Normandy, which were to be held as fiefs of France; and Philip, thinking that this was unreasonable, determined to make peace. Bedford died just as the terms of peace were being settled. Charles had to make an abject apology for the murder at Montereau, and had to agree to allow the Burgundians complete independence during the lifetime of the Duke, who received Macon, Auxerre and Ponthieu. The Anglo–Burgundian alliance was over, and the end was in sight for the English occupation.

However, despite the end of the struggle with the Burgundians, and the prospect of a general peace, France was weak. *Ecorcheurs*, the Flayers, private bands of lawless soldiers, had destroyed whole districts. Nevertheless, Charles, helped now by Richemont, by his brother-in-law of Maine and by the Bastard of Orléans, his half-brother, and by popular uprisings against the English, began to make ground. In 1437 Paris fell to Charles VII, although he did not remain there. England was tired of war. There were only a few thousand English troops in France. But they were enabled to hold on, owing to Charles's lethargy. Perhaps this may appear in a less critical light when one notices his energy in dealing with the Praguerie, a rebellion so called after a similar rising in Prague. In this rebellion the Dauphin and Bourbon attempted to depose the King, which could only have resulted in France falling once again into the hands of rebellious and insubordinate nobles. Charles's determination to prevent this was something new, and the rebellion collapsed. The Dauphin was virtually exiled to his domain of Dauphiné.

But Charles still disliked war. He avoided pitched battles with the English. He had enough to do, bribing or defeating those who conspired to get rid of him, and trying to solve the problem of the *Ecorcheurs*, and setting the administration in order. Gradually these aims were achieved, for the crown's success was the sole hope of all those who hated anarchy. The army was disciplined and paid for by the *taille* and the new *aides*, and in 1440 and 1441 Evreux and Pontoise were taken. Henry VI wanted peace, and in negotiations in 1444, although the war was not ended, a truce was made. This Treaty of Tours gave France an opportunity to recover. Taxes were collected regularly, and the crown's financial position was strengthened. The mercenaries were expelled from France, and new cavalry regiments, *compagnies d'ordonnance*, of 600 men, were founded as the basis of a national standing army. To them were added *compagnies de petite ordonnance*, auxiliary infantrymen and archers. These were paid for by a heavy *taille*, and there was a heavy expense, too, in guns. An artillery force was built up by Jean and Gaspard Bureau, and it was to prove its value at Châtillon in 1453.

War began again in 1449, and soon the English lost Caen, were defeated at Formigny (in 1450, when Normandy became French for ever), and lost Bordeaux and Bayonne. After Châtillon, the war was over. Charles, the victor of the Hundred Years' War, is hardly recognizable as the former Dauphin of Bourges, but by this time he had become Charles *le bien servi*. Those who served him so well were Jacques Cœur, the great financier of Montpellier, Jean Bureau and Pierre de Brézé. They enabled him to defeat the English, to thwart the plans of Philip of Burgundy who was trying to build up a strong state on the eastern frontier of France, and to try his hand at gaining territories in Italy. His counsellors were often bourgeois, just as those of Philip IV had been. The States General declined in powers and in importance. When Charles died in 1461, a despotic monarchy had been restored to France. His son, Louis XI, loved power and was an unscrupulous despot. His father had created the means for him to be one, although Louis had, for years, done nothing but oppose his father and wish for his early death. Louis was treacherous, and known as the Spider; but he was a successful king, original and gifted, and far more intelligent than his contemporaries.

As Dauphin, he had been helped by Philip of Burgundy. Immediately he became King, he made it clear that he regarded Burgundy only as an enemy. He reclaimed Ponthieu for 400,000 crowns, as the Treaty of Arras permitted, but which Burgundy did not wish to lose. He encouraged the people of Liége to rebel against their Bishop, Burgundy's nephew; and he showed both his ability and his good luck when dealing with a rebellion of nobles, grandiloquently called the League of the Public Weal, and led by Bourbon and Burgundy. The rebellion was faced squarely by Louis, who brought one party to heel in the Bourbonnais, and then coolly fought another at Montlhéry, in 1465. Having done so, and held on to Paris, he ceased fighting to resolve the problem by diplomacy. His brother Charles, Duke of Berry, was given Normandy. Burgundy's son, Charolais, received the Somme towns. The other rebels received nothing by this Treaty of Conflans.

As soon as the trouble was over, Louis took Normandy back and began to cause trouble again for Burgundy in Liége. Charles the Bold was now Duke (1467), in succession to Philip; but the ruler's identity mattered little. Trouble with Burgundy was inevitable. Both sides were trying to gain Edward IV of England as an ally. Burgundy succeeded, in 1468, when Charles married Margaret of York. However, Louis was not to be perturbed. For the moment, peace was necessary, and he thought, perhaps foolishly, that he had a better chance of making peace in person, which may explain why he rode to see Charles at Péronne, on Burgundian territory. As talks began, news came through of a rebellion in Liége, which had been instigated by Louis's agents. The infuriated Charles forced the King of France to go to Liége to witness the punishment of the rebels, and to sign the humiliating Treaty of Péronne. Among other things, Louis had to promise to give Champagne and Brie to Charles of Berry. But he had no intention of keeping his promises. To Louis, treaties were worthless scraps of paper—a fact which made it difficult for his contemporaries to understand him or to deal with him in any normal way. He gave Charles Guienne instead, for this was much less dangerous than allowing him to have the key territory of Champagne. And he managed to hold off the other problems by a diplomacy which made it difficult for Burgundy ever to keep an ally for long. He even averted the threat from England by making the Treaty of Péquigny in 1475, by which Edward was bribed to make a seven years' truce.

In fact, Louis had only to wait to allow Charles the Bold's ambitions to ruin him. Charles wanted Alsace and Lorraine, but this aroused the hostility of the Swiss, with whom Louis made terms. The result was that in 1476 and 1477 the Swiss defeated Charles at Grandson, Morat and Nancy. In the last of these battles, Charles was killed, and the serious threat to France by the Burgundian power had gone. Gradually, various Burgundian territories came under Louis's rule. Inexplicably, he did not follow up his first intention of marrying the Dauphin to Charles's daughter, Mary. Instead, she married Maximilian of Austria in 1477, and so Louis did not gain Flanders, for the Hapsburg power menacingly came into the Netherlands as a result of this marriage, a catastrophic alliance for France. Warfare followed, but, after the indecisive battle of Guinegate in Flanders in 1479, Louis decided to make terms. Mary's daughter, Margaret, was betrothed to the Dauphin, and Mary's son, Philip, was to rule Flanders. Louis had gained Burgundy, but Flanders was lost. Even so, Louis had won a great victory for France. He also gained Anjou and Maine, when its ruling house died out; and took Provence too.

He became strong in Navarre through a diplomatic marriage, but gained little more in Spain than Roussillon. He was also interested in Savoy, and made alliances with the Medici and Sforza families. At home, he helped towns and trade, worked his officials hard, and ruled of his *bon plaisir*. Undoubtedly, he had made mistakes, but he had emerged triumphant despite them all, except perhaps in not preventing the marriage between Mary of Burgundy and Maximilian. The arrival of Hapsburg power in the Netherlands was to have important consequences. When Louis XV, in the eighteenth century, saw the tombs of Charles the Bold and Mary in Bruges, in the Church of Our Lady, he is reported to have said that they were "the cause of all our wars".

Louis XI's legendary reputation, seen, for example, in Scott's novel, *Quentin Durward*, has followed him ever since. Yet he was not so much a "terrifying gargoyle" as a great statesman of the Machiavellian type, "the shrewdest in getting out of a tight spot", as de Commynes said. His incredible character may be seen from his keeping offending nobles in cages, while he carried leaden images of saints in his cap in a form of overt religiosity. He was a subtle negotiator, who planned his life to return to France all that she had lost. With "utter good sense", he did so. With Louis, the Middle Ages come to an end, for it was his son, Charles VIII, who began the campaigns in Italy which indicate a new kind of monarchy and a new variety of royal ambition. Louis had completed French territorial unification and had created an absolutism foreign to the political ideals of medieval society. Towards the end of his life, the sinister aspects became paramount. He lived withdrawn and obsessed by fear, surrounded by archers, in gloomy Plessis.

Another noticeable change in French policy is that, after the Avignon Papacy, from 1307 to 1377, during which time the Popes had been closely connected with French political problems, there had come the period of the Great Schism and the Conciliar movement, when France appeared to be less closely involved than one would have assumed. France had, at first, supported Clement VII, the Avignon anti-Pope, but had then become neutral, hoping for an end of the Schism. Eventually, when Martin V became Pope in 1417 and the Schism was over, France took little interest in Papal affairs, and the Papacy itself was too concerned in building up the "Papal monarchy" to be much interested in the work of Charles VII and Louis XI. On the other hand, the University of Paris was greatly concerned with furthering reform and the unity of the Church and, after 1417, the French clergy were among the foremost reformers who wished to reduce the absolute power of the popes. For example, in 1438, there was the Pragmatic Sanction which reduced Papal rights in France, and although Louis XI abolished it, the French church remained independent or Gallican. The importance of Rome had declined, and it is significant that during the Hundred Years' War many churches and monasteries were ruined and despoiled.

The universities were of growing importance in the medieval period. The University of Paris, growing out of the Cathedral school of Notre Dame, existed before 1200, but received its first charter from Philip Augustus in that year. It grew in reputation for theology, medicine, law and the arts, and became a great centre for Dominicans and Franciscans. Its first college was founded by Robert de Sorbonne in 1257. Some of the most famous students at Paris, which became the mother University for western Europe, were Bonaventura, Thomas Aquinas and Duns Scotus. There were thirteen other universities in France, but most were founded in the fifteenth century. Exceptions were Montpellier (1289), Toulouse (1230) and Avignon (1303).

French medieval architecture was very different in the south, which was far more strongly influenced by the classical Roman tradition, from that in the north. The Romanesque style began to be replaced in the twelfth century in the Capetian domain; but examples of earlier work at Avignon, Arles, Toulouse, Autun, Le Puy and Vézelay should be compared with the early French Gothic in Paris, Chartres, Bourges and Reims, to its final flowering at Amiens. A revival came in the fifteenth century in the flamboyancy of the last period of Gothic architecture, as at Rouen and Albi. The sculpture of medieval France was important, although, of course, its subjects were almost entirely religious. So were those of its paintings, but in the Duke of Berry's breviary, *les Très Riches Heures* (early fifteenth century) one may see the work of the de Limbourg brothers, giving a taste of what was best in the world of French medieval art. The student can do no better than to visit the Cluny museum in the rue du Sommerard, just off the Boulevard Saint-Michel in Paris, to obtain material for the study of French medieval art. Its treasures include, in the medieval town house of the Abbots of Cluny, the arts, crafts, tapestries and toys of medieval Paris. Perhaps its finest possession is the tapestry of The Lady of the Unicorn.

The literature of the period 1420 to 1483 includes, of course, the work of Philippe de Commynes (1445–1511), who served first Philip of Burgundy and then Louis XI. His *Mémoires*, however, although concerned with the years reviewed in this chapter, were not written until about 1490. He is important as the first genuine French historian. Of interest also is the anonymous *Livre des Faicts de Jacques de Lalaing*, and de la Marche's *Le Chevalier Délibéré*. De la Sale, who died in about 1460, wrote *Le Petit Jehan de Saintré*, and literary interest abounds in *Les Quinze Joyes de Mariage* and *Les Cent Nouvelles nouvelles*, a collection of stories written in about 1460. De Villon produced *Le Testament* in about 1462, and also some *ballades*, while Charles d'Orléans was writing lyric poetry at Blois after his return from captivity in London. Charles had an incredible career. He was rescued alive from under a heap of dead at Agincourt. He married Richard II's widow and made Blois a brilliant focus for such writers as Villon. The sparkle of his beloved Loire shines through his lyrics. The stage was set for the Renaissance by these writers of prose and verse, producing their work in a time of great political difficulty and uncertainty.

## RECOMMENDED READING

*Joan of Arc*. Lucien Fabre. Odhams, 1954.

*Louis XI: The Legend and the Man*. P. M. Kendall. *History Today*, Vol. II, No. 8, 1961.

*Medieval France*. Joan Evans. Oxford, 1925.

*Medieval France*. Ed. A. Tilley. Cambridge University Press, 1922.
    Chapter 2—History, by C. V. Langlois.
    Chapter 6—Universities, by A. G. Little.
    Chapter 9—Architecture, by T. G. Jackson.
    Chapter 10—Sculpture and Painting, by M. R. James.

*Mémoires*. Philippe de Commynes. (English translation in Bohn's Classical Library.)

*The Cathedral Builders*. Jean Gimpel. Evergreen Profile Book, 1961.

*The Dawn of a New Era, 1250–1453*. E. P. Cheyney. Harper, U.S.A., 1936.

*The Wandering Scholars*. Helen Waddell. Pelican, 1954.

*Saint Joan of Arc*. V. Sackville-West. Penguin, 1955.

## CHAPTER 5

# *France from Charles VIII to the Rise of Catherine de' Medici*

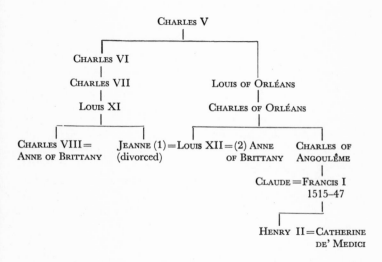

LOUIS XI, after a four years' illness, died in 1483. His son, Charles VIII, came to the throne as a 13-year-old, and, for the next nine years, was the puppet of his sister, Anne of Beaujeu, a practical politician like the late King Louis. Charles, by comparison, was a romantic weakling, who seemed to have inherited none of his father's qualities. Anne formed a council of fifteen royal princes, of whom the most important was Louis of Orléans, the future Louis XII. The States General, assembled in 1484, drew up a list of grievances and protests against the *taille*; but nothing came

45

of it. The government was too strong, and the only reason for the
assembly of the States seems to have been that Anne was looking
for popular support against rivals like Louis of Orléans. Times
were not easy, for peace was not yet secure in Burgundy, and
Brittany was still an independent fief. The Duke of Brittany,
Francis, was an old man, and had no son. His eldest daughter,
Anne, was therefore the heiress to the Duchy, and suitors were
not lacking. They included Louis of Orléans and the Emperor
Maximilian. The latter, indeed, became betrothed to her, but
when a French force invaded, the betrothal was repudiated, and
Anne was quickly married off to Charles—a triumph for the
methods of Louis XI, as practised by his daughter.

Charles, by this dynastic marriage, was now King of all
France, and he seized the opportunity to become ruler as well
(1491). Immediately, he began to show an interest in foreign
affairs, partly to show himself to Anne in an heroic light. This
delicate, undersized man rode to battle on a vast war horse,
wearing a blue cloak spangled with stars, like a hero of the
*chansons de geste*. By this time, France, Spain and England had
emerged as nation states, but Italy had not. She was still a
collection of communes in the north, the Papal states in the
centre and Naples in the south. The latter was ruled by the
Spanish house of Aragon. This Spanish claim to dominance in
Sicily and Naples was rivalled by a Valois claim—Charles of
Maine, ruling in Sicily, had bequeathed his title to Louis XI. In
law, the French claim was weak, but it was accompanied by the
Orléans family claim to Milan, inherited by Louis of Orléans
from an ancestral connexion with the Visconti. However, temporarily, the claim was dormant, for Charles was an ally of the
Milanese rulers, the Sforza family. If and when the French were
to press their claim, there would be trouble with the maritime
republic of Venice. Genoa and Florence were also important,
geographically and politically; and it so happened that it was an
appeal for help from a reforming party in Florence which decided Charles to intervene in Italian affairs. The decision to do
so was a foolish one, for French power ought to have been

deployed on the Spanish frontier or in Burgundy, rather than in Italy.

Charles's advisers were certainly against his extravagant plans for an Italian campaign. Maximilian was pleased, no doubt, that the decision had been taken, and Henry VII of England saw his opportunity to invade French territory. But Charles was determined to do what he had planned. He made the Treaty of Etaples in 1492, bribing Henry to leave France with 745,000 crowns. The Spaniards were given Roussillon to persuade them to remain neutral; and even Maximilian was given Artois and Franch Comté, which had been ceded to France when it was projected that Charles should marry Maximilian's daughter. Having completed his diplomatic arrangements, Charles set out from Vienne in 1494, and marched through Florence and Rome to Naples, which surrendered to him. But back in northern Italy, the rival powers joined in the League of Venice, which, on Charles's return, forced him to battle at Fornovo. His victory there enabled him to withdraw safely into France, but the results of his campaign disappeared overnight. It was while he was planning a second expedition, in 1498, that Charles died, and Louis of Orléans became Louis XII. The military results of the Italian campaigns of Charles VIII soon disappeared, but France continued to have a political and social preoccupation with Italy. Italian poisons, pastry cooks, architects and gardeners were imported into France, and Italianate castles, such as Amboise, and gardens like those at Langeais became the fashion.

Louis XII's first action was to get rid of his wife, Jeanne, whom he had been forced to marry by Louis XI, and to marry Charles's widow to keep Brittany still within the French realm. This done, he turned to Italian affairs, to enforce his claim to Milan. He made his invasion safe by negotiating terms with Philip of Flanders, the Swiss, the Papacy and the Venetians; and went on to take Milan in 1499. Although Ludovico Sforza regained the city the following year, he soon lost it again and was taken to France as a captive. In the dungeon of gloomy Loches one can still see the drawings he made on the walls. The next step was for Louis to negotiate a partition of Sicily and Naples with Ferdinand of Aragon, and, with an agreement made, Naples was taken and its ruler given a pension. But it was unlikely that a Franco–Spanish agreement would last; and before long there was a quarrel which resulted in a series of defeats for France, culminating in the Spanish victory of the Garigliano. At the same time, Pope Alexander VI died, and was succeeded, first by Pius III and then, soon afterwards, by Pope Julius II, the great patron of the Renaissance artists. Julius used his influence to negotiate a peace between France and Spain, and the peace was used by Louis to make an alliance with the Emperor. One of the terms agreed was that Louis should have his title to Milan recognized; in return, Louis's daughter, Claude, was betrothed to the Emperor's grandson, Charles.

These terms were embodied in the Treaties of Blois (1504), and by them Louis was committed to an attack on Venice, largely on behalf of Julius II. The treaties were not observed, however. In 1505 Claude was betrothed to Francis of Angoulême, the heir-presumptive. Maximilian was angry, but the situation changed when Maximilian's son, Philip, died. The Emperor, intent on interfering in Italy, discovered that the main obstacle to his plans was the Venetian republic, and he therefore made a coalition with France and Spain to attack the Venetians. This League of Cambrai was, in fact, not in the best interests of France, had Louis been able to see it. However, he did his part. Venice was defeated at Agnadello; and, almost immediately, Julius II withdrew from the League and began negotiations for a new anti-French alliance. When it was formed, it consisted of the Papacy, Venice, Spain and England, and was called the Holy League.

Louis appointed Gaston de Foix to command the French armies, and he was an excellent commander. He defeated the Spaniards at Valeggio, sacked Brescia, and moved on Ravenna, destroying a Spanish force *en route* (1512). Unluckily, de Foix was killed in this engagement, and the French had to withdraw themselves from Italy altogether, partly because of a strong threat from the Swiss. It was a difficult time for Louis, for Ferdinand had just taken Navarre, and the French lacked the forces to deal with this new threat. When the French moved into Italy again in 1513, they were defeated by the Swiss at Novara. In the same year, they lost the battle of the Spurs at Guinegate against an invading English army. Obviously, Louis badly needed a breathing space.

He therefore made peace with Henry VIII, and, being now widowed, married Henry's sister, Mary, a girl in her teens who was besotted with Charles Brandon, one of her gentlemen-in-waiting. This marriage was a death warrant for the aged and sickly Louis. Mary led him such a hectic life that in a few weeks he died (January 1515). Mary, with scandalous speed, married Brandon, whom her obliging brother elevated to a dukedom. No one could say that Louis's Italian ambitions had brought France anything but disaster, but at home his reign may be counted as a success. His government had instituted various legal reforms; and, despite the heavy taxes necessitated by the wars, he had been a popular king. Louis was succeeded by his second cousin, Francis I, *le roi chevalier*, "magnanime, débonnaire et libéral", as de Serres described him. With him, the Renaissance arrived in France. He was the patron of Leonardo da Vinci, the builder of Fontainebleau and, encouraged by du Bellay, the founder of the Collège de France. He was the personification of the French spirit—and also a despot, a Macchiavellian statesman, a voluptuary and a flamboyant wit.

His father had died when Francis was a baby, and he had been brought up by his mother, Louise of Savoy, and his sister, Margaret. It was plain that he should marry Louis's daughter, Claude, to prevent Brittany being lost again to the French throne; but this marriage did not take place until Anne of Brittany, who hated him and his family, died in 1514. The following year, Francis came to the throne. His mother had enormous influence over him. He began by earning his reputation as *le roi chevalier*, which he was not always to deserve, by leading another invasion of Italy and defeating the Swiss at Marignano. An imaginative piece of romanticism followed when Bayard, *le chevalier sans peur et sans reproche*, knighted the young king on the field of battle.

A French government was established in Milan, which Massimiliano Sforza gave up, in return for a pension. Terms were made with Pope Leo X at Bologna—a Concordat by which the Pope was to receive revenues from the French Church, while Francis was to have the right to nominate its bishops, which gave the King considerable political control of the Church. This strange reversal of functions had one unfortunate result in the future. French bishops tended to be men of noble birth, completely out of touch with the ordinary priesthood.

In 1519 Maximilian died. Despite the bribes of Francis to the Electors, the Imperial title went to Charles of Austria, who was already a rival to France as the ruler of Aragon. The election meant that the rivalry with the Hapsburgs, already begun at the time of the marriage of Maximilian and Mary in 1477, now flowered into an opposition which was to be a great theme in European history for more than two centuries. Charles V was to rule Spain, the Netherlands, Austria, Naples and parts of America. He was to be a cautious and conservative ruler, very different from the French "King of the Renaissance". Francis, however, in view of the build up in power of his rival, looked for an ally, and found one in Henry VIII—the occasion being celebrated by the famous, and meaningless, Field of the Cloth of Gold in 1520. When war began in 1521 Henry VIII reversed his alliance and joined in against Francis, who lost Milan, was defeated at Bicocca and then, betrayed by Charles de Bourbon, Constable of France, lost again at Pavia in 1525. As he said, "Tout est perdu hors l'honneur". Francis was captured by the Emperor, and Louise ruled as regent while he was in Spain. He was ill-equipped for adversity, and fell ill, but not until he promised to give up Burgundy was Francis released. Although he sent his sons into captivity in his stead, and one of them, the future Henry II, was embittered by the harsh imprisonment, Francis had no intention of keeping his word. War went on until the Peace of Cambrai in 1529. When it ended, Bourbon was dead, and Rome had been sacked by the mutinous Imperial troops. Indeed, Francis might have had more successes in the later years of the war, had he been willing to grant concessions to his ally, Andrea Doria, the Admiral of Genoa. As it was, Naples was saved for the Emperor. The French troops suffered from a severe epidemic, and Doria went back to Genoa and established a republic there, free from French rule.

By the Treaty of Cambrai, France gave up her claims in Italy, Artois and Flanders, and Francis promised to pay Charles V 2,000,000 crowns, which necessitated a *grosse taille*. Meantime, he made another alliance with Henry VIII, for the annulment of whose marriage with Catherine of Aragon he even pleaded with the Pope. But Francis was willing to negotiate with any power for an alliance—with German Protestant princes, with the Pope, and even with the Sultan Suleiman of Turkey, who was about to invade Hungary. The news of a Franco–Turkish alliance shocked Europe, but, although that particular friendship came to nothing, Francis was setting a precedent which was frequently followed in after years by other French kings and ministers. In this period of peace, Francis placed his trust in Montmorency. Negotiations were carried on successfully, and the French army was reconstructed on the lines foreshadowed by Charles VII. There was even an attempt at reconciliation with the Emperor, which came to nothing. War broke out again in 1536, and yet again in 1542, but the fighting tended to be in Provence, Picardy and the Pyrenees, although there was one French victory in Italy—at Ceresole in 1544—which was not worth the winning. Charles V, eventually nearly bankrupt and war-weary, offered peace terms at Crépy.

Francis's achievements were few. No doubt, he had shown some military successes, but his policies, like his court and government, were dominated by his mother and sister; by favourites like Bonnivet and Montmorency; and by his mistresses, women like Françoise de Chateaubriand and Madame d'Etampes, and even Diane de Poitiers, the Dauphin's mistress. His favourite of all his advisers was undoubtedly his sister, Margaret, later Queen of Navarre, the author of the *Heptameron* (1559). She was the patron of the poets of the *Pléiade*. Francis was not sympathetic to religious reform. His government persecuted many like Calvin, who fled to Geneva, and was responsible for the massacre of the Vaudois in 1545, and the burning of Protestants at Meaux. The gay young man, *magnanime, débonnaire*, gave way to a mean and selfish old voluptuary. Francis died in 1547 and was succeeded by Henry II, who was dominated by Diane de Poitiers, the Duchess of Valentinois, who was twice his age. Henry had no affection for his wife, Catherine de' Medici, who often only remained at court because Diane had no strong objections! The reign of Henry II is therefore largely concerned with Diane, and with the struggle for power of the Guise and Montmorency families.

The Montmorency family, led by the old Constable and his nephews, the Colignys, were important in the earlier years of the reign. The Guises, from Lorraine, were more significant in the later years. They were led, at first, by Anthony and his brother, the Cardinal John. They were followed by Francis, Duke of Lorraine from 1550, a good soldier, and his brother, the Cardinal Charles, a Church diplomat who did valuable work at the Council of Trent. Another brother was Louis, Cardinal of Guise. Their sister Mary married James V of Scotland and became the mother of Mary, Queen of Scots. Her marriage to the Dauphin in 1558 completed the triumph of Guise family importance. As a family, their character and ability were in strong contrast to the last Valois kings. Henry II was an athlete—it is unlikely that he would have matured into a wise king, but he certainly did not do so before his death, which occurred in his thirties, through an accidental wound in the lists, at a tournament. He left a family of delicate and decadent half-Italian children. Their mother, Catherine, was named *Madame Serpent* by the French.

Henry had inherited several problems—the rivalry of the Emperor, the growing importance of Protestantism and the insoluble and misunderstood question of rising prices, which was to perplex other sixteenth-century monarchs, not least Elizabeth I. He also had to take into account the various ambitions and policies of his advisers. Foremost among them was Diane de Poitiers, the beautiful widow of Louis de Brézé, Seneschal of

Normandy. She was a politician, a lover of power and influence, and Henry became infatuated with her while still Dauphin. He remained so for the rest of his life. She found political allies where she could—either among the Guises or with Montmorency—but she always knew how to control her obstinate royal lover. She was violently anti-Protestant. She took what money and property she could, including that confiscated from Protestants, or from Madame d'Etampes, or even money from the royal treasury. She virtually stole the château of Chenonceaux from its owner. She was always on the watch for shifts in the balance of power between the rival parties at court. The only subject on which they were all agreed was the repression of heresy.

Montmorency advised Henry against intervention in Italy; and peace was maintained until 1551, when a plan was made to help the German Lutheran princes in their struggle with the Emperor. French forces set out and occupied Metz, Toul and Verdun; but the Imperial troops then attacked Metz and took Thérouanne. Montmorency, a poor soldier, retired. A French success followed at Renty, but this led to a quarrel between Francis of Guise and Coligny, each claiming the victory as his own. French hopes in Italy proved to be useless, although the terms of the Treaty of Vaucelles in 1556 made it seem that France had been waging a completely successful war. The Guises wanted the war to continue, and, supported by Diane, their policy was followed. War was renewed in 1557, with the last Valois attack on Italy. Montmorency, back in office, led an army eastwards which was defeated at Saint-Quentin, and France was only saved from utter defeat at the hands of Charles V's successor, Philip II, by the return of Francis of Guise from Italy, and by the determination of Catherine de' Medici, who rallied the people of Paris. The only French triumph came early in 1558, when Guise took Calais, the last English possession in France.

The Guises now ceased to be supporters of Diane, turning instead to Queen Catherine. The Duchess promptly returned to her old alliance with Montmorency, and, between them, they gained Henry's support to make the Treaty of Cateau-Cambrésis. Peace was made, but France retained few of her recent acquisitions. The treaty even proposed a marriage alliance between Valois and Hapsburg. It seemed that Diane had reversed French foreign policy, which had been more or less consistent on this point since 1519. But the financial and religious problems of the monarchy, which could be seen in the growth of Calvinism and even trouble in the *Parlement de Paris*, were to ensure that there would be no great Valois–Hapsburg alliance to force a counter-Reformation on Europe. Although the proxy marriage between Philip of Spain and Henry's daughter, Elizabeth, took place in 1559, the King met his death during the celebrations. Diane was left stranded, her power gone. She had to retire, to watch the once despised Catherine de' Medici rule in France. She was almost as pitiable as Mary, Queen of Scots, who, when the Scots had been defeated by Protector Somerset at Pinkie Cleugh in 1547, took refuge in France, married the Dauphin, became Queen, and saw her husband die only seventeen months after his accession.

The France of this period, under the new absolute monarchy of the Valois, took an active, if somewhat imitative, part in the Renaissance. She produced a Greek scholar in Guillaume Budé, and there were other great humanists in Etienne Dolet and Lefèvre d'Etaples, who prepared the way for religious reformers like Calvin. The latter's *L'Institution de la religion chrétienne* appeared in French in 1541, and he found it wiser to move to Geneva, which became the focus of the reform movement. Dolet himself died at the stake for heresy. It was the age, too, of François Rabelais (1490–1553), Voltaire's "drunken philosopher", whose *Gargantua* and *Pantagruel* were published from 1532 onwards, to bring a new kind of fantastic and ribald writing to literature. Like many later French writers, Rabelais was a satirist, concerned and involved with all the intellectual problems of the day, a man with an enthusiasm for living which was the keynote of the Renaissance. The *Heptameron* of Francis I's sister, Margaret d'Angoulême, has been mentioned above; she also wrote metaphysical poetry, as in *Le Miroir de l'âme pécheresse*. One of her friends was Bonaventure des Périers, and other novelists of the period were de Troges and Noël du Fail. Even tragedians were making their appearance, a sign of literary sophistication. The first were de Baif and Bochetel, but there was nothing original in their work translated from the Greek. Clément Marot (1495–1544) wrote *rondeaux, ballades* and *chansons*—a mixture of the old medieval forms with an admixture of the new Italian humanism. A contemporary was Antoine Heroët, another member of the literary group which surrounded Margaret. At Lyons there was Maurice Scève, leader of a group much influenced by the fourteenth-century writings of Petrarch. Much more important was Joachim du Bellay (1522–60), a Latin scholar, a sonneteer and a member of that movement called *La Pléiade*, which included Ronsard and Jodelle. With them, the Renaissance had arrived in French literature.

## RECOMMENDED READING

*Diane of Poitiers and the Reign of Henry II*. J. H. M. SALMON. *History Today*, Vol. 12, No. 2, p. 77 (February 1962).

*Francis the First: le Roi Chevalier*. J. H. M. SALMON. *History Today*, Vol. 8, No. 5, p. 295 (May 1958).

*The Century of the Renaissance*. L. BATTIFOL (translated by E. F. BUCKLEY). Heinemann, 1916.

*The New Cambridge Modern History*, Vol. I: *The Renaissance* (1957).
    Chapter III, by Hans Baron—Fifteenth Century Civilisation and the Renaissance.
    Chapter X, by R. Doucet. France under Charles VIII and Louis XII.
    Vol. II: *The Reformation* (1958).
    Chapter XI, by F. C. Spooner—The Hapsburg–Valois Struggle.

*The World of Humanism, 1453–1517*. M. P. GILMORE. Harper, U.S.A.

## CHAPTER 6

## *Protestant and Catholic—France in the Days of Catherine de' Medici*

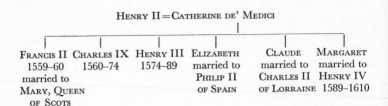

HENRY II = CATHERINE DE' MEDICI

| FRANCIS II 1559–60 married to MARY, QUEEN OF SCOTS | CHARLES IX 1560–74 | HENRY III 1574–89 | ELIZABETH married to PHILIP II OF SPAIN | CLAUDE married to CHARLES II OF LORRAINE | MARGARET married to HENRY IV 1589–1610 |

FROM 1562 to 1598 France was engaged in futile religious wars, and the country was largely ruined as a result. It was unfortunate for France that it was also a period of weak kings, dominated by their mother, Catherine de' Medici, or by the leaders of the various factions in the state. Not until all the parties were exhausted by war was peace made; and at the end of it all, France reverted to catholicism, for the Protestants never stood a real chance of permanent victory in a country where the monarchy had such a strong vested interest in the Roman Church, or where the capital city was always staunchly anti-Protestant. The only unity in the period can be found in the life of Catherine de' Medici; for even the Protestant Huguenot party was often fighting for political rather than purely Calvinist principles.

Admittedly, catherine's career is well worthy of study, for, although handicapped by her sex, her bourgeois origins and her Italian nationality, and although, ultimately, her policies were a disastrous failure, she was an interesting example of a Renaissance politician. She was an intelligent woman, but no statesman.

Her ambitions were always for herself or for her children, and never for France. She was the daughter of Lorenzo de' Medici, the man to whom Macchiavelli dedicated *Il Principe*. Her childhood was spent as a puppet in the complicated politics of northern Italy, the Italy of the Renaissance; and from it she learned only pretence and cynicism. She was married at the age of 14 to the future Henry II, who was contemptuous of her; and her failure to produce children for nine years nearly ended in her being divorced. But she bided her time, and the death of her husband in 1559 gave her the opportunity she needed. Her son, Francis II, aged 15, was an invalid and a minor. He was married to Mary, Queen of Scots, and was thus influenced by Mary's powerful Guise uncles. Diane de Poitiers was banished from the court, and power passed to Francis of Guise, his brother John, Cardinal of Lorraine, and to their ally for the moment, Catherine. The Guises were Roman Catholics, protagonists of a policy of repressing the Protestants, and of building up an alliance with the Hapsburgs.

Opposed to them were Anthony, the husband of Jeanne d'Albret, Queen of Navarre; and, more important by far, his younger brother, Louis I of Condé. These were members of the Bourbon family, and Huguenots. Thus religion became a political question. Also on the Calvinist side were the three Châtillon brothers, nephews of the Constable, Montmorency. The second of the three was Gaspard de Coligny, a convinced Huguenot. Coligny and Condé were determined not to leave the person of the young King in the clutches of the Guises, and it was this which led to the Conspiracy of Amboise in 1560. Condé claimed that his brother, Anthony, as first Prince of the royal blood, should be the Regent during Francis's minority. His plan was, therefore, to kidnap the King at Amboise—and it was directed against the Guises, not against the boy ruler of France. It was a political movement, not a religious one. Indeed, the Calvinist faith taught passive obedience and non-resistance at this stage. However, the plot failed. It was badly organized, it was betrayed, and about 1200 men were hanged or drowned as a result.

Many were hanged from the turrets of Amboise with the young Valois princes looking on.

However, the revenge of the Guises brought them unpopularity, and Catherine could see how much opposition there was to her allies. She therefore turned against the Guises, decided in favour of a policy of religious toleration, did away with the Inquisition, and appointed her friend, Michel de l'Hôpital, as Chancellor. She turned for advice to Coligny and ordered a complete cessation of religious persecution. She called an assembly at Fontainebleau, to hear arguments for and against toleration, and the States General to meet at Meaux (December 1560). But any attempt at stopping the political and religious rivalry of Guise and Bourbon was hopeless. Although Condé had denied all knowledge of the Amboise plot, and had escaped punishment, the Guises were not to be dismissed from power so easily. They arranged that the States General should meet at Orléans instead of Meaux, gathered evidence that Condé was plotting another Huguenot rebellion, ordered that he should be tried, and gained a conviction and order for his death for treason. However, just at this moment, Francis II was dying. Catherine saw that his brother Charles, very definitely a minor, would need a Regent. This Regent must almost inevitably be Anthony of Navarre, Condé's brother. She therefore persuaded Navarre to renounce the Regency in her favour, in return for Condé's release and oblivion for the recent "Protestant" plotting. The dying boy was blamed for the unauthorized arrest of Condé, Catherine was confirmed in power on the accession of Charles IX, and the Guises were, once again, out of favour, although Catherine allowed them to remain at court so that they would not spend their time plotting in opposition. She believed that she could best hold on to power by playing off the Guises against the Bourbons. It is not surprising that she became known as *La Reine politique*.

Unfortunately, this meant playing off the Catholics against the Protestants. If she withheld support from the Guises, then the Catholics of France might rise up against her, and she would lose power; but if she supported the Guises, they might become too strong for her to control. Although she cared little for religion herself, she knew that she must temporize and compromise. This meant that her policies must always tend to be negative, and, in the end, her negative subtlety got her nowhere. However, at this point, in 1560, Catherine returned to her policy of toleration, believing, possibly, that the Huguenots were stronger than they were. When the States General met, de l'Hôpital explained that the struggle between the Guises and Bourbons was over, and that religious toleration was the order of the day. Few deputies believed him, but the Ordonnance d'Orléans was made, an attempt to enforce conciliation. The Huguenot leaders were disturbed that Navarre had forfeited his undoubted right to the Regency in return for the empty title of Lieutenant-General. But Anthony was weak, and Catherine knew him to be pliable. The Calvinists were disgusted with him. However, the Queen Mother's policy of conciliation was tried out, and her "partial toleration" proved to be a superficial answer to a difficult problem. Montmorency, putting his religious beliefs before family unity, went over to the Catholic Guises, and in 1561 he, Saint-André and Guise formed a Triumvirate which appealed to Catherine to support Catholicism.

Her reply was the Colloquy of Poissy, an attempt to heal religious problems by discussion. The Calvinist viewpoint was to be put by Theodor Beza, the Catholic by Cardinal John of Lorraine. As could easily be foreseen, the Colloquy was a dismal failure. Catherine despaired when no compromise could be reached—hardly surprising in an age when few believed in toleration for the opposition. However, Catherine issued, owing to the influence of de l'Hôpital, an edict giving religious liberty to Huguenots outside city walls, or in private houses. This temporary policy was sufficient to cause tumult and civil war. The enraged Catholics turned to the Guises for leadership, which was speedily forthcoming. Catherine, who "had no idea what dogma meant", had unleashed religious war. She gave the impression that she supported Calvinism, yet she had no religious principles at all.

Guise looked around for allies—even among the German Lutheran princes, thus proving that his own ideas were purely political—and the Triumvirate organized a party for the defence of catholicism against all comers. Even Navarre went over to the Catholic cause—the Huguenots called him Julian the Apostate, or Turncoat. Catherine herself, still feeling that Huguenot power was strong enough to be eventually victorious, asked Coligny to say what support he could muster. The Huguenots began military preparations, persuaded that they were fighting on the King's side, while the Catholics also prepared to take up arms.

Then, on 1 March 1562, came the Massacre of Vassy. Some of Guise's men killed about thirty Huguenots, worshipping illegally within a town, and war began. Huguenots were massacred in Cahors and Tours, and the Triumvirs seized Charles IX, dismissed de l'Hôpital and forced Catherine to give up her hopes of support from Condé and Coligny. Indeed, when Condé published her letter to him, asking for support, she gave her full support to the Triumvirs. She may not have known it, but she was now supporting the side which was bound to triumph. The Huguenots were few in number—probably never more than a tenth of the population of France. What gave them the appearance of strength was that they consisted largely of the landed gentry and well-to-do townsmen. Their military strength was considerable. They normally had strong cavalry forces. This meant that they were difficult to subdue, but, on the other hand, they were never likely to convert France to Calvinism. The importance of the Huguenots was always a political one. They were against absolute royal power, they believed in constitutional reform, they were enemies of the Guises—but as a religious force they were negligible, despite the excellent Calvinist organization, which excelled even the organization of the Roman Church.

Condé and Coligny led the Huguenots into war. Their capital was Orléans. Tours, Blois and Rouen declared for them, while their great stronghold of La Rochelle dominated the west. Foolishly, Condé negotiated for help from England, promising Elizabeth the eventual return of Calais. Guise was infuriated by this lack of patriotic feeling, especially as he had captured this town for France! The war began with the siege of the Protestant town of Rouen, but its most serious battle was at Dreux, where Saint-André was killed, and Montmorency was captured. Navarre was already dead. However, Guise managed to capture Condé and to defeat Coligny; and when the siege of Orléans began, the Protestant cause seemed lost. Then came a stroke of fortune. In 1563 Guise was assassinated, to the ill-concealed delight of Coligny. But the only gainer was Catherine. With her Triumvirs gone, she was left in power. Once again, she determined to try for conciliation, although she no longer overestimated the strength of the Protestant cause. Some freedom was given to the Huguenots by the Edict of 1563, while a war was declared on England which Elizabeth hastened to terminate by the Treaty of Troyes in 1564.

However, peace was not to last. The Huguenots were dissatisfied, while catholicism had been roused to defend itself. Mob violence continued. The Huguenots, too, were suspicious of Catherine after the events of 1562, and especially when she met the Duke of Alva, the Spanish minister, at Bayonne. Undoubtedly, however, all that the irreligious Queen Mother wanted was to keep control of her son, Charles IX, and to keep order in France. She wanted a Gallican church—Catholic, but not too dependent upon Rome. She did not want to share her power with Coligny in the way she had had to share it with Guise. But she could not keep the peace for ever by her usual negative duplicity. In September 1567 the Protestants put a plan into operation to kidnap Charles at Meaux, and, although Catherine spirited him away to Paris, war had begun again. In this second war, Montmorency was killed at Saint-Denis, and Condé besieged Paris, but officially peace was made again in March 1568, by the terms of Longjumeau. This did not mean that the fighting was over. In the various districts of France, local Leagues continued the murders, massacres and mêlées.

Catherine, at long last, had made up her mind that the Huguenots were aiming at political revolution. She was determined not to allow them to rule in France, and they, knowing her determination, made plans for the renewal of the struggle in their fortress of La Rochelle. By this time, Catherine had another problem. Charles IX was beginning to want to be free of his mother's tutelage, while she was bringing to the forefront of affairs his younger brother, Henry of Anjou, possibly as a counterpoise. The late Francis of Guise was also being replaced by his son, the young Henry of Guise. War broke out for the third time in the late summer of 1568. This bloodthirsty struggle was one of Catholic victories. At Jarnac, Condé was killed, and the leadership of the Huguenots passed to Coligny. He, in turn, was defeated at Moncontour, although he did have some success in a campaign in the Rhône valley. War weariness and near-bankruptcy caused peace to be made in 1570 at Saint-Germain. A new party—the Politiques—mostly moderate Catholics, and led by Francis de Montmorency, wanted peace.

Catherine also had plans to marry her daughter Margaret to the Protestant Henry of Navarre, son of Anthony of Bourbon and Jeanne d'Albret, as well as a scheme to marry Charles to the Protestant Elizabeth of England. For the moment, she wanted to keep the Huguenots complaisant. Coligny himself wanted to turn French martial ardour against Spain, while the Guises remained loyal to their old idea of friendship with the Hapsburgs. Charles IX determined to be independent of his mother for once, and began to turn to Coligny for advice. This, of course, was a cardinal sin in the eyes of such a possessive mother. She must get rid of Coligny. To her cynical mind, any method would suffice. She may, although it is improbable, have poisoned Jeanne d'Albret, the Huguenot widow of Anthony of Navarre, at this time. Certainly she made plans to dispose of Coligny, and, on 22 August 1572, the Calvinist leader was wounded in an attempted assassination. But he did not die. Charles remained loyal to his friend; and, possibly in desperation, Catherine decided to set in train a plan which culminated in the infamous massacre of St. Bartholomew (24 August 1572).

She managed to persuade the King that here, with all the Huguenot leaders in Paris for the marriage of Margaret and Henry, was an opportunity never to be missed. She told him of her responsibility for the attempted assassination of Coligny, and, frightened by Catherine's prophecies of what might occur, the King gave orders for the murder of all the Huguenots in Paris. Henry of Guise murdered Coligny, and something like 10,000 Protestants were murdered in the capital and the Provinces. The killers wore white arm-bands to safeguard themselves from massacre; and the Seine and other rivers became choked with Huguenot corpses. In Paris, only Henry of Navarre and Henry, Prince of Condé, were permitted to survive. Catherine must bear the responsibility for the events, although it seems certain that the massacre was not long premeditated. From the point of view of one who wished to destroy Calvinism, the massacre was a failure. It was a success for the Guises, for Catherine and, indeed, for Spain, now free from Coligny's threat of war. But it did not prevent a fourth religious war, when La Rochelle was besieged. The wars were to be ended, not by Catherine, but by the action of the moderate Politiques; and the struggle was still going on when Charles IX died in 1574, still filled with remorse at the dreadful events of the St. Bartholomew massacre and at the death of his friend, Coligny. Even young Henry of Navarre, to save himself, had briefly embraced catholicism.

The beginning of the second half of the sixteenth century is still within the confines of the French Renaissance. Théodore Beza, the Calvinist writer and apologist, has already been mentioned. Muret and Dorat, younger poets of the *Pléiade*, were at work, but it was still primarily an age of religious controversy, in literature as well as in political action. Montaigne was learning law and, in 1568, retiring to his château to begin the studies which were soon to bear fruit. Amyot was beginning to produce his translations of Plutarch, which were to have such an influence on Montaigne and Racine. The ordinary people of the day were being described by Noël du Fail, whose *Les Baliverneries* appeared in 1548; and the stories of Bouchet were being read. Jodelle's tragedy, *Cléopâtre captive*, was produced—the first original work of its kind in French literature—followed rapidly by La Péruse's *Médée* and the work of de la Taille and Grévin. In 1562 de la Taille wrote *Saül le furieux* on an Old Testament theme, and it was published in 1572 with a preface which discussed the rules of tragic writing. This work established a tradition of taking Biblical themes for tragedy, as well as the subjects so favoured by classical authors. Robert Garnier was producing tragic plays of poetic merit, which, like the work of other dramatists, were being produced by companies of travelling players. It is possible that plays were being produced in the first French theatre—the Hôtel de Bourgogne in Paris. The first French comedy was Jodelle's *Eugène* (1552), and others, by Grévin and Belleau, for example, followed swiftly, often based upon the Italian *commedia dell'arte*. It was the Italian actors, with their stock characters, who were to have a great influence upon the French theatre, and who eventually, were to produce plays in the Hôtel de Bourgogne and to become part of the Opéra-Comique.

In poetry, this was the age of the Pléiade—Ronsard, de Baïf, Dorat, Belleau, Jodelle and du Bellay. Between them, they developed new poetic ideas, linked poetry with humanism and classical writing, and wrote lyric verse, chiefly in sonnet form. Their leader was Ronsard, whose pastoral *Amours* appeared in 1556, while his *Sonnets pour Hélène* were produced before 1578. His friend was du Bellay, the first great French sonneteer, who died in 1560. These men were indicative of the survival and development of literature in France at a time when religious and political conflict were as bitter as at almost any other point in history.

### RECOMMENDED READING

*Catherine dei Medici and the French Wars of Religion.* J. H. M. SALMON. *History Today*, Vol. VI, No. 5, pp. 297 (May, 1956).
*Europe in the Sixteenth Century, 1494–1598.* A. H. JOHNSON. Chapter IX, pp. 387–448. Rivingtons.
*The Age of Catherine de Medici.* J. E. NEALE. Jonathan Cape, 1943.
*The Wars of Religion in France, 1559–1576.* J. W. THOMPSON. Constable, 1958.

## CHAPTER 7

# *The End of the Valois Line, and the Reign of Henry IV*

WHEN Charles IX died in 1574, his brother of Anjou was not in France. The previous year, the ambitious Catherine had secured his election as King of Poland, and he was in that country, rather against his will. Now it was time for him to return to France, to take the throne; but during his absence Catherine assumed the Regency again. The moderates, the Politiques, wanted to destroy her power and influence, and she was very conscious of this threat. Above all, they wanted to gain the adherence of another of her sons, the Duke of Alençon, who, jealous of her domination and of his elder brother, besides being a friend of the late Admiral Coligny, was only too willing to escape from her and to join these men. Catherine learned of a plot to achieve his departure from court, and struck out immediately. She imprisoned him, along with Francis de Montmorency; and so created a very difficult situation for Henry III on his eventual arrival in France. It was unfortunate for Catherine that, when Montmorency was caught, his brother Damville was not; for the latter was an intelligent and successful leader of the Politiques. He promptly joined the Huguenots, and, using his position as Governor of the Languedoc, set up a more or less independent state in the south of France, claiming to owe allegiance to Condé, who was safely away in Germany at the time.

Damville was, therefore, a dangerous man, with sufficient power to withstand Henry III, and able, it seemed, to divide France into two, for his word was law south of the River Loire.

Henry III's finances were non-existent, and Catherine discovered that none of the financiers of Lyons, Venice or Florence would dare to advance money on the credit of the King of France. As there was no money to pay the royal army, and as Alençon, who had escaped, and Henry of Navarre both managed to join the rebels in the south, the new King had no choice but to give way to the inevitable. With a threatened invasion of France by Condé facing him as well, Henry made terms by the Peace of Monsieur in 1576. He had to express his sorrow at the events of the Massacre of St. Bartholomew, and religious freedom was awarded to the Huguenots, except in Paris itself. Eight towns, *Places de sûreté*, were given to them, and Condé was bought by being given the Governorship of Picardy. Once more, a policy of appeasement was being tried; and appeasement was a sign of the political and financial weakness of the monarch. It might have worked if Henry had been a strong monarch, but this he could lay no claim to be. In character, perhaps, he was something like King John of England. On some occasions he would be energetic, on others, slack. He would have fits of macabre religious enthusiasm, followed by weeks when the pursuit of pleasure was all his interest. Of all Catherine's sons, he was the favourite; but he was also the one whom she could not always control, and of whom she was sometimes afraid. He filled his court with his favourite companions, dandies, "Princes of Sodom", who were his *mignons*, completely dependent upon him. Later, he developed a passion for poodles, and was surrounded by scores of them. At the same time, there were occasions when he showed determination and ability; but he could never keep it up. Sustained resolution was not his strong point.

The danger of a weak and bankrupt monarch being on the throne was shown when, once again, two parties began to emerge, threatening to destroy France and the Valois monarchy. A Catholic League was re-formed, led by Henry of Guise, one of whose ambitions was to take the throne for himself. The King could not control it, and so he joined it, but his military strength, although augmented by the forces of the League, was incapable of defeating the Huguenots sufficiently thoroughly to solve the religious problem once and for all. The Protestants were beaten, however, and their religious liberties were curtailed by the Peace of Bergerac and the Edict of Poitiers of 1577. But they regarded this as a temporary setback only. They were determined to secure a more favourable situation than this, and the struggle went on, if somewhat fitfully. A leader like Coligny was what the Huguenots badly needed. Alençon, who was now the Duke of Anjou, was unfitted for the task, and, in any case, he was more concerned with wooing Elizabeth of England to further his ambitions.

While he was in England, being called "my frog" by the masterful Queen, Guise was paying court in a different way and in a different place. He was becoming the agent of Philip II of Spain, accepting Spanish money and generally learning the role of traitor. It appears that he had the idea, not only of using Philip's money to restore France to the Catholic faith with himself as King, but also of installing his friend, Don John of Austria, as King of England, Scotland and the Netherlands. His chimerical plans came to nothing. Philip did not trust Guise as far as the latter thought, and in any case, the death of Don John put an end to the scheme. Even Guise's own party could not feel completely confident of one whose Spanish alliance was suspected of treachery.

With the death of Alençon (Anjou) in 1584, the situation changed again, for Henry of Navarre, a known Protestant, was now heir-presumptive. He had escaped from Catherine's control in 1576, under which he had been since the St. Bartholomew massacre, and had gone to La Rochelle. As heir-apparent, he could hope to unite the Huguenots and Politiques, and this fact, along with the prospect of a heretic being seated one day on the French throne, roused the Catholics. What they needed was a rival candidate for the throne, and they produced one, not in Guise himself, but in the Cardinal Bourbon, possibly because of the general suspicions of the motives of Guise. The Catholic leader, however, had not renounced his ambitions. He had hoped to lead the attack on England on Philip II's behalf, but, when this proved to be impossible, he led the Catholic demand for the acceptance of the Cardinal as heir-presumptive. Something had to be done to placate the Catholics, and so Catherine stepped into the picture again. She announced the Treaty of Nemours, by which drastic penalties were to be exacted of the Huguenots. Once again, the King was to spike Guise's guns by appearing to be the leader of the Catholic cause.

The result of this decision was the War of the Three Henries. It was clear that the King did not want the Catholic cause to triumph, for this would mean a victory for Guise. Catherine spent some of her energies trying to persuade Navarre to accept the Catholic faith. She, too, had no wish to see a Guise triumph. Her blandishments failed. In the fighting, Navarre won a victory at Coutras in 1587, but Guise won a counter-balancing battle, the effect of which was ruined when Henry III decided to make terms with the rebels. But by this time, it was becoming clear that Henry III mattered less, in the struggle for power in France, than did Henry of Navarre and Henry of Guise. The latter had begun to act almost as independently as any monarch. For political and religious reasons, he was prepared to aggravate the Catholic sympathies of the citizens of Paris against the King. Henry III was accused of treachery to his faith and to his subjects, not only by Guise but by the latter's sister, Madame de Montpensier. A rebellion against the King was fostered and encouraged, and it was timed to coincide with the attack of the Spanish Armada on the shores of Britain. There was to be a double Catholic triumph, and Guise, disobeying the King's orders to stay away from Paris, deliberately rode into the city. The people were triumphant. The propaganda of Madame de Montpensier had been effective, and the citizens were ready for the Day of Barricades. The King was furious at this threat to his power in his own palace, and Guise might well have been killed on the spot, had it not been for the intervention of Catherine de' Medici. The Catholic leader appeared again next day at court, with hundreds of supporters. It was clear that he was meditating

a *coup d'état*, and that Henry's life was not safe. The King, therefore, escaped to Chartres, and Guise, his plans having gone
awry, reverted to his original scheme of getting the Cardinal
declared heir-apparent.

This the last of the Valois agreed to, in the Edict of Union of
July 1588. But the King was determined to regain his lost
powers, and, when he found no support even from the States
General called at Blois, he planned individual action, without
even consulting his mother. It was made considerably easier for
him, when the news arrived of the defeat of the Armada. Philip
was in no position to protect his ally, Guise, at that point.
Henry made his arrangements, and, on the pretext of a royal
council, called Guise into his room at Blois. It was the signal for
assassination. The Cardinal Louis of Guise was also murdered on
the following day. Catherine was shocked by the proceedings—
perhaps because she could foresee that the King had gone too
far, perhaps because she had not been asked for her opinion. In
any case, she was dying.

Henry III thought that his problems were over; "Enfin, je
suis roi", he is reported to have said. But he was no longer
regarded as King in Paris. The people openly called him a
murderer. There were public celebrations at the christening of
Guise's posthumous son. The Pope declared the King excom-
municate, and the theologians of the University of Paris stated
their view that no Frenchman need feel bound to obey the King.
Guise's brother was openly in rebellion against the crown. It was
clear that Henry must appeal for the support of the Huguenots.
This Navarre was prepared to give, and the two men met at
Plessis. Having agreed to besiege Paris, the attack was set on
foot, but the end had come for the Valois. The King of France
was assassinated by a friar, Jacques Clément. It was the end of a
dynasty, and the end of the France of Catherine de' Medici. It
was the occasion for the accession of a Protestant King. But the
religious wars and the statecraft of Catherine had sadly injured
France. The monarchy was bankrupt, the state knew no economic
progress at a time when other countries were making rapid

strides in this direction, and the rule of the Queen Mother had left a ruined country for Henry IV to attempt to govern.

Henry IV, the grandson of Margaret d'Angoulême, and the son of Anthony of Bourbon and the Calvinist, Jeanne d'Albret, had been born in Béarn in 1553. His life story has been interpreted in many ways by historians; on the one hand he appears as the man to whom Paris was worth a Mass, the man to whom principle mattered far less than the expediency of the moment: on the other he is the hero-King, the chivalrous Gascon wit. To the men of his time, he appeared in varying guises. To the Protestants, he was a traitor to their cause. To the Catholics, he was an insincere convert to their faith. To the Politiques, he was a King who was prepared to be reasonable, to rebuild a united France against the threat of Spanish ambitions. Later historians have seen him as a despot, as a patriot, or even as a liberal innovator. Certainly he was an able business man, the supporter of Sully, a brave King with a knowledge of statecraft, a sympathy with the ordinary people, and a real sense of humour, who wanted every Frenchman to have a "chicken in the pot".

His father, who should have been Regent of France, ended his life fighting for the Catholics against the Huguenots, of whose party he had been a member. His mother had been a convinced Protestant, which explains why Catherine de' Medici had kept the young prince at her own court. As a young man, he had eventually escaped, and had joined Coligny, along with the son of Louis of Condé. It was part of Catherine's plan to make terms with the Protestants which had been the cause of Henry's marriage to her daughter, Margaret, the celebrations of which had been the occasion of the St. Bartholomew massacre. This marriage, however, was never successful. Henry left Margaret when he rejoined the rebellious Huguenots in 1576, and eventually divorced her in 1599. During those years of Medici domination, he had learned wisdom. He had criticized his fellow Protestants who suggested forming independent Huguenot districts on the Swiss model, and he had supported Damville, the moderate Politique who governed the Languedoc. Despite his protestantism, he realized, perhaps, that catholicism could never be replaced as the faith of most Frenchmen, and that, in any case, questions of religion could never be settled by war. Admittedly, Henry was an able soldier; but reason and diplomacy were, in his eyes, the better weapons.

He had become the heir to the throne on the death of Alençon in 1584, but he knew that his rights to the throne would never be willingly accepted by the Catholics. In fact, in the following year, he was excommunicated by Pope Sixtus V; but he published a most moderate claim to the throne on the grounds of hereditary right, which excited the sympathy of those moderate Catholics who knew Henry and his patriotism. Many Frenchmen were as tired of the foolish and effeminate Valois kings as they were of the religious wars, the rule of Catherine and the influence of the Spanish King. To them, Henry of Navarre, a soldier and leader of men, offered the prospect of the restoration of national pride and unity. On the assassination of Henry III in 1589, Navarre claimed the throne, despite the undisguised threats of Philip of Spain, who hoped to marry the Infanta to a French prince, and the claims to the title which were hopefully put forward by the Prince of Savoy and the Duke of Mercœur.

The attitude of the Papacy was, of course, significant; and although Sixtus V had no liking for the Bourbon Protestant, he hoped that Henry might see the political advantages of being converted again to catholicism. His successor, Clement VIII, who feared that the French Church might go the way of the English one, was also only too willing to persuade Henry to accept catholicism. The new King did not want to incur the enmity of his Protestant allies, for, as yet, he could hope for little support from the French Catholics. Indeed, the Catholic League, the people of Paris, and the forces of Spain were all ranged against him, and he could expect help only from the Huguenots and from Damville. Henry also had the advantage, which might only be temporary, that the French Catholics were not united, and that he had their candidate for the throne, the Cardinal Charles of Bourbon, a prisoner. In Paris, the Council of Sixteen, dominated by the more fanatical Roman priests, were ruling. Outside it, the Catholics were led by Henry of Guise's brother, Charles of Mayenne, who disliked the prospect of Spanish domination as much as did any other Frenchman.

In the fighting which followed, Mayenne was beaten in battle at Arques in 1589, and Henry followed this with a splendid victory at Ivry in March 1590. Mayenne's army was much larger, and the day seemed lost, until Henry dashed into the thick of the battle, crying, "Rally round my white plume". He then set about the siege of Paris, which lasted long enough to reduce the inhabitants to complete starvation. However, his army was too small to hope to capture the city, and when the Duke of Parma sent a force from the Netherlands, Henry withdrew his troops, while the Parisians brought in supplies of food and were strengthened by Spanish forces, which regarrisoned the city. Life was still most unpleasant, however, within its walls. The Council of Sixteen instituted a Reign of Terror under the leadership of Bussy Leclerc, against all who were suspected of Politique opinions. Members of the Parlement of Paris were proscribed, and the ambitions of the Council became so great that Mayenne had to step in and hang some of them, *pour encourager les autres*.

The war went on, still. Henry was defeated by Parma at Aumâle in 1592, but the latter died of a wound received in the fighting there, and Henry was freed from the worry of Parma's presence in France—an important fact, for the Spaniard was a better soldier than Navarre. In 1593 Mayenne decided to call the States General to sound public opinion on the question of the succession to the throne, and Henry decided to make an appeal to the patriotic sentiments of France. He let it be known that he was contemplating a return to the Catholic faith, just at a time when more and more moderates were conscious of a growing resentment of Spanish influence in France. Their feelings could be seen in the publication of the *Satyre Menipée*, and, while the powers and the influence of the ultra-Catholics declined, negotiations went on which culminated in a temporary peace for a few months at the end of 1593, and Henry's public conversion to the Catholic faith at a ceremony in Saint-Denis Cathedral in July of that year. The moderate forces managed to end the Terror of the Sixteen in Paris, and Henry led his forces into the city in March of 1594, while the foreign troops were permitted to withdraw.

The policy then adopted by the King was indicative of his keen desire to establish peace. He wanted to prevent the Guise faction from continuing the struggle, and was willing to forget the activities of the Council of Sixteen, Madame de Montpensier, and his other rivals. He wanted them to unite in opposition to the national enemy, Spain, against which country he declared war in 1595. Unfortunately, the Guise party in the provinces had to be bribed and persuaded to give up their hopes, while Henry began a campaign against the Spaniards. This had considerable success at first, culminating in the victory of Fontaine-Française; but Henry's strength, as yet, was insufficient to win a long-drawn-out war with a great power. He managed to get Mayenne to come to terms with him at home, but it was not until 1598 that he managed to pacify the last of his Guise opponents—Mercœur. Meanwhile, he made an alliance with Elizabeth I by the Treaty of Greenwich, but lost Amiens to the Spanish forces. Eventually, as both he and Philip saw the need for peace, Henry made the Treaty of Vervins. This was followed very soon by the famous Edict of Nantes of 1698, which ended the religious wars of the sixteenth century by giving toleration to the Calvinists, who were awarded also certain guarantees, including the control of certain great towns, and separate representation in the French *parlements*. These were councils of lawyers in each province, on which the Huguenots obtained representation. There were several Huguenot judges on the chief benches, and thus unfair verdicts caused by religious bias were less likely.

Henry could now devote his attention to giving good order and government to his kingdom. His victory had been made possible, partly by his own abilities and partly because moderate Catholics were prepared to put the nation before the absolute maintenance of their religion; the separatism of the century had done nothing for France but to ruin her economy and to let the Spanish power in. Now peace was made; plainly the Huguenots did not like Henry's defection, but even they were convinced of Henry's determination to give internal peace to France. In this, he was aided by Maximilian de Béthune, Duke of Sully. With this able administrator, Henry was able to ignore the institution of the States General, and to do without the support of the *parlements*. Instead, the Conseil du Roi was revived, and its inner Conseil d'Affaires. Sully's abilities as a business man were shown in his work as Surintendant des Finances, in which office he helped to reduce the crown's fiscal deficit, to make it possible for the financiers of Europe to be willing to lend money again at reasonable rates to the King, and to clean up the corrupt system of tax gathering in France. Admittedly, it was difficult to make the burdensome *taille* fall more equitably, and to deal with the problem of exemptions, for so long purchased by the rich. Sully even increased the *gabelle*, another unfair tax; and he found it difficult to introduce free trade and more indirect taxation. But much was done to encourage commerce and agriculture, the marshlands near Bordeaux were drained, and there were many schemes for irrigation, afforestation and public works. The silk industry of Lyons was founded, and Sully's chief claim to fame is in the overhauling and cleansing of the old system of finances, rather than in the introduction of anything new. He did not agree with the ideas of Bartholomew Laffemas, the Controller General of Commerce, but these were to come to fruition later in the days of Colbert.

Henry's private life changed considerably over the years. In 1599 he divorced his first wife, Margaret of Valois; and he might have married his mistress, Gabrielle d'Estrées, had she not died in the same year. In fact, in 1600 he married Marie de' Medici and took another mistress, Henriette d'Entragues. A Dauphin was born in 1601. Henry showed his determination to keep the unity of France in the way in which he dealt with several plots against his régime. There were conspiracies led by Biron, his general; and by Bouillon, a discontented Protestant; but the King knew what was going on, and was willing to pardon offenders after a spell in prison.

In foreign affairs, Henry was always conscious of the Hapsburg power which surrounded his kingdom. This explains his interest in the affairs of Savoy and Switzerland, through whose territories Spanish troops must pass if they wished to travel direct from the Netherlands to Italy. It helps to explain why he wanted the land around the rivers Rhône and Saône, as well as for the additional protection of Lyons. It makes it clear why he negotiated a treaty with the Swiss in 1602, to gain the use of the majority of the Alpine passes for France. He wanted to make French power important in Italy again, which was seen in his support for Clement VIII in the matter of Ferrara. He supported the United Provinces in their struggle with Spain, as a matter of course; indeed, he would have liked to acquire the Spanish Netherlands, even if it had meant a marriage with the Infanta in order to accomplish this.

However, it was his dislike of the Hapsburg power which led him to a policy on which he embarked just before his death, and which, had it been continued, might have proved fatal to all that he had achieved in his reign. Partly because of the excuse of the quarrel over the question of succession to Cleve-Jülich and Berg, and partly because of a personal quarrel with the Prince of Condé, whose wife he wished to have as mistress, and who fled to Brussels, Henry determined to renew war on the Hapsburgs. He appointed Marie de' Medici as Regent, and, just on the eve of leaving Paris, went to see Sully. On the way, he was stabbed by François Ravaillac, a religious fanatic, and killed. His death prevented a full-scale war, which, if it had been begun by Henry IV, might have made a very great difference to his reputation in after years. That reputation was very high, especially, perhaps surprisingly, in Paris, where he had been responsible for the Pont Neuf, the Place Dauphine, and the Place Royale. After his death, he became and remained the most popular of French Kings—which he certainly was not during his lifetime. His Vert Galant statue remained undestroyed throughout the Revolution of 1789.

The period is one of specific interest to the student of French literature. In the 1580's Montaigne produced his experiments, his *Essais*, discussing the ideas of other writers and comparing them with his own philosophy, and thus becoming the father of a literary genre. Jean Bodin produced some political ideas— mostly anti-Macchiavellian—in the *Six livres de la République* in 1576. Literary historians are concerned with the first work of its kind, on that subject, by Etienne Pasquier, while those who want a colourful, if inaccurate, account of court intrigues in the sixteenth century must go to Brantôme's *Mémoires*. Among the earliest French novels, recognizable as such, were the works of de Verville, especially his *Les Aventures de Floride*; but more interesting developments were to be seen in d'Urfé's *L'Astrée*, published in parts from 1607 onwards, on the themes of love.

Garnier's tragedy, *Antigone*, published in 1580, was of considerable influence, not only on French, but also on English writers; and in the field of poetry, Ronsard was followed by the much less important Philippe Desportes. However, work of better quality was coming from de Sponde and de la Ceppède. Their contemporary, du Bartas, was not so highly regarded in France, perhaps because of his Protestantism, but he may have had a considerable influence on Milton. In a period when the growth of protestantism and its effects on France were so important, one must notice Agrippa d'Aubigné, a personal friend of Henry IV and a staunch Huguenot. Ironically, he was to be the grandfather of Louis XIV's Madame de Maintenon, who was to play such an important part in the revocation of the Edict of Nantes. D'Aubigné's *Les Tragiques* is the great work of the Huguenot minority in the field of literature; among other things, it takes the wars of religion as its theme. So does the same author's *Histoire Universelle*, and, if protestantism had grown in France as it did in England, his literary influence might have been as great as that of Milton. Desportes was followed, as court poet, by the much more significant figure of Malherbe. His odes on ceremonial occasions and rigid, dignified, religious verses were not so important, though, as his reputation as a teacher. His "Classical" rulings on literary matters influenced French writing for a long time. Perhaps more notice should be taken of his contemporaries, Régnier, the satirist, and de la Fresnaye.

## RECOMMENDED READING

*Henri of Navarre: the Conclusion of the French Wars of Religion.* J. H. M. SALMON. *History Today,* Vol. VI, No. 6, p. 387 (June 1956).

*The Huguenots: a Study of Minority.* J. B. MORRALL. Part One—*History Today,* Vol. XI, No. 3, p. 191 (March 1961).

Part Two—*History Today,* Vol. XI, No. 4, p. 271 (April 1961) (covering events in the seventeenth century and onwards).

*The Ascendancy of France, 1598–1715.* H. O. WAKEMAN. Rivingtons, 1936, pp. 14–38.

*The French Wars of Religion: Their Political Aspects.* E. ARMSTRONG. Blackwell, 1904.

# CHAPTER 8

## *France under Marie de' Medici, and the Creation of French Power by Richelieu*

WHEN Henry IV was assassinated in 1610, the fortunes of France took a severe turn for the worse. All his policies were abandoned under the regency of his widow, who ruled on behalf of her son, Louis XIII, who came to the throne as an 8-year-old boy. Marie de' Medici had never taken a part in the government of the country while her husband had lived, and she had no sympathy with his ideas, or with his minister, Sully. Her career naturally draws comparisons with that of her predecessor, Catherine de' Medici, a distant cousin; but there is little that one can say in Marie's favour. Admittedly, she was married to Henry because of the vast indebtedness of the French monarchy to the Florentine bankers, and she had had to bring up her six children along with half a dozen of her husband's illegitimate offspring. But she had no idea of statecraft, she wasted money on a grand scale, and she reversed completely Henry's anti-Hapsburg plans without a thought of their value to France.

Very soon, Sully lost all his power and influence, which went to the adventurer Concini, the Italian husband of Marie's confidante, Leonora Galigaï. Between them, Marie and Concini bribed those members of the royal family who might cause trouble—men like Condé and Soissons. Henry IV's alliance with Savoy was forgotten, and negotiations began with Spain, to end the war and to create a Hapsburg–Bourbon marriage alliance. This was too much for Sully, who resigned; the extreme Catholics saw that fortune had turned in their favour, and the Huguenots,

78

fearful of the future, prepared for a renewal of trouble, electing Sully's son-in-law, Rohan, as their leader. In fact, this was a period of which the Catholics of France should be proud, for it

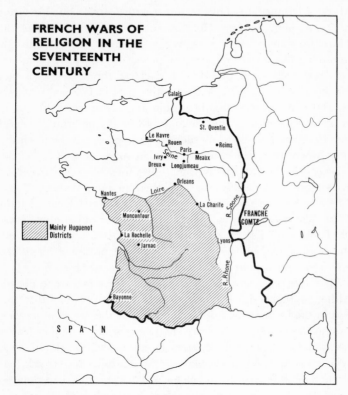

MAP 4

was the time of men like Cardinal de la Rochefoucauld, Cardinal Bérulle, who founded the Oratorians; St. Vincent de Paul, missioner to the sick, the poor, and galley slaves; and of François de Sales, the author of the important and influential *Introduction à la vie dévote*.

However, even the Catholics might have been suspicious, to say the least, of a sudden intimation of the adoption of a pro-Spanish foreign policy, and so the negotiations over a marriage alliance were kept secret. Knowing that she would need allies, Marie attempted to come to terms with Condé; but his terms were too high for her. He was not as powerful, perhaps, as Marie imagined; but she was prepared to make some concessions in order to maintain her grasp of power, a grasp that remained very real even when, in 1614, she declared the King was of age. She encouraged him to take no active part in political matters; all that mattered was that he should amuse himself. In the same year, partly owing to the demands of Condé, the States General met in Paris. There was no thought of co-operation between the rival interests in the assembly, which made it simple for the Queen Mother to make vague promises on their *cahiers* of grievances and suggestions, and then to send them packing. There was to be no other assembly of the States General until 1789. There was no other possibility of public opinion declaring itself, short of riots or revolution, for the *Parlement* was merely the council of Paris lawyers, and when it protested about the changed foreign policy, was told to mind its own business.

In 1615 the plans for the Spanish marriage went ahead. Although Marie did her best to persuade the princes that this was in the best interests of France, even to the extent of making Condé the Governor of Berry, it was clear that opinion feared the possible extension of Spanish influence. Condé, indeed, rebelled and was imprisoned in the Bastille. It seemed that France might return to the chaos which Henry IV had done so much to clear. Marie was incapable, it seemed, of discerning the problems her policy would create. For example, Henry IV's ally, Charles Emmanuel of Savoy, despairing of the new French attitude to Spain, made an alliance with Venice, which could prove to be dangerous to French interests. A good deal of un-popularity was attached to Concini, now the Maréchal d'Ancre; his reckless extravagance was unlikely to endear him to the moderates and patriots. Even if part of his ambition was for his adopted country, which seems unlikely, no tears were shed, except by his wife and by Marie, when he was assassinated in April 1617. The event occurred because of the jealousy felt by the young King's new favourite, Luynes, the King's falconer, who persuaded Louis to give orders that Concini should be shot. Within weeks, Concini's wife was burned for embezzlement of public funds and sorcery. Luynes was in power, and Marie realized that her hey-day was over. The King was now to be reckoned with, and he was always to be an uncertain factor for the rest of his life.

Luynes was as well hated by the nobility as Concini had been, even though he did call an assembly of Notables to discuss such reforms as the abolition of the *paulette*. Many decided that their best plan was to leave court, and even Marie, under surveillance at Blois, escaped and joined those who decided to rebel against the new régime. She was taken prisoner eventually, and terms were made with the rebels after their defeat at Ponts de Cé in 1618, but it was not long before she recaptured some of her old influence over her son. The foreign situation was something which Luynes, a mere intriguer, could not grasp. On the death of the Emperor, there was trouble in Germany. The two religious groups were represented by the Catholic Archduke Ferdinand and the Protestant Frederick, Elector Palatine. On the election of Ferdinand, Luynes made a useless intervention in the Treaty of Ulm, which attempted to make peace between the Catholics and Protestants in the Empire, except those of Austria and Bohemia. This tacit approval of the struggle between these two was, in reality, of great assistance to the Hapsburg power; and when Frederick, now King of Bohemia, led a Protestant army against the Catholics in 1621, he was utterly defeated because of a lack of allies. The Thirty Years' War had become inevitable, partly owing to the stupidity of Luynes. He was no more successful at home, when trouble broke out with the Huguenots over the restoration of catholicism in Béarn; and it was in a campaign against them that Luynes was killed outside Montauban in 1621.

The loss of his adviser resulted in a temporary return to favour of the King's mother, and of the appointment as chief minister of the equally useless Sillery. Condé, newly converted to catholicism, also found favour; and it was partly his responsibility that war against the Huguenots was continued. Their defeat resulted in the Treaty of Montpellier, by which they were left with only two fortified towns—Montauban and La Rochelle. Sillery was replaced by La Vieuville, whose only claim to fame is that he introduced Richelieu into the Royal Council in April 1624. Armand-Jean du Plessis, born in 1585, a member of a poor but aristocratic family from Poitou, and whose father had been Grand Prévôt at court and a *politique*, had given up the idea of being a soldier in order to inherit the family's church preferments. He became Bishop of Luçon in 1607, and became a friend of the founder of Jansenism, the Abbé de Saint-Cyran, and also of the Capucin, Father Joseph, who, in after years, was his adviser in many matters. He deliberately set himself to gain political promotion, first under Henry IV and then under Marie's regency, by good service, flattery or any other weapon which lay to hand. These arts of the statesman succeeded, eventually, in gaining him a post as Secretary of State under the regency, although it seemed that he might lose all his powers when Luynes got rid of all those who had supported Concini.

However, he emerged as the mediator between the supporters of Luynes and their opponents, was given the title of Cardinal in 1622, when aged only 37, and became the darling of the Catholic party, the *dévots*. Richelieu became a member of the Council and undermined La Vieuville's authority, demanding pre-eminence over the others because of his position of Cardinal. The King had been somewhat doubtful as to the wisdom of giving him power, but it was not long before Richelieu had made himself indispensable, not only as the royal minister, but as the leader of the anti-Hapsburg party. The foreign policy of France was to revert to what it had been under Henry IV. Richelieu's determination to face the Hapsburg power, and to make international esteem and power the main aim of the government, meant that he had to be subtle, and to ensure that internal religious problems were to be dealt with effectively. In his own words, he said that he would destroy the Huguenots, destroy the pride of the great, compel all Frenchmen to serve the King, and to make the name of the King great in Europe.

In achieving these ends, Richelieu was preparing the way for the government by an absolute despot which France was to see in the reign of Louis XIV. There were to be no great nobles ruling as governors in the provinces, ready at any time to be a threat to the royal power. In fact, the aristocracy of France was to lose most of its political power, even though it retained its social privileges. The Huguenots lost their power, too, not merely because they were a religious minority, or because Richelieu detested their faith, but because they were a political nuisance, a threat to the unity of France. And such a unity was necessary if Richelieu was to make France able to make a stand against the Hapsburgs. To the Cardinal, political motives were more significant than religious ones, and his attitudes were to decide the form of French policy for decades. Attitudes were, perhaps, more important than administrative actions, for he was not greatly concerned with the detail of government.

Once Richelieu was in power, his commanding position was but rarely threatened. The only person who might have succeeded in displacing him was Marie de' Medici; and, although she attempted it, she never succeeded. Although she badly wanted to regain the power she had lost, her apparent determination to destroy the royal power out of personal selfishness was sufficient to ensure that Richelieu, the man to whom the royal power was everything, should withstand her. For example, in 1630 Marie de' Medici tried to get the King to agree to the dismissal of the Cardinal, who promptly offered to resign; this so distressed Louis that Richelieu was promptly confirmed in office as *premier ministre*. Within a few months, Marie renewed her effort to get the dismissal of her former servant. Again there was a threat of resignation—indeed, Richelieu thought that his career had ended, and Marie and her friends were openly rejoicing—

but Louis, thinking the matter over, sent for the Cardinal again. This was the celebrated occasion of the Day of Dupes.

On Richelieu's accession to power, the Catholic forces in the Thirty Years' War, led by Tilly and Maximilian of Bavaria, were triumphant. Richelieu was determined to stop the revival of the Austrian Hapsburgs, led by the Emperor Ferdinand II, and to do this he was even willing to sacrifice Catholic victory in the Empire. First, he decided to try to cut the communication lines between these Hapsburgs and Spain. The most important link in these lines was the district of the Valtelline, connecting Milan with the Tyrol. The Catholic Valtellinois were nominally under the suzerainty of the Protestant Grey Leagues. Using the religious problem as an excuse, Richelieu made an alliance with the Grisons League and Venice, to subdue the Valtellinois and, incidentally, to expel the Spanish forces who had got into the district owing to the stupidity of Luynes. For a time, the policy was successful; the valley was taken by Richelieu's troops, but the Spaniards persuaded the Huguenots to cause trouble in France, a Protestant revolt began in the Languedoc, and the Cardinal had to turn his attention to this threat. The Huguenots were defeated, but Richelieu had to come to terms with Spain over the Valtelline. He had lost control of this important link, and he was determined that the political independence of the Huguenots should not interfere with his policies again. The French Protestants had no allies. Spain had, of course, defaulted, when Richelieu had signed a treaty with her. On the other hand, the Protestants were as annoyed as many Catholic patriots that the Cardinal had made peace with the Hapsburgs. At first, it seemed that Richelieu was being too gentle with the Huguenots, too, and so a plot took shape, led by Gaston of Orléans, Louis XIII's brother. Richelieu dealt with this danger rapidly, and turned to deal with the Protestant mischief again. He began to besiege the Huguenots in La Rochelle, and by this time they had obtained some foreign support. This came from England, whose small force was led by Buckingham, and which besieged the royal forts outside the Huguenot stronghold. Richelieu's determination to take La Rochelle was equalled by Buckingham's incompetence, and the Protestants surrendered in October 1628, but only after a desperate fourteen-month defence had reduced them to eating rats and boot leather.

Richelieu's strength was greater than ever. He had become minister of navigation and commerce, as well as being chief minister, and the old posts of Constable and Admiral, which had been held by unreliable princes of the royal blood in the past, were abolished. But the Hapsburg problem remained, and when Mantua and Montferrat were inherited by the French Duke of Nevers, an excuse for war was presented yet again to the Spaniards. Louis took a force to attack Turin, which succeeded in detaching Savoy from the Spanish cause, and Richelieu set up an anti-Spanish Italian League, another example of his policy of checks and balances in foreign affairs. But he had not forgotten that the Huguenot menace to political solidarity remained. The King commanded a force which took the Protestant stronghold of Privas in the valley of the Rhône, and the Paix de Grâce of 1629 provided Richelieu's final settlement of the problem. Rohan had surrendered; there were to be no more Protestant *places de sureté*; and yet the Huguenots were to be allowed religious toleration so long as they gave no trouble to the government. Richelieu, although a cardinal, was no persecuting tyrant.

The Italian question was still in hand. Charles Emmanuel of Savoy joined with the Spaniards again, and a force under Spinola attacked Casale, while Mantua was besieged. Richelieu saw that Savoy might be more easily dealt with than Spain. A French force took Pignerolo, partly because of its strategic significance, with the Imperial forces holding the Valtelline. However, the death of Charles Emmanuel in 1630, and the transference of power to the Duchess Christina, enabled a truce to be made, while Richelieu turned to the question of intervention in the Thirty Years' War. While Maximilian and Tilly had been enjoying victory, Ferdinand II had seemed to be an unimportant member of the Catholic side. However, he had taken Wallenstein into his service in 1624, empowered to recruit and finance his own army. Wallenstein's military successes, of course, were likely to create a strong Hapsburg dominion, and this was the reason for Richelieu's decision to take a more active part in German affairs. The collapse of opposition to the Catholic forces in Germany also caused concern to Gustavus Adolphus of Sweden. Richelieu determined to support the Swedes, and at the same time he sent an embassy to the Diet of Ratisbon, which had met to elect Ferdinand's son as King of the Romans. The Diet concerned itself with other matters, one of which was the dismissal of Wallenstein, and, perhaps because of Father Joseph's diplomacy, an alliance between France and Maximilian of Bavaria, and an Italian settlement which was of considerable benefit to Richelieu's plans.

The Imperial forces left Grisons, and all conquests were restored. At the same time, a treaty with Savoy obtained for France La Perosa and Pignerolo. Richelieu's triumph over the interests of Ferdinand can only be explained by the Emperor's concern at the intervention of Gustavus Adolphus, who had made an agreement with the Cardinal at the Treaty of Bärwalde in 1631. The same year saw the departure of Marie de' Medici; discovered plotting again, she was sent to Compiègne. Escaping from custody there, she went to Flanders and was never allowed back on French territory. Her pernicious influence on Louis XIII was over. Richelieu's power grew even stronger with the departure of Guise, the execution of Montmorency for raising a rebellion and the capture and incarceration of Gaston for plotting against Louis with Charles IV of Lorraine.

Prospects in Germany were now brighter for the anti-Hapsburg allies. The Rhineland princes were mustered on Richelieu's side, while Gustavus had had an important success against Tilly at the battle of Breitenfeld. However, Richelieu was concerned that Gustavus should devote his activities to fighting only the Emperor's forces, and he was furious when the Swedish King turned to the Rhine valley instead of making an attack on Vienna. It did not ease the situation when Gustavus offered France Flanders, Lorraine and Alsace, for the Cardinal knew that he must court

Catholic opinion, which would scarcely approve of these gifts from the Protestant. However, events were moving fast. Trèves and Lorraine made an alliance with France, Gustavus turned away from the Rhine valley to attack Bavaria, and killed Tilly at the passage of the Lech. He entered Munich, and the Catholics had no alternative but to recall their best soldier, Wallenstein, who took Lützen on the Elbe, and there met Gustavus in battle. The Swedish King was killed, and the balance of power in Germany was restored. The Empire was saved—but Richelieu's embarrassing ally was no more. The Swedes were defeated at Nördlingen in 1634, and Wallenstein, tempted to turn traitor to the Emperor by Richelieu, was assassinated.

But the war was not over. Spain was still fighting the Dutch, and Richelieu, seeing this as a threat to the frontiers of France, took Lorraine—inevitably coming into conflict with the Emperor. War was declared on Spain in 1635, although war was not officially declared on the Emperor until 1638. It was fortunate that the Swedes were still present in Germany, and still a considerable menace to the Imperial forces, for the French army proved to be of little value. Its 150,000 men were sadly lacking in experience and organization. In fact, it was not until Richelieu was dead, and the command of the French forces had passed to Condé and the young Turenne, that the French began to have any real successes. In the early years of French intervention, Richelieu learned what failure meant. In 1637 the Valtelline was given up; the Spaniards were victorious in the Pyrenees; Spanish forces entered north-eastern France and took Corbie; only the determination of Louis XIII prevented a large-scale evacuation of Paris. So great was the threat to Richelieu's prestige that rebellion was likely in some of the provinces.

Luckily, things began to change in 1638. An Imperial army was defeated at Rheinfelden by Bernard of Saxe-Weimar, commander of the Protestant Swedish mercenaries after the death of Gustavus, and Turenne had his first success against Charles of Lorraine. Richelieu's position seemed stronger, too, with the birth of a Dauphin, despite the death of his counsellor, Father

Joseph, who might have succeeded the Cardinal had he lived. The Capucin was replaced by Mazarin, an Italian confidential secretary, whom Richelieu had trained to take over all his policies, and who was to be the next in the line of the great ministers of the *ancien régime*. In 1639 the Spanish forces at sea were defeated by the Dutch under van Tromp, and the death of Bernard was of service to France because his mercenary army went over to the service of Louis XIII. In 1640 the Spanish forces were pushed out of Piedmont, and Turin was taken; and within a year, a revolt in Spain made it easier for the French to push on and to take Roussillon. The Swedes also were having some success, and threatening Vienna. Just as the fortunes of France were beginning to look more promising, Richelieu died. Within a few months, in 1643, Louis XIII followed him to the grave. But the international situation showed how important France had become. Lorraine, Alsace and Roussillon were French. Savoy was dependent on France, and the Spanish power was not overwhelming as it had been thirty years before.

Richelieu had achieved what he had set out to do, giving France defensible boundaries, although in doing so he had laid the foundations of the absolute despotism which was to be the feature of French government for the next century and a half. His ambitions for France and the monarchy had quadrupled the still inequitable taxes. With all his great ability, he had done little for trade, commercial sea power and the colonization which was to make France's near neighbour, England, so much the greater power in the end. Even the *Cent Associés*, which had been given a charter to found a colony in Canada in 1628, never came to very much. However, he had struck a severe blow at the powers of the nobles; he had prudently dealt with any opposition to the centralized tyranny which he had built up within the framework of existing institutions and methods of government. He had made the crown absolute in practice, and had instituted a system of travelling *intendants*, or government agents, and spies. His success can best be seen by comparing the state of the monarchy in the time of Catherine and Marie de'

Medici with what it achieved under Louis XIV. But the importance of his creation of a central despotism, which made his name so great in the history of France, must not make us forget his importance as a patron of learning, the rebuilder of the Sorbonne, the man who persuaded Louis XIII to issue Letters Patent to the Academy and the founder of the French Navy. He has also been described as the founder of modern journalism, in his use of the *Gazette* as a means of propaganda. Politically, he may be described as a successful Wolsey; yet he never established a complete ascendancy over the King he served. His power and wealth were seen in the model town which was built to house his *entourage*, and his notable collection of antiques.

In literary matters, the early part of the seventeenth century, so significant politically, is important for the invention of a new system of philosophical reasoning by Descartes, whose *Le Discours de la Méthode* appeared in 1637. He is famous for his comment *Cogito, ergo sum*. Important also were Bishop Cornelius Jansen, whose *Augustinus* presented predestination to the Catholic mind, and whose theories were to cause raging controversy in the future; and also Jean Rotrou, du Ryer, Tristan L'Hermite, Saint-Sorlin, Saint-Evremond, and Scarron, who, among others, wrote for the famous comic actor, Jodelet. The novelist de Gomberville produced his *Polexandre* in 1637, and Sorel wrote *Le Berger extravagant*, an influential parody on *L'Astrée*. It was the time of the Marquise de Rambouillet's literary salon—her famous *chambre bleue*. She and those like her—educated and well-bred women—had a great influence on European culture, particularly as the *salon* influence was to spread to English society in the eighteenth century. Richelieu's own *Mémoires* must not be forgotten, nor his importance as a subject to French writers. But without doubt the most important figure was Corneille, the Rouen citizen whose *Le Cid* also appeared in 1637. It may be noted that this play glorified both duelling and Spain, and might have been banned by Richelieu, had he been as despotic in literary matters as in political. Corneille's first comedy, *Mélite*, appeared in 1630, and was followed by several others in

D

that decade. His tragedy, *Médée*, was performed in 1635, and *Le Cid* was followed by a series of plays on Roman themes in the 1640's. Corneille was to have a vast influence on French classical drama. It was significant, however, that French writing in the future was to be directed and disciplined by the Academy which was the brain-child of Richelieu.


## RECOMMENDED READING

*An Introduction to Seventeenth Century France.* J. LOUGH. Longmans, 1954.

*Cardinal Richelieu.* J. H. M. SALMON. *History Today*, Vol. IX, No. 10, p. 643 (October 1959).

*Marie de Medicis and her Court.* L. BATTIFOL. Chatto & Windus, 1908.

*Marie de Médicis as Queen and Regent of France.* J. H. M. SALMON. *History Today*, Vol. XIII, No. 5, p. 295 (May 1963).

*Richelieu and his Rise to Power.* C. J. BURCKHARDT. Allen & Unwin, 1940.

*Richelieu and the French Monarchy.* C. V. WEDGWOOD. English Universities Press, 1949.

*The Thirty Years War.* C. V. WEDGWOOD. Jonathan Cape, 1938.

CHAPTER 9

## Mazarin and the Years of the Fronde

BEFORE Richelieu died, he had made it clear to the King that his successor ought to be Cardinal Giulio Mazarin, a Sicilian who had been in the Papal service in Rome, Spain, and eventually in France as Papal Nuncio. He had become an intimate friend of Richelieu, who had helped him to obtain the red hat; and he had shown himself to be anti-Spanish in his sympathies. It is notable that Richelieu cared little for public opinion. He might have known that a foreign-born minister would be unpopular, and this was certainly true in the period of the *Fronde*. In fact, there was little difference in the aims and ambitions of the two cardinals, although Richelieu's patriotism compares well with Mazarin's naked opportunism and self-seeking; and there was a remarkable dissimilarity in their characters and their methods. Where Richelieu had been imperious and dominating, Mazarin was supple and pliant, a dissimulating actor. The harsh rule of the older man was replaced by the superficially easy but extremely cunning control of the Italian. Mazarin's true abilities could only be seen when men realized how he was generally the victor, the survivor, the indispensable minister; and how he maintained his authority for two decades, until his death. That a man so guilty of nepotism should survive can only be explained by his abilities, and by the close relationship which he built up with the Queen Mother, Anne of Austria.

Mazarin had another great advantage in his success in choosing and in trusting servants: men like Colbert and Le Tellier were his *protégés*. And yet Mazarin's régime was one of the strangest that France ever knew. He has been described as a *condottiere* in diplomacy, and yet he was Richelieu's chosen successor. Educated by the Jesuits and at Madrid, his enemies never quite knew how to deal with him, and he managed to maintain a stable central authority during the years of a minority which might have resulted in France returning to a state of chronic anarchy. One can only speculate about Mazarin's relationship with Anne of Austria. She was an affectionate, but not particularly attractive, woman, and there has been considerable controversy about whether she married her chief minister or not. Certainly their relationship seems to have been more than platonic, and perhaps it would seem that her real affection and marriage to the lay-cardinal is the only explanation for the influence which Mazarin was able to exercise, even when he was absent from court. Whatever the truth may be, the Cardinal was a difficult man for his contemporaries to understand or to struggle against. The Italian elegance set new standards at court; his expensive and ostentatious way of life offended the Jansenists as much as his seemingly empty foppishness puzzled his political opponents.

On the death of Louis XIII, Mazarin became a member of the short-lived Council of Regency. Shortly afterwards, he became the leading minister, and those who thought that the days of Richelieu were over, and all his policies were to be reversed, returned to court. However, the anti-Richelieu party soon found a new enemy in Mazarin, and among its leaders were the Duke of Beaufort, the Marquis de Châteauneuf and the Duchess de Chevreuse, often called the *Maréchale des Frondeuses*. This group of intriguers, the *Importants*, could have been a threat to Anne and to the safety of France; but Mazarin had the measure of them. On the other hand, there was political trouble in these years of Louis XIV's minority which was partly the result of the policies and characters of Anne and Mazarin. The Cardinal's career as *chef du conseil* opened with a continuation of the war. The French forces in Alsace were in a useful position, and there was a plan to take the Rhine territories from Basle to Mainz, which would have been a first-rate defence for Champagne and the eastern frontier. The plan necessitated the capture of Rocroi, a town which was being besieged by Spanish forces. Despite the advice of his council of war, this was done, quite brilliantly, by the 20-year-old Duke of Enghien, later to be known as the great Condé. There was a triumph for the French cavalry over the Spanish infantry, at Rocroi in May of 1643, and the news did something to establish Mazarin in power. Orders were sent to take Thionville and to establish contact with Guébriant's army, and Enghien even managed to get sufficiently far to menace the safety of the Electorate of Trèves. But just as the plan appeared to be approaching a successful conclusion, Enghien, intent upon affairs in Paris, returned to the capital. This was unfortunate in more than one sense, for it led to the death of Guébriant in the siege of Rottweil, and to a French defeat at Tuttlingen. Mazarin was now faced with the problems of military failure just at the time when he had to overcome the *Importants*, but fortunately he was able to have Beaufort, an eminent person by any standard, imprisoned in Vincennes, which gave him time to turn his attention to the war. He needed all the support that Anne could give him, for Beaufort and others had been planning to murder him; but it was just at this moment that Anne had moved into the Palais Royal, with Mazarin living next door. If a marriage occurred, it may have taken place at this time.

The command of the army was given to William the Silent's grandson, Turenne, and to Condé. Between them, they organized a campaign around Freiburg which resulted in French successes. Speyer, Mainz and Worms were occupied, while Mazarin was using his diplomatic talents to persuade the Swedes to use the subsidies which France was sending, not to quarrel with other northern powers, but to attack the enemy in Germany. The Swedish army invaded Bohemia as a result, and Vienna itself was threatened. Turenne took his forces across the Rhine, and, despite a defeat at Marienthal, went on, with Condé's help, to win the battle of Nordlingen in 1645. The other events of the war were not quite as clear cut. There were interminable sieges in the Netherlands, possibly because Mazarin was determined to gain what he could for France in that area. He may even have hoped to win the Spanish Netherlands for France; but any such ambition would have been frustrated by the Dutch to the north. In any case, the Dutch were concerned when the French took Dunkirk, and even began to negotiate with their old enemies, the Spaniards. In fact, a treaty was made between Spain and Holland in 1647, and this was something which Mazarin had not foreseen and which was a serious blow to his diplomacy.

Fortunately for Mazarin, France was more successful in other ways. In a remarkable campaign, Turenne marched down the Rhine and crossed it to join the Swedes at Friedberg, and then, by long marches, managed to get a strategical advantage over the Imperialist forces and to reach the outskirts of Munich. Maximilian, to avoid the capture of his capital, made terms by the Treaty of Ulm in 1647, and left the Emperor in the lurch. It would have been possible for Turenne to attack Vienna, had it not been for the fact that final negotiations for the end of the war were delicately poised. The approaching Treaty of Westphalia possibly prevented Turenne from winning a resounding victory. In Italy, despite the election of Innocent X as Pope, which was not what Mazarin had hoped for, Mazarin was encouraged by an anti-Spanish rebellion in Naples. The last weeks of the long struggle in Europe saw another victory for Turenne at Zusmershausen against Maximilian, who had seen fit to ignore the Treaty of Ulm once the immediate French threat had disappeared; and a victory for Condé at Lens against the Archduke Leopold. The Emperor, believing that the French strength was too much for him to overcome at this stage in the war, duly agreed to the Treaties of Westphalia, which ended the Thirty Years' War in 1648, and left France demonstrably in the ascendant—an ascendancy which was to be yet more emphasized in the Peace of the Pyrenees, in 1661.

By the terms of the Treaties of Westphalia, France was given the three Bishoprics, and Pignerolo, Breisach on the Rhine, and Alsace, which meant that the French frontier was now on the Rhine, thus fulfilling Richelieu's final aim. French ambitions were furthered still more by the Religious Peace of Augsburg of 1555, which extended religious toleration in the Empire, and gave greater independence of the Emperor to the German states. In other words, France and the Princes of the Empire had gained a considerable triumph over the Emperor. The terms of peace were a triumph for the *divide and rule* policies of Richelieu and Mazarin. The Austrian Hapsburgs had been weakened and the Spanish Hapsburgs were left without allies. France had become the arbiter of Europe, and had gained considerably in territory.

It is remarkable that Mazarin's triumph should have been so real when he had so little ability as an administrator and finance minister. Even at this moment of French triumph, there was hatred for the man who burdened France so heavily with taxation and yet could not afford to pay his troops. He tried to introduce all kinds of new taxation, but failed. There were riots in Paris, and Mazarin must have realized that his victories had been purchased at the cost of national poverty and misery. Mazarin himself was bankrupt of ideas for reform. Indeed, there might well have been a revolution in France at this time, as there was in England; but whereas the English discontent was mirrored in and led by Parliament, there was no such French equivalent. The States General were no more, and the *Parlement* was a selfish and privileged assembly of lawyers, which yet had little power.

Admittedly, in 1648, the *Parlement* did cause trouble over the question of the *paulette*, so named after Paulet, Sully's minister who had invented a *droit annuel* of a sixtieth of the purchase price of judicial offices. Now the magistrates were ordered to pay a sum equal to four years' salary for a renewal of their privileges, and there was even an *arrêt d'union*, an agreement signed by delegates from the civil courts. A meeting in the Chambre Saint-Louis put forward demands for freedom, popular consent to taxation and the abolition of the *Intendants*, but there was no national unity of sentiment behind these demands, and when Mazarin decided to compromise, the field was ready for his intrigues, which would end in his eventual triumph.

He was given a good start when the news came through of Condé's victory at Lens, and he ordered the arrest of the reformer Broussel. This was the signal for rioting in Paris, where there was sufficient hatred for Mazarin to stir the mob. Among the trouble-makers were the future Cardinal de Retz and the Duc de Longueville. So violent were the rioters that the government was forced to release Broussel, and Mazarin ordered the court to leave Paris for Rueil, until Condé should arrive. The city prepared for a siege, but the Cardinal opened negotiations, and recognized the Chambre Saint-Louis. The government returned to Paris, and it appeared that Mazarin had suffered a serious blow. However, he was plotting still, and angling for the support of Condé, who had adopted a neutral attitude. That winter was marked by the publication of pamphlets, *mazarinades*, criticizing and condemning the rule of the Queen and her Cardinal.

But Anne would not agree to the dismissal of her chief minister, and it was soon evident that fighting must break out. The court moved to Saint-Germain-en-Laye, and France saw the outbreak of the so-called "War of the Public Weal". The leaders of the *Fronde*, as it was known, were Condé's brother, Conti, and Longueville. It was a rebellion of princes throughout. The *frondeurs* (literally, "slingers", children throwing stones) were not engaged in a real war. The middle classes who were at first disposed to support them, soon wanted the security of peace, even when Turenne and Bouillon ignored Mazarin's bribes and joined the rebellion. Fortunately for the government, the army remained loyal; Condé quelled the troubles in Charenton, and the *bourgeois* members of the *Fronde* made the peace of Rueil, ending the first rebellion. The court went back to Paris again, but the peace was not final, and Mazarin and the Queen went to Compiègne while Condé dealt with troubles in the provinces (1649–50). Gradually, law and order were restored in the capital, and it became possible for the young Louis XIV, Anne and Mazarin to return to the capital in August 1650.

The man who had made this possible was Condé; but when he saw that Mazarin was still the ruler of France, and that he had not gained power for himself, he decided to initiate a second *Fronde*, one which the Cardinal would be unable to overcome. However, Condé was no diplomat, and he soon made enemies of his possible supporters, like Beaufort. Before long, he was imprisoned in Vincennes with Conti and Longueville. The *frondeurs* were leaderless, although Turenne invaded France from the Netherlands and threatened to attack Paris itself. Fortunately for the government, Turenne was defeated at Rethel, but although Mazarin seemed to be triumphant, he lost, at that moment, the support of a new ally at court, Madame de Chévreuse, and left the court to go to Bruhl. With his disappearance from the government, the excuse for rebellion had gone. Although Anne was shaken by his defection, it was soon plain that the Cardinal had made a wise move in the game of politics. The anti-Mazarin party turned its enmity against Condé, the other contender for supreme power in France. Thinking that this was his opportunity, the Cardinal returned to court—but he had reappeared too soon. Immediately, the *status quo* was resumed. Fighting went on between the royal forces and armies led by Nemours, Beaufort and Condé. Frenchmen were scandalized when they realized that the latter, a Prince of the Blood and the victor of Rocroi, was serving the interests of the national enemy, Spain. Condé even managed to take Paris, but as the only point of unity among the various *frondeurs* was a hatred for Mazarin, there could be no decisive success for them. When Mazarin withdrew once again from the direction of affairs, the *Fronde* collapsed, and the King returned to Paris. The wars of the *Fronde* were finished. However, a permanent fear of the mob in Paris remained in the mind of the young Louis, who had seen his palace invaded. This probably explains his building of Versailles when he attained his majority.

In February 1653, however, Mazarin returned yet again to take his place in affairs of state; there had been no change, despite the five years of this cruel and pointless civil war. All that had happened was that France had suffered inevitable reverses. Tuscany and Casale had gone; so had Dunkirk, Gravelines and Catalonia. Even another "Calais" was created when Mazarin, seeking friends, made an alliance with the Protector Cromwell, which resulted in Mardyke being captured and handed over to republican England. Dunkirk suffered the same fate, after Turenne had defeated Don John of Austria and Condé at the battle of the Dunes. Spain was nearly defeated, and Mazarin knew that there was a good chance of Philip IV agreeing to a peace treaty if this included a marriage between Louis XIV and the Infanta, who might well inherit the Spanish throne. Arrangements were therefore made. The plan that Louis should marry Mazarin's niece, Marie de Mancini, was dropped. By the Peace of the Pyrenees, the Cardinal agreed that Condé should keep his liberty; the French ally, the King of Portugal, was abandoned; France lost some territory in the Netherlands and in Franche Comté; but the marriage with the Infanta was a considerable dynastic gain, and France also obtained Lorraine, Artois and Roussillon. The dynastic agreement eventually brought Spain into the Bourbon family and, although the Peace terms were much criticized, it is difficult to see how else the war might satisfactorily have been ended. Mazarin himself died at the moment of triumph, in March 1661.

He had achieved all that a diplomatic intriguer could. France was the great power of Europe, despite war, devastation, plague and poverty. His successes were entirely in the fields of war and international diplomacy, and France owed nothing else to him. But there were other interests in Mazarin's France. Gallicanism had been growing, despite the rise of Jansenism. Cornelius Jansen had died in 1638, but his *Augustinus* had been published posthumously in 1640, and his ideas had taken root at the Cistercian monastery of Port-Royal in Paris. These had included austerity, penitence, and a strict evangelical discipline, which naturally aroused opposition among the worldly and ambitious clergy. In 1643 d'Arnauld's *La fréquente Communion* had given Jansen's philosophy a much wider circulation. Pascal's *Lettres Provinciales*, published after his conversion to Jansenism in 1646, had brought great ability to the new cause. But it was not to last. The Sorbonne's orthodox philosophers condemned *Augustinus*, and so did the Pope in 1653. The Jansenists began to be persecuted, but persecution was no longer a popular weapon in the late seventeenth century, and Pope Clement IX ordered that the oppression should cease (1669). However, by this time, the great days of Jansenism had gone; so, perhaps, had the great days of religious and spiritual conflict.

In the literary landscape, one may note the death of Descartes in 1650, and that of the free-thinking Gassendi, the forerunner of Voltaire and Montesquieu, in 1655. Other contemporary *libertins* were le Vayer and Cyrano de Bergerac. The latter was to be romanticized 250 years later by Rostand, but the original Cyrano was a considerable satirist in his own right, an opponent of religious orthodoxy. These sceptics were, of course, the very opposite of Pascal, whom we have already mentioned. He was interested, as were so many men of letters in the seventeenth century, in mathematics and science as well as in literary and religious controversy. His incomplete *Les Pensées*, although disjointed, show him to have been a profound as well as an ironic and logical thinker. It was also the period of Vangelas, the grammarian, who did much to establish the standards of the French language; and of de Balzac's *Dissertations critiques* and elegantly stylish letters.

De la Rochefoucauld (1613–80), who fought for the *Fronde* against Mazarin, was producing maxims and epigrams, besides his famous *Mémoires* in 1662. Among his friends was the Marquise de Sévigné, whose garrulous letters recorded much of the events and spirit of the times. The Cardinal de Retz, another *frondeur*, recorded the events in which he took a leading part. Among novelists, la Calprenède succeeded de Gomberville, publishing *Cassandre* from 1642 to 1645, and *Cléopâtre* from 1646 to 1657. The Marquise de Rambouillet was followed, as the great salon hostess, by Mlle de Scudéry, who wrote popular novels containing characters which were very thinly disguised portraits of important people. But it was in drama that French literature was beginning to flourish. Villiers produced his Don Juan play, *Festin de Pierre*, in 1659, and Corneille was producing *Le Menteur*,

*Héraclius* and *Sertorius*. Rotrou, employed by the Hôtel de Bourgogne, wrote various works like *Saint Genest*, and du Ryer and
L'Hermite were still at work. It was not yet the age of Racine,
who was being educated at the monastery of Port-Royal during
Louis XIV's minority. But there was considerable interest in
Saint-Evremond's parody on the Académie Française, *Les Aca-
démistes*, and de Bergerac's *Le Pédant joué*.

The most important figure was Molière (Jean-Baptiste
Poquelin), the Parisian actor who began to write in 1653, under
the patronage of Orléans. His company produced plays in
Richelieu's theatre in the Palais-Royal, and were accorded
Louis XIV's special protection. Molière's *L'École des maris* and
*L'École des femmes* came to the public attention just after the death
of Mazarin, and his greatest period was yet to come. It was not a
great period for poetry, but one may note Saint-Amant, Scarron
and his *Virgile travesti*, and d'Assouci and his *Ovide en belle humeur*.

### RECOMMENDED READING

*Cardinal Mazarin and the Fronde*. J. H. M. SALMON. *History Today*, Vol. VII,
   No. 7, p. 458 (July 1957).
*Letters of Mazarin*. BRUNET. Paris, 1896.
*Mazarin, Soutien de l'État*. J. BOULENGER. Paris, 1929.
*Mémoires* of Colbert. Paris, 1861.
*The Ascendancy of France, 1598–1715*. H. O. WAKEMAN. (Chapter 7.) Rivingtons,
   1936.

## CHAPTER 10

# Louis XIV and the Establishment of Absolutism

THE young Louis XIV took over the reins of power in 1660. Despite all the criticisms of Mazarin's policy, that statesman had bequeathed a powerful state to the King, who was to fashion a new kind of government for the admiration of Europe. The continent had seen vast changes during the Thirty Years' War and the decade following. Whereas at the beginning of the struggle, there had been a clear-cut division between the Catholic and Hapsburg party on the one hand, and the Protestant party on the other, the war ended with Catholic France fighting Catholic Spain. The conflict had almost become one of nationalism versus nationalism, rather than of Catholic versus Protestant. Religion was no longer the chief concern of the great powers.

It is tempting to see the division as one of absolutism on the one hand, and Puritan republicanism on the other; but this does not give a fair or a complete picture, for, although the Catholic countries tended to develop royal absolutism, such a feature was not unknown in some Protestant states. However, in France it may be claimed with justification that the Church was now subservient to the state, and that this was inevitable with the growth of royal despotism. This growth was the great achievement of Louis, who worked hard at the business of being a king. He knew the importance of royal dignity, and of the public impression created by his great court at Versailles. It is, of course, with Versailles, its etiquette, ceremony, scandals and the routine of monarchy that most people today associate his reign.

Certain factors helped to create this new system, which was to become, eventually, what we call the *ancien régime*. First of all, the nobles, although retaining all the trappings of power, and being welcome at court, lost the substance of what political influence they had previously enjoyed. Admittedly, they were exempted from the burden of taxation, but they were of little political importance during Louis's reign. He had profited from his knowledge of the period of the *Frondes*, which had engraved upon him, at an impressionable age, the vital need to control both the nobility and the Parisian crowds which could become their tool. The middle classes were not in a position to demand a share in the government, and, so long as Louis gave France unity and strength, were unlikely to prove troublesome. In any case, the bourgeoisie were badly hit by the religious persecution which was to follow the revocation of the Edict of Nantes.

The *Parlement* continued to exist, but had little real power. This was drawn into the hands of Louis and of his ministers and *Intendants*, royal executive officials, travelling on circuit. The Council of State, a little group of powerful royal officials, supervised the work of lesser councils for home affairs, financial affairs, etc. Louis and his bourgeois officials were the only men that mattered. In the early part of the reign the chief minister was Colbert, who came of merchant stock despite his attempts to prove an ancestry of Scottish gentility. He rose to power when Fouquet, a friend of Mazarin, was disgraced on account of his accumulation of private wealth, and sentenced to life imprisonment. Jean-Baptiste Colbert, of Reims, had entered the service of Mazarin, and then that of Louis XIV, and is remembered for his, perhaps idealistic, determination to promote the industry and trade of France by government action. He could see that financial order and periodic budgets were essential to bring an end to the fiscal problems of France.

Colbert's ambitions to reform the taxation system, his moves to prevent fraud and to put some kind of order into the chaos of the national debt, were not always successful. There was considerable resistance to his plans to reduce the interest payable on the state's debts, but he managed to repudiate some of the older ones. He is an important figure in economic history because of his

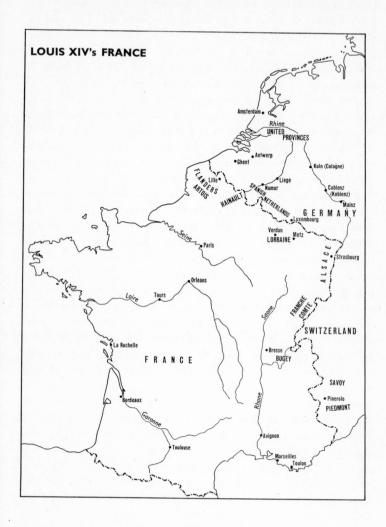

MAP 5

development of state industries, protected by tariffs, in such fields as shipbuilding, silk weaving, linen production, furniture making, and tapestry. This last industry was carried on at the famous *Gobelins* works, founded in the fifteenth century and bought for the crown in 1667. He also tried to encourage more trade by ordering the improvement of roads and building of canals, such as the canal from the Mediterranean to the Bay of Biscay, opened in 1681. Uniform weights and measures were also among his improvements; but most of his schemes were opposed, either by interested parties, such as the silk merchants of Lyons, or even the peasants, who could see little prospect of any improvement in their lot. It was one of Colbert's determinations to keep wages low; and his only plan to solve the problem of unemployment was to send the workless to the galleys. In fact, there was little that was new in Colbert's schemes—but they were new to France. On occasions, army regiments had to be called in to restore order when his schemes led to rioting.

His reorganization schemes were mostly carried out in the period from 1661 to 1672. After that date, Louis began policies which resulted in France being engaged in war for most of the rest of his reign. Colbert's plans were forgotten and Colbert himself ceased to be the most important member of the royal councils. His place was taken by the war minister, Louvois, who was as great a reformer in military matters, introducing new weapons like the bayonet and flintlock musket, and building new depots for a reorganized army. One of Louvois's inspectors was the strict Martinet, whose name has passed even into the English language. Through the work of servants like Colbert and Louvois, and by a strict control of them, Louis had created a despotic and centralized administration. "L'Etat, c'est moi", may not have been Louis's own words, but they adequately summarize the situation he was striving to create. All that Louis wanted was to make France, and therefore himself, more glorious. To do this, he was prepared to work himself and his officials as hard as was humanly possible; he attended to administrative detail with what has been described as a "deliberate and appalling thoroughness", and worked longer hours than most modern government officials would consider possible.

Louis could never bring himself to trust his servants; he was always cynical and slow to understand new ideas. He suffered from dyspepsia and a complete lack of a sense of humour. He could not tolerate the idea of being placed in embarrassing situations—either by his ministers or by avoidable circumstances. At least he could learn some things from history, and this may well explain his determination to avoid employing an over-powerful or unpopular chief minister, and to create a court at Versailles, away from the Paris mob which had forced him, as a child, to seek refuge in the provinces. However, Louis never seemed to learn the necessity of limiting his expenditure. Nor was he willing to tolerate the existence of persons and institutions which seemed to prejudice the creation of a completely central-ized state. Local immunities in the provinces were attacked, as were the municipalities and the *états*, by his *Intendants*. Eventually, the Huguenots were to suffer persecution for essentially the same reason.

It is difficult to see whether or not Louis understood the sig-nificance of Colbert's schemes, except to see that here was a man who might make France richer, and therefore its King more able to play the part of the greatest ruler in Europe. But when Colbert attempted the reform of the *gabelle*, the *aides*, the *taille*, or to establish corn-growing in areas where there was insufficient, or to protect infant industries with high tariffs, one can imagine Louis believing that these were interests suited only to a bourgeois mind. Certainly he failed to realize the true importance of Colbert's schemes to build new ships, to create arsenals and harbours at Brest, Rochefort and Toulon, for various later events proved that Louis could see no great purpose in using or de-veloping sea power. His determination to win his wars on land was to set a pattern for France which benefited Britain enor-mously. In fact, it was as advantageous for Britain as Louis's lack of interest in colonization and in merchant ventures like the French East India Company. Colbert's hundred warships were rarely used to much effect.

After the death of Colbert in 1683, and that of Louvois in 1691, there were no famous men among Louis's counsellors. Perhaps this was one of the reasons for the decay of the French bureaucracy; it was certainly a reason for the failure of France to develop along constitutional and commercial lines that might have enabled her to compete more successfully with the growing power of England. Apart from territorial aggrandizement and the cause of Bourbon glory, Louis's sole interest after Colbert's death seems to have been in the establishment of a France united in every particular, but especially in administration and in religion. Although there was some trouble with the Gallican Church, on the whole the machinery of the established faith was subservient to Louis' régime. Certainly the Jesuits supported the crown even more than they did the Papacy. However, the Huguenots were regarded with little sympathy by Louis XIV. Both as heretics and as democrats addicted to republicanism, he detested them. The Protestants began to feel his hostility in 1669, when the *chambres mi-parties*, which helped to guarantee Huguenot legal rights, were abolished. But the real attack began after 1684, in which year Louis married his mistress, Madame de Maintenon, and came more and more under the influence of the Jesuit, La Chaise, who instructed her to press the view that Louis's soul was endangered while he permitted privileges to heretics. All sorts of measures were set on foot to make life intolerable for the Huguenots—the *dragonnades*, by which troops were quartered on known Protestant households; by the removal of Huguenot children from their parents' care; and by persecution and outrage. The final step was taken in 1685, with the revocation of Henry IV's Edict of Nantes. The results of this tragic act were that, in the face of persecution in which thousands were killed, thousands of other French Protestants migrated to Brandenburg, the Netherlands and England. As Protestantism, throughout western Europe, was the religion of the growing middle class, it was unfortunate that Louis got rid of his merchants and industrialists, who took their skills to countries which were France's greatest rivals. It was also a misfortune that no alternative religion was permissible to the growing number of scientific and political thinkers who found themselves unable to accept catholicism. Louis's rigidity forced them into atheism, to the detriment of the post-revolutionary France, of which many leaders were atheists.

The loss of potential wealth was particularly important when Louis was about to embark upon a policy of foreign ambition and inevitable war. At the beginning of his period of rule, it was clear that he was determined to be friendly with Charles II of England, recently restored to the throne, but to be unfriendly towards Spain. Louis had no strong feelings about keeping the peace with Rome, for war nearly developed with the Pope. But with England, Louis felt that he could exert enough influence on the almost bankrupt Charles to ensure a thorough-going sub-ordination to French interests. He purchased Dunkirk for cash from Charles, and also arranged to claim the reversion of the Duchy of Lorraine from its ruler, Charles, despite his lack of legal right to do so. In Spain, Louis's wife, Queen Maria Theresa, had had some claims to the succession until the birth of the future ruler, Charles II. Louis was even prepared to support the view that she was the true ruler of the Netherlands, through her descent from Philip IV. This claim might have turned out to be important, in Louis's estimation; for the Dutch, in their rivalry with England, were prepared to accept any help that France might give. Indeed, a treaty was made between de Witt and Louis in 1662. But the outbreak of war between England and Holland in 1665 put Louis in a difficult situation.

He did not want to engage in a naval war, especially with his friend Charles II. Louis had little sympathy with the Protestant Dutch, and in any case Philip IV, on his death, deliberately excluded Maria Theresa's claims. Louis's solution was to declare war, but to do nothing of any account for the Dutch. In fact, he soon commenced to negotiate peace with Charles II, for by this time he had decided on war with Spain. In any case, the Anglo-Dutch war was ending. The Dutch, having succeeded in burning the English fleet in the Medway, were negotiating the Treaty of Breda with England. Louis began his campaigns against the Spanish Netherlands in 1667. Successfully, he besieged and took towns like Courtrai and Lille. The Dutch became anxious, especially when they heard that Louis had made a treaty to partition the Spanish dominions, if Charles II of Spain were to die without an heir. The treaty was with the Emperor. The Dutch, therefore, were prepared to forget their rivalry with the English, and the result was a Triple Alliance between Holland, England and Sweden, to protect themselves from French attack. This piece of diplomatic determination was sufficient to incline Louis to make terms with the Dutch and, by the Treaty of Aix-la-Chapelle of 1668, peace terms were offered which he hoped would satisfy the Dutch temporarily and so end the Triple Alliance. The alliance was a weak one in any case, for Charles II was always eager to remain on good terms with the French King, although his increasingly Whig Parliaments disliked Charles's French leanings.

It appears, however, that Louis was determined to break the Dutch power when opportunity offered; and in the next few years the French armed forces were strengthened and rebuilt. Louis was not idle in the diplomatic field, either. He made the Treaty of Dover of 1670, with its secret clauses, with Charles II, who abandoned his Dutch alliance for hard cash; and followed it up with a secret treaty with the Swedes in 1672. The Triple Alliance was gone, while the French army was increased to a size of nearly 300,000 men. Louvois and his assistants developed new methods of infantry training and built a strong artillery force, while Vauban, the great military engineer, planned and constructed great fortresses. With Turenne and Condé to lead his armies, Louis went to war in 1672. The Rhine was crossed and Amsterdam was threatened. The Dutch, however, struck back. The English and French fleets were defeated by de Ruyter at Southwold Bay, but Holland itself was only saved by the opening of the sluices to flood the countryside before the advancing French.

De Witt offered terms, but this was to be the only occasion when the French were to be offered surrender. Shortly afterwards de Witt and his brother were murdered, and the government was taken over by William of Orange, the descendant of the heroic William the Silent. Meanwhile, Louis continued his campaign of slow and deliberate sieges. Despite Turenne's success in defeating Brandenburg, de Ruyter won three sea battles against the French, and William gathered sufficient strength to push the French out of Dutch territory. He even managed to bring together a coalition of anti-French powers: Spain, Austria, Brunswick and Brandenburg, which were joined by England in 1674. The war continued, for Louis considered his armies perfectly capable of dealing with this grouping of powers. Turenne was fighting in the Rhineland, taking Alsace and winning battles at Sinsheim and Colmar before his death in 1675. Condé was concerned in siege warfare in Flanders, while there were even French victories at sea, against de Ruyter in the Mediterranean. William suffered a defeat at Cassel and the picture seemed a very favourable one for Louis.

Then came an interesting diplomatic development. Charles II permitted his niece, Mary, to marry William of Orange. The threat of a close Anglo-Dutch maritime alliance may have impelled Louis to make a determined attack, and his troops moved on Antwerp. They did not reach the city, and moves were being made for peace. William was glad enough to arrange a period of peace, as was Charles of Spain, and in 1678 the Treaties of Nymegen brought the fighting to an end. William, however, did not like the way in which the Nymegen negotiations showed the weaknesses of Holland, nor the undeniable fact that the peace was a triumph for Louis. The French King could hardly claim that he had achieved all that he wanted, yet all the same he had emerged with considerable advantages and a much enhanced prestige. Yet one cannot ignore the fact that Holland was undefeated. Indeed, the opportunity to defeat the Dutch had been lost, and they had gained their barrier fortresses on the frontier.

France needed a period of peace, and Louis needed to gain the friendly alliance of some of his neighbours, or, at least, their neutrality. This was probably the reason for his alliance with Brandenburg, for he had given up all hope, by now, of securing much support from England. Nevertheless, Louis's aggressive tendencies persisted. He used the general unwillingness of Europe to renew the war as an opportunity to take cities like Metz and Strasbourg. But this unwillingness did not mean that the western European nations were not alarmed, and an alliance between Spain and England was followed by the building of a Quadruple Alliance between the Empire, Spain, Holland and Sweden. Fortunately for the French, it was just at this time that the Turks were threatening Vienna (1683). Louis was unwilling to regard this as a serious threat to his plans in western Europe, and he offered no help to the Austrians. They were rescued by the Poles, under Sobieski. Louis was more concerned with going to war with Spain—a short war, soon ended by the Treaty of Ratisbon, by which France obtained several towns and Luxemburg.

Ratisbon was probably the peak of Louis's success. In any case, the first part of his reign was over, and a new pattern was visible in the political life of France. Colbert was dead; Louis had married Madame de Maintenon; the Edict of Nantes had been revoked; Paris was giving way to the glories of Versailles, where the talk was of Lulli and Le Nôtre. It could be guessed that Louis was conscious of the failure to carry through the reforms which Colbert had suggested. The growth in the national debt was a weakness, only concealed by the façade of royalty which might be mistaken for national strength. Even the great French army, reformed and administered so well, had not been as successful as might have been hoped. One sign of Louis's change of attitude, already mentioned above, was the determination to achieve a united, monolithic French society. The problem of Jansenism, which had appeared again, had to be left unsettled, but Louis was foolish enough to follow his inclinations, and those of his wife and of Père La Chaise, his confessor, and to revoke the Edict of Nantes on 22 October 1685. No doubt, had there been a referendum, Louis's action would have had the support of most Frenchmen. The middle classes, where Protestantism was strong, were unpopular; on the other hand, there was no serious doubt of their loyalty to France. This was no safeguard for them; it is possible that 800,000 fled from France once the persecutions began.

The consequences were important outside France, too. Opinion in other countries hardened against Louis. The alliance between France and Brandenburg was rapidly broken. The persecution of Protestants made James II's position in England completely untenable, even if the other factors in the English "Revolution" of 1688 are not taken into account. Louvois found that it was impossible to restore French industries or to expect any confidence in French commerce among foreign merchants and bankers. Louis's policies, which were always aggressive, made a renewal of war inevitable. His attack on Genoa, the persecution of the Vaudois, the quarrel with Pope Innocent XI, all these made it impossible for Europe to settle to a period of peace. The diplomatic scene began to change with the formation of the League of Augsburg and the defeat of the Turkish invaders of eastern Europe at Mohacs and Belgrade. At last the Emperor could take a more active share in western diplomacy and the prospects of war. But the most serious threat to Louis was to come with the enforced abdication of James II of England and the arrival in England of a new Protestant monarch—William of Orange, whose energies were centred on checking the power of France by a European alliance.

At first, with the renewal of war, it might have been possible for Louis to hope for a limited war, perhaps confined to a struggle with the Empire. William's Grand Alliance of 1689, an alliance of Protestant and anti-Hapsburg powers, put an end to any such hopes. Similarly, a naval success at Beachy Head may have encouraged Louis to suppose that it might be possible to restore James to the English throne, until the defeat of his fleet in the battle of La Hogue in 1692 made any French expectations in this direction completely hopeless. Indeed, this defeat for the French at sea meant that William could turn his entire attention to the battlefields of Europe. Opposed to William was an able French commander, Luxembourg, but, despite successes for the French at Steinkirk and Neerwinden, William and his allies went on fighting implacably until terms were made at Ryswick in 1697. This settlement was important diplomatically, for William was recognized as King of England; but from other points of view it was a mere stalemate peace, for neither side had been able to gain much, in glory or in territory, in the fighting. Yet another phase in Louis's reign had come to an end. Luxembourg and Louvois were dead, and a new political and diplomatic problem was coming to the fore—the question of the Spanish succession.

It was clear that Charles II of Spain could not last much longer, and this brother-in-law of the French King had no direct heir. It had been a matter of concern among diplomats for years. There were various possible claimants. Although Louis's wife, Maria Theresa, had renounced her claims, this renunciation might very well be revoked. Her sister Margaret had passed a claim to her daughter, married to the Elector of Bavaria; and she in turn had passed the claim to her son, the Electoral Prince. In addition, Leopold hoped that the Archduke Charles, a son by his second marriage, might be considered as a compromise candidate. By a first Partition Treaty in 1698, the Spanish King's territories were to be divided between the Electoral Prince (who was to become King of Spain), a member of the French royal family, and the Archduke Charles. Then, in 1699, the Bavarian prince died. A second Partition Treaty, made in 1700, decided that the Archduke should become King of Spain, while France was to obtain Naples, Sicily and Milan. But all these negotiations came to nothing when Charles died, and left a will in which Louis's grandson, Philip, was to receive the whole kingdom and empire. After very slight hesitation, Louis accepted, on his grandson's behalf, and Europe was plunged into war. As Louis could have said, "Il n'y a plus de Pyrénées"; but the comment is mythical. It might have been possible for the war to have been between France and Austria only; but Louis made no attempt to persuade England that France and Spain would never come under one single ruler. Within three months all hopes of peace had gone.

William took immediate steps to restore the Grand Alliance of England, Holland and the German princes. It seemed that France had some better hopes in this struggle than the last, for, with the Spanish Netherlands in French hands, a direct attack on Holland was more possible. Certainly this may explain the lack of enthusiasm among the Dutch for doing more than defend their own territories—which was to infuriate Marlborough more than once in the years ahead. It was fortunate for the allies that they had Prince Eugène and the Duke of Marlborough to command their forces; and unfortunate for the French that their own military leadership was inept, with the exception of that provided by Villars. At the start, there were French successes in Germany, but Marlborough saved Liége from capture by the French. But the great event of the war was soon to come, the event which upset all Louis's designs in the east. Marlborough led his forces on their great march down the Rhine and Danube, fooling his allies and the French into believing that this was to be an attack on France. Instead, he swerved south to save threatened Vienna, defeated Tallard at Blenheim and saved Austria, the beaten French general spending the rest of the war in Nottingham, where his house still stands. England's hitherto negligible military prestige was vastly enhanced. The French had been virtually unbeatable for half a century.

Blenheim was followed by defeats for the French at Ramillies (1706), where Villeroy met his master, at Oudenarde (1708) and at Malplaquet (1709). These defeats, despite Villars making Malplaquet a pyrrhic victory for the allies, made certain that Louis had few hopes of emerging victorious from the struggle. However, it was still possible that his grandson, Philip, might retain the Spanish throne, if the war ended in a stalemate. This, in fact, was what occurred. The defeat of the Whig party in England by Marlborough's Tory opponents was one of the causes of the beginning of peace negotiations. Although the war went on, the Grand Alliance was beginning to fall apart, and Villars was even able to win the battle of Denain in 1712 against Eugène, fighting now without English aid. By the various treaties which made up the Treaty of Utrecht in 1713, France received more than she might have hoped for if Marlborough's campaigns had continued, and if the English landed gentry had not been so intent upon peace at almost any price. Bourbon support for the Stuarts came to an end, and Louis agreed to safeguards against any possibility of Philip—who did gain recognition as King of Spain—or his descendants inheriting the French throne. England augmented her overseas possessions by taking Minorca and Gibraltar from Spain, and also obtained entry to the slave trade with the Spanish–American colonies. Louis gave up certain territories to the Dutch, who obtained possession of barrier fortresses like Namur, Ypres, and Knocke. It could easily have happened that France, defeated so often by Marlborough, would have lost far more; but disunity among the allies made it possible for Louis to retain French prestige. Perhaps it was not clear to him that the English gains were to add vastly to the power of his great rival. He must have been relieved when the Emperor made peace, agreeing to terms at Rastadt in 1714. He could congratulate himself on losing few territories of importance, and on gaining the Spanish throne for his grandson. Presumably, there was no serious self condemnation in his mind, on account of the economic difficulties of a France which was near to a state of famine.

Louis died on 1 September 1715, at the age of 77. He had been on the throne for seventy-two years, and had established the most complete royal despotism for centuries. He had had some able servants in the earlier years of his reign, but, on the whole, he had failed to use the abilities of men like Vauban, the economist and famous military engineer. Louis's marriage to Maria Theresa had resulted in only one son, although there had been several daughters. There had been illegitimate children by his mistresses. But on his death, there was only one surviving legitimate heir, apart from Philip of Spain, who was excluded from the succession. The heir was a 5-year-old great-grandson, and therefore, after a dispute with an illegitimate claimant to the Regency, the Duke of Maine, it was settled that the control of the kingdom should pass to the Duke of Orléans, nephew of the late *Roi Soleil*.

Louis XIV had had his admirers—perhaps too many of them. Even Voltaire had made some favourable remarks. But lessons like that of the *Fronde* had taught him to be an absolute king. He had never forgotten the flight from Paris when he was a child; and this may have been the reason for his determination to build his capital at the former hunting lodge of Versailles. He distrusted the Parisian mob. The famous rigid court etiquette at Versailles had its purpose. It made the monarchy a public spectacle—"a perpetual ballet", as Professor Cobban has called it. The palace was a setting for the sun king. In Voltaire's words, it was also a grand caravanserai, filled with human misery and discomfort. At Versailles, Louis held his court and ruled his kingdom. He did what he could to enhance the glory of France, but he equated it with the glory of the monarchy, and he became master of the *métier du roi*. Another way of putting it is, of course, that he was the "greatest of Postmasters", with his ineradicable passion for detail. Unfortunately, his craftsmanship had not created what France needed. Apart from the critical economic state of the kingdom, a situation had been created in which an aristocracy existed, but for purely decorative reasons, so that it had no political power or responsibility. All the offices of state could be, and were, bought and sold. Absolute power had corrupted the monarchy and the state. They lacked a sense of social responsibility, partly because the life at Versailles separated the nobles from their estates, which were often maladministered by agents. Often the sole aim was to extort cash to provide further display at Versailles.

Louis XIV's long reign was marked, as one might expect, by important literary developments and personalities. Early in the period, the Marquise de Sévigné emerged as a significant figure, reporting the gossip of her times for her friends and for posterity.

Jean de la Bruyère (1645–96) produced *Les Caractères ou les Mœurs de ce siècle* in 1688, criticizing the Versailles society of which he was a hanger on. His portraits were often satirical, but not very effectively; however, his prose was brilliantly written. Other writers of the early period were Mme de Lafayette (*Mémoires de la Cour de France pour les années 1688 et 1689*) and Bussy-Rabutin (*L'Histoire amoureuse des Gaules*). Saint-Simon appeared later on the scene (1675–1755), but his portraits of the French court, written from 1740 onwards, are essential to students of Versailles in the reign of *Le Roi Soleil*. A vastly different writer was Fénelon (1651–1715), a Quietist in religious matters, whose ideas on education and reform gave hints of future developments. His *Les Aventures de Télémaque* appeared in 1699. It greatly influenced progressive rulers, such as Frederick the Great of Prussia.

Novelists were at work, including Antoine Furetière (1619–88) and Alain-René Lesage, but the latter's *Gil Blas de Santillane* did not appear until the end of Louis XIV's reign. Much more important in the literature of France were Pierre Corneille's younger brother, Thomas, who was writing comedies, tragedies and even libretti for Lully's operas; and Jean Racine, the greatest of classical tragedy writers (1639–99). His *Phèdre* appeared in 1677. He was appointed royal historian to Louis XIV, as well as producing plays of the quality of *Andromaque* and his only comedy, *Les Plaideurs*. Racine overshadowed his contemporaries, such as Boyer, Quinault and Crébillon. However, another great man of letters and the theatre produced his greatest work early in the reign. This was Molière (1622–73), whose *Tartuffe* was produced in 1664. *Don Juan* appeared in 1665 and *Le Misanthrope* in 1666, the latter probably Molière's most important play. He produced farces like *Le Médecin malgré lui*, followed by *Les Femmes savantes* in 1672, and *Le Malade imaginaire* in 1673, just before his death. He was a brilliant writer and a dramatist of European significance. Other comic writers for the stage included Dancourt and Regnard.

Among poets, an important place belongs to Jean de la Fontaine (1621–95), whose *Fables* appeared between 1688 and

1694, a concise and cynical writer whose polished phrases have had a universal attraction. Boileau (1636–1711) was a significant critic as well as a poet. His *Réflexions sur Longin* appeared in 1694; his poetry indicates a French love of clarity and illumination rather than a desire to produce work of lyrical beauty. The figure of Bossuet (1627–1704), a great preacher, orator and controversialist, the defender of religious orthodoxy, was of more interest to his contemporaries than to later generations. It may be concluded from the literary scene in Louis's reign that it was difficult for any literature or art to flourish that was not connected with, or produced within, the magic circle of that great court at Versailles. In all literature there is a noticeable decrease in creative vigour towards the end of the reign.

## RECOMMENDED READING

*Le Siècle de Louis XIV.* VOLTAIRE. Tr. M. P. POLLACK. Dent, 1958.

*Louis XIV and the Greatness of France.* M. ASHLEY. English Universities Press, 1946.

*Mémoires of Mme de la Fayette.* Harrap, 1958.

*Mémoires of Saint-Simon.* Cassell, 1955.

*New Cambridge Modern History,* Vol. V. *The Ascendancy of France, 1648–1688.* (Chapters I, IX, X, and XI by F. L. Carsten, G. Zeller, J. Lough and D. Ogg.)

*The Art of Kingship–Louis XIV: a Reconsideration.* ALFRED COBBAN. *History Today,* Vol. IV, No. 3, p. 149 (March 1954).

CHAPTER 11

# Louis XV and the Decline of the French Monarchy, 1715–74

THE history of the reign of Louix XV is largely the history of the decline of France; and the decline is one which was caused largely by the defects of the King himself, defects which were shown in every sphere of activity, foreign and domestic. A capacity for indecision was bound to ruin the machinery of centralized administration built up by Mazarin and his successors. The history of the reign is the history of the failure of the *ancien régime* to adapt itself to the forces of change; and as a result, Louis XV saw the defeat of France, particularly in the Seven Years' War, and the end of French hopes of expansion in America and in India. It might be claimed that the *ancien régime* was ruined because Louis XV was too bored to deal with the business of being a king.

When Louis XIV died in September 1715, there were few who genuinely mourned his passing. Despite the undoubted splendour and power of France, there could have been little genuine feeling for the great king, either among the aristocracy which had lost all its political power, or among the people, who felt the burden of debt which Louis's ambitious foreign policies had created. The accession of a mere child created certain problems, which, to a certain extent, had been foreseen by the *Grand Monarque*. Owing to a series of unfortunate deaths, the King's nephew, Philip of Orléans, was separated from the throne only by the child-King, who might easily die of the smallpox, as had the other members of the royal family. Gossip had it that Philip had poisoned them, and certainly Louis XIV was sufficiently

118

aware of the character of his nephew to appoint a Council of Regency which would include the Duke of Maine, who was to protect the young King and to see to his education. But the late King's wishes were ignored by the *Parlement*, acting in its function of supreme court, and Philip was elected sole regent, to the fury of Maine and of Madame de Maintenon.

Philip had one defect which he shared with the new King, or with the man that the new King was to become; in the words of his mother, Philip was "bored by everything". In the words of Saint-Simon, his gods were "avarice, debauchery and ambition". Philip held the Regency for eight years, and introduced France to a relaxation of the rigid Versailles discipline which rapidly degenerated because of the Regent's scepticism, imprudence and debauchery. Louis XIV's reactionary period soon gave way to an age of immorality and speculation, the age of Dubois and Law. It is possible that the Regent intended to give France certain inestimable advantages, on his accession to power. He may have realized that France needed, above all, peace and a relaxation of the central control imposed by Louis XIV's ministers. He may have been convinced of the necessity of a serious attempt to solve France's financial difficulties. There was an enormous and chronic deficit, and steps were taken to remedy this. The armed forces were cut down; the coinage was debased; interest rates were lowered; and official peculation was to be inquired into, while the old national debts were reduced by the introduction of new *billets d'état*.

In foreign affairs, Philip was very conscious of the possible threat from Philip of Spain. Despite the obligations of the treaty which forbade him from claiming the French throne, Philip was aware of the late King's dictum, that the Pyrenees no longer existed, and the Regent wanted to make sure that the Treaty of Utrecht's provisions were maintained. He and Dubois were conscious of the ability and ambitions of the Spanish minister, Alberoni. Dubois, formerly Orléans's tutor, now an *abbé*, was of importance as one of the Regent's principal advisers. The Regent and Dubois were so concerned to prevent Philip of Spain from thinking of upsetting the agreement made at Utrecht, that they made an alliance with England. Part of the price they paid for such an agreement with the Hanoverian King of England was that James, the Stuart pretender, was exiled from France. In addition, the fortifications of Mardyke were razed. The resulting Triple Alliance between France, England and Holland aroused some critical comment in France, where England was regarded as the traditional enemy, but it was a sensible diplomatic step. The alliance became quadruple in 1718 with the accession to its ranks of the Emperor, for Spain had attacked Sicily and Sardinia. However, the fighting did not last long, for Spain made peace once French armies invaded her territory, and her fleet had been destroyed by the English under Byng at Cape Passaro. Not only were any possible Spanish ambitions destroyed, but Philip dismissed Alberoni, his ablest servant. Once this situation had been reached—a satisfactory one for France—the "un-natural" alliance with the maritime powers came to an end. A treaty between France and Spain in 1721, by which the young King Louis XV was to marry the Infanta, restored a more normal feeling to the political scene. However, the marriage plan came to an end in 1725, when the unfortunate Spanish princess was sent back to Madrid.

Orléans, in fact, showed some ability as a statesman; he had courage and ability, too, in war, as he had shown as a young man in Spain. But he was incurably a dilettante, and incurably indolent, indifferent to insult and to criticism. In courtly circles, it was a period of informality, sexual corruption, libertinism. As Professor Salmon remarks: "the formality of Versailles was deserted for the liberal Parisian manners of the Palais-Royal." Certainly the Regent believed in various kinds of freedom. The previously banned *Télémaque* by Fénelon was published openly. Writers like Voltaire were permitted to satirize the régime. The Jesuits, so important in the exercise of Louis XIV's power, were ousted by the Gallicans and Jansenists, until Orléans decided to ignore the views of the majority of the French people, and revert to supporting the Jesuits—this for the benefit of Dubois, who had hopes of becoming a cardinal. The Regent himself had no interest whatever in religion and theology, although he had a great knowledge of all kinds of current intellectual ideas and attitudes.

One of his interests was of immediate importance to the government and economy of France. It was daily more necessary to achieve some kind of solution to the financial difficulties in which the state found itself. This explains the remarkable episode in French history of the theorist and gambler, John Law. This Edinburgh Scot had some knowledge of the universally accepted mercantilism of the day, some acquaintance with the banking systems in use in Europe. He believed that commerce could be encouraged with more credit and what he called circulation. He was an advocate of paper money and a state bank which would remove unnecessary restrictions on trade. The Regent allowed him to open a bank in Paris which would issue bills redeemable in cash, and in 1718 this became a state bank. Undoubtedly, Law's *Système* helped to stimulate commerce and to reduce the national debt, and in 1717 he founded a company which was to develop Louisiana in North America with the help of the cash accruing to a state tobacco monopoly. Other companies were taken over, and became the *Compagnie des Indes*. By 1720 Law was Controller-General, with a monopoly of the right to coin money; and his company was able to advance the crown a vast sum, without the backing of a sound capital investment, at 3 per cent. There was frantic dealing in shares in Paris, just as there was in England with the contemporary "South Sea Bubble". All kinds of activities came under the economic umbrella of the plausible Scottish adventurer. Colonists were recruited to be sent out to Arkansas; criminals were deported to New Orleans, named in honour of the Regent. Share prices went up by nearly fortyfold in the last six months of 1719; but this kind of speculation could not last. Prices began to fall, and panic spread through the investing classes in the early months of 1720. Food prices went up to famine level, and the government passed several edicts attempting to stop the collapse of the *Système*.

E

The whole of what was called the Mississippi scheme came to an abrupt end. By the summer of 1720 the bubble had burst, and, although Law was a man of considerable personal courage, and had faith in his own ideas, by December he had left France. Fortunately for the Regent, he, as ruler, escaped censure; and the Pâris brothers, established financiers who had criticized Law from the first, were called in to rescue the French economy from the wreckage. A survey of the wealth of the nation was carried out; many who had made profits during Law's boom were fined heavily, and steps were taken to restore the credit of the government. While this was in process, the Regency came to an end. Louis, at the age of 13, became King in more than name. Shortly afterwards, Orléans and Dubois died, and a new régime came to France. It is difficult to have much sympathy with Philip of Orléans. His court was noted for its depravity, and his family was little better. The aristocracy of the court, men like the Duke of Richelieu, led debased and scandalous lives. Elegance and extravagance went hand in hand with immorality. The aristocratic councils, set up by the Regent to replace Louis XIV's ministers, achieved very little, with the possible exceptions of those for internal and marine affairs. The Regent could do little— and was probably unwilling to do much—to reduce the privileges, especially financial privileges, of the nobility and of the Church. The collapse of Law's schemes, along with the final dissolution of the government by councils, saw the Regent revert to the despotism of the former King. The sole triumph of his period was the success of Dubois as foreign minister, although there was much to be said for Philip's action in expelling the *Parlement* from Paris when it criticized Dubois so freely.

Once Dubois was dead, and the young King began to reign in his own right, the Duke of Bourbon became first minister of state. This thoroughly incompetent statesman is remembered for the continuation of the persecution of the unorthodox in matters of religion. This persecution was accompanied by the breaking of the betrothal of Louis to the Infanta of Spain, and the arrangement instead of a royal marriage with Maria Leczinska of Poland, an unattractive woman several years older than the King. She was known as Unigenita at the court of France, after the Papal bull which was such a bone of contention between Jesuits and Jansenists, because she was a strong supporter of the Jesuit order. Also in Bourbon's ministry was the devaluation of the currency and the establishment by one of the Pâris family of a 2 per cent tax—the *cinquantième*. The opposition to these measures was sufficient to ensure the overthrow of Bourbon and his replacement by Bishop Fleury, who subsequently became a cardinal. Fleury had once been Louis's tutor, and he was now in his seventies; but he was to be chief minister for nearly seventeen years. His determination to cling to office despite advancing senility was not good for France. On the other hand, his policies were usually aimed at keeping the peace, and France began to spend less on her armies and the navy. He was, for his time, an honest man and not without ability in financial affairs. He fixed the value of the currency, reduced interest on state debts, and did what he could to encourage commerce. The building of roads by means of the *corvée*, a demand for forced labour, did much for the merchants of France. But despite these achievements, Fleury was not a genuine reformer, either of the government or its administration. Religious persecution continued, and the tax farmers took over, once again, the collection of taxes of which they had been deprived under the Orléans régime.

The King Fleury served was growing up to be a grave disappointment for those who had hoped for change. He was an idle and immoral young man, who seemed to be incapable of making a real effort to learn the tasks and responsibilities of a monarch. In fact, he lacked the determination to make any prolonged efforts; he suffered from a continual boredom, and hated the business of state and the etiquette of the court, in which Louis XIV had delighted so much. This defect of character goes far to explain the lack of progress and reform in eighteenth-century France. The King was incapable—as were most of his ministers—of taking decisions in favour of any change in the thoroughly corrupt and corrupting system from which France suffered throughout the period. Only war could arouse the King from his lethargy, and despite his bravery, even this activity was temporary. All that could be said for him was that he looked the part of a king. He made no attempt to make war on the real enemy of French society: privilege.

Fleury had certain characteristics in common with his English contemporary, Robert Walpole. For a time, the two worked together in an atmosphere of surprising amity. Part of the explanation may be that both men were determined on a policy of peace. Spain, after the collapse of the projected alliance through marriage, had made a treaty with Austria, by which she guaranteed the Pragmatic Sanction, so dear to the Emperor, on behalf of his daughter and heiress, Maria Theresa. So France made the Treaty of Hanover in 1725 with Prussia and England, but it was unlikely that such an odd alliance would last, and after the collapse of the Austria–Spanish friendship, France was not slow to make a treaty with Spain. Curiously, this was a treaty which included England and Holland as well, in reply to the Austrian alliance with Prussia in 1728. It was not surprising when normality returned with a renewal of the Family Compact with Spain in 1733. War soon followed—the War of the Polish Succession, a war in which France became engaged because one of the claimants for the Polish throne was Stanislas, a former monarch of Poland, and father of Louis XV's queen. The other claimant was Augustus, supported by the governments of Austria and Russia. This excuse for international rivalry was the motive for a French attack upon the Austrian possessions in Italy, and the war was conducted by some astonishingly aged French generals. Villars was over 80. It is scarcely surprising that he died in the attack on Turin in 1734, nor that the elderly commander of the French forces in the Rhineland, Berwick, after taking Lorraine, died while besieging Philippsburg in the same year. But despite some French triumphs, Fleury wanted peace, and his negotiations succeeded in obtaining this in 1735 at the Treaty of Vienna (ratified in 1738).

From the French point of view, the treaty was not unprofitable. Stanislas was to rule in Lorraine; on his death, the land would revert to France. Yet there was criticism from all quarters for the pacific Cardinal, and especially from Chauvelin, who had been unaware of the negotiations for peace. The critics believed that if France had gone on fighting, the gains at the conference table would have been considerably greater. Fleury, however, was no gambler. He knew that France might not do so well if the campaigning had continued, and that France was in no position, from the financial point of view, to waste money on military glory. Taxation was high already, and there was a shortage of bread. Besides, all the signs were that yet another war was about to break out—this time over the Austrian Succession. War broke out between England and Spain in 1739—the so-called War of Jenkins's Ear—over commercial rivalry between the two countries in the New World; and this was soon merged in the war which developed after the death of the Emperor in 1740, leaving only a daughter to succeed him. Most of the powers of Europe had agreed to the Pragmatic Sanction (public guarantee) which safeguarded Maria Theresa's rights to the throne; but the new ruler of Prussia, Frederick, decided to ignore any promises made by his father, and ordered his armies to march into Silesia. This attempt to grab territory was too much for the self-discipline of the French, enemies of Austria for so many generations. Fouquet's grandson, Belleisle, was achieving power in place of the peace-loving Fleury, and he was determined to use the opportunity to smash Austria. Frederick made an alliance with France, and the war opened with French attacks on Westphalia and Bohemia.

Prague was taken, and all might have gone well had it been possible for France to trust her new ally. Unfortunately, this was impossible. Frederick brought Austria to the brink of absolute defeat, and then, by the Treaty of Breslau of 1742, accepted Silesia from Maria Theresa, and made peace. France was left to fight Austria alone, and the Austrians began to claim a string of successes, at Linz, Munich and Prague. Walpole had lost power in England (1742) and Fleury was to die in 1743. Austria's ally, England, mounted attacks with the Dutch along the River Main, and that courageous Hanoverian monarch, George II of England, even took personal command of the English troops at Dettingen, the last occasion on which an English king did so. In fact, it was unfortunate for the French that they lost this battle—they did not deserve to do so. But this conglomeration of enemies proved to be too much for France, especially as her Spanish ally demanded her intervention in Italy. Here England and Austria had an ally in Sardinia, and the French, finding these entanglements and obligations involving her in too great a strain upon her resources, renewed her terms of friendship with Frederick of Prussia, temporarily forgiving his earlier treachery. The French foreign minister, d'Argenson, was partly to blame for this difficult situation, and the future was unpromising. However, the struggle continued. Attacking moves were made in Flanders, the only area where it was possible for France to threaten the northern powers. Tournai was besieged, and Louis, with his general, Saxe, attacked the English under Cumberland and defeated them at Fontenoy, where Cumberland won admiration by the steadiness of his retreating army. There were also some successes in Italy, as at Bassignano, where Maillebois did well with a combined force of French and Spanish troops. The prospects brightened when the English were forced to retire from active participation in the land war in order to deal with the Stuart invasion of the Forty-Five. Indeed, Austria was now prepared to negotiate with Prussia again, or failing that, with d'Argenson, in order to isolate Frederick.

The French minister was unwilling to take this chance of peace. He was determined to crush the power of Maria Theresa if he could, and he saw no reason for making terms which would enable the Austrians to recover Silesia. And it was at this point that Frederick, determined to prevent any such contingency, attacked Saxony and did so well that the Austrians made peace with him a second time (Dresden, 1745). Prussia withdrew from the war, yet again, and once again the Austrians could turn the full weight of their armies upon the French. With Charles Emmanuel of Sardinia, the Austrians defeated the French at Piacenza, and Louis ordered the evacuation of all French forces from the Italian peninsula. Even this was insufficient, for Provence was invaded, and the war began to go badly again for the French. Despite the successes of Saxe in the north, where Brussels and Antwerp fell to his forces, and where Cumberland was defeated at Lauffeldt, in 1747, it was ridiculous to suppose that France might emerge unscathed from the war. The lack of sea power meant that no serious victories could be expected against England. This was particularly so in regard to French possessions and interests overseas. Although a few Frenchmen like La Bourdonnais were conscious of the importance of sea power, it was never realized as being significant by the government.

La Bourdonnais and Dupleix did manage to take Madras in the fighting in India, and Dupleix even managed to besiege Fort St. David; but the lack of support for his forces was shown when Dupleix himself was besieged in Pondicherry, and when the war came to an end, Madras was returned to the English. At the same time, the English returned Louisbourg, on Cape Breton Island, the key to the estuary of the St. Lawrence, which they had captured by an attack from the sea. Apart from these sideshows, little happened outside Europe in the war; but in the next struggle between England and France, both Canada and the French factories in India were to be lost. By the end of 1747, the war was approaching a condition of stalemate, and d'Argenson began negotiations for peace. Terms were agreed on and, at Aix-la-Chapelle, peace was signed in 1748. All the French conquests were lost, and the Dutch were strengthened by the return of their Barrier fortresses. The only gain for Louis was that Austria was weakened. The other powers all made significant gains, and the wastage of wealth, manpower and prestige brought little pride to France. Eight years of peace followed before the next struggle for power in which France was engaged. These were the years of Machault, the Controller-General, and of the Marquise de Pompadour.

Madame de Pompadour, a gifted courtesan with artistic and literary interests, had become the King's mistress in 1745, and, under her influence, the royal treasury was used more and more for the sole purpose of "keeping Versailles in carnival". Possibly because of her misuse of public funds, she was concerned with the chaotic state of the nation's finances, and she encouraged Machault to do what he could to remedy matters. The privileges of the aristocrats and the clergy, of the officials, the tax farmers and of the excepted districts were all inquired into. However, there was considerable protest by those who might be affected by any reforms; and Machault's introduction of a *vingtième* tax was sufficient to provoke enough public dissent for Louis to get cold feet and to withdraw support from his minister. Machault resigned in 1757, as did yet another reformer, d'Argenson, younger brother of the former foreign minister, who had attempted a reform of the army.

D'Argenson had exerted considerable influence over the King in the matter of the struggle between Jansenists and Jesuits. He had strongly supported the latter, while the Jansenists had had the support of the *Parlements*. So strong was the feeling between the two parties that there had nearly been outbreaks of fighting in 1754—largely provoked by the *Parlements*. Louis had realized the danger, and had gone to some trouble to conciliate the Gallican leaders, even though this had caused him to be highly criticized by the Jesuits and their supporters. There was even an attempt to assassinate Louis in 1757. The King was sufficiently frightened by this to drop any ideas he might have had for introducing reforms along the lines which Machault had suggested, and perhaps this was another step towards the inevitable revolution. By this time, the faults of the régime were becoming clear and obvious to everyone. Not only were the faults clear to the governing classes, but to everyone else as well. Voltaire, Rousseau and Montesquieu were at work, criticizing the government and social system of France in all their works. The first volume of the famous *Encyclopédie* had appeared in 1751, and Montesquieu's *Esprit des Lois* in 1748. The *Encylopédie*'s political importance was that it disseminated advanced political ideas under the guise of general information, and was so popular among intellectuals and even at court that bans imposed on reading it were speedily broken.

In the 1750's the Diplomatic Revolution also occurred. Frederick of Prussia had made an alliance with the Hanoverian George II of England, and France had gone against tradition to make terms of friendship with Maria Theresa of Austria, who felt that her previous treaty with England had failed to protect her interests or her territories. The Family Compact with Spain was to be preserved, not only to provide Louis with a much needed ally on the battlefield, but also because Spanish sea power might turn out to be of inestimable value in a war against England. By the Treaty of Versailles of 1757, terms were made with Austria which were indicative of Louis's determination to defeat England. The Austrians were to be subsidized by the French in a war which was to go on until Austria had recovered Silesia. All that seemed likely to accrue to France were Minorca, Dunkirk and a few Flemish towns. It seemed that Louis was forced into this alliance because Austria was his only possible choice if Britain was to be defeated. Louis seemed unaware of the fact that French hopes of success against her great rival were slender. Frederick's abilities in land war were well known, and British sea power seemed unlikely to be overcome despite the prospect of Spanish help. In addition, although Montcalm in Canada had some ability, the other French commanders, Paulmy, de Moras and Bernis, had as their sole qualifications for office the fact that they were Madame de Pompadour's nominations.

When the Seven Years' War broke out in 1756, fortune seemed to be in favour of the Austrians and the French. The former gained an important victory over the Prussians at Kolin in June 1757, and followed this up with another at Prague. The French forces moved across the Rhine to mount an attack upon Hanover, and defeated a force under Cumberland at Hastenbeck. But this period of success was not to last. The French advantage was lost at Klosterseven, and an unfortunate change in the command replaced d'Estrées, who had done so well at Hastenbeck, by Richelieu. Although the Austrians went on to gain another victory over Frederick at Rossbach, he gained his revenge only a few weeks later at Leuthen. This victory put an end to any hopes of a speedy victory over the Prussians, and as it was plainly obvious that Richelieu was incompetent, he was deprived of the French command, which now went to Clermont, a descendant of Condé. However, even Clermont was beaten—this time by Ferdinand of Brunswick, Cumberland's successor—at Crefeld, and the command changed hands again. Now Contades was the commander of the French troops.

So far, little had been heard of the strength of England, but the English year of victories was at hand. There was a curtain-raiser in Canada in 1758, when Amherst and Wolfe took Louisbourg, that key to the St. Lawrence that had been returned to France in 1748. Montcalm, after some early triumphs, lost Fort Duquesne, the most important of the French fortresses in the line which stretched down the Ohio River to the Mississippi, thereby cutting through the territories into which the thirteen English colonies would, one day, expand. Fort Duquesne was renamed Fort Pitt, after the new Prime Minister whose genius, especially in choosing leaders, was to play its part in the defeat of France. But the impressive list of British victories was to appear in 1759. Montcalm was killed in the battle by which Quebec—and Canada—were lost to Wolfe on the Plains of Abraham. Wolfe's successor, Murray, took Montreal. Several West Indian islands, like Guadeloupe, fell to English naval forces. Ferdinand of Brunswick defeated the French at Minden, and the French fleets were defeated by the English under Boscawen and Hawke. The latter's victory over the Brest fleet at Quiberon Bay turned out to be a decisive one for the fortunes of France in India and in Canada. The new chief minister, Choiseul, was forced to recognize that a continuation of the struggle could mean only further defeat.

French fortunes in India were also on the downward path. There had been fighting since 1751, when a puppet of the

French governor, Dupleix, had laid claim to the throne of the Carnatic, and had besieged its capital, Arcot. Clive, however, had led a force of troops in the pay of the East India Company in 1751, and had retaken it and then held on in the face of a determined siege, led by Dupleix. His success in the struggle against the French had led to the recall of Dupleix in 1754, and Clive's great victory at Plassey against the Nawab, Surajah Dowlah, in 1756, had put Bengal under British control. The French had continued the struggle during the Seven Years' War. Their representative in India, de Lally Tollendal, had begun well in fighting at Arcot and at Fort St. David, but the end of French ambitions in India came in 1760, with Tollendal's defeat at Wandewash, where the victory went to the English commander, Eyre Coote. In the following year, the most important surviving French factory in India, Pondicherry, was surrendered to the English. The only reason for the eviction of the French from India, apart from the genius of Clive and of his assistants like Lawrence, was the fact that the French had insufficient sea power to be able to support Dupleix and Tollendal.

Negotiations for peace were set on foot in 1761. By this time Spain, mindful of her obligations under the Family Compact, had decided to enter the war—but only in time to suffer along with her ally when the Treaty of Paris was made. Frederick of Prussia had gone on campaigning vigorously, despite a defeat at the hands of a Russian army at Kunersdorf. Even Choiseul was encouraged by French successes at Cassel and Korbach, and by the fact that Frederick was in difficulties. However, fortune smiled on the Prussian King when a new Czar came to the Russian throne in 1762, a Czar who happened to be an admirer of Frederick. This accident of fate made peace terms even more necessary, and the political situation in England made the negotiations somewhat more manageable. Pitt had resigned in 1761, over his determination to declare war on Spain and to continue the war as vigorously as before, in the face of opposition from the new King, George III, and opposition from his colleagues in the government. As a result, the Treaty of Paris was signed in 1763, and Louis had to agree to the loss of Minorca, Senegal, Canada, the factories in India, and Louisiana. The latter went to Spain, as some compensation for that unfortunate ally's loss of territories to the English. Louis's most important war had ended in disaster. After nearly half a century on the throne, he was unable to point to any enhancement of the power and prestige of France which might balance the bankruptcy of his governments in domestic and financial affairs.

The reign of Louis XV was to continue for another eleven years. For the first seven of them, Choiseul was still in power, and, during that time, despite some attempts to reform the armed forces, little enough was done to set on foot the reforms of which France stood so much in need. The financial problems were no nearer to being solved, and the domestic situation was not made easier by the revival of the ambitions of the *Parlements*, which seemed determined to obstruct the King in every way. Jansenism began to revive, and it was also a time of persecution for the Protestants, which Voltaire scathingly condemned as being unworthy of the civilization of the eighteenth century in the powerful and sophisticated state of France. The Jesuits suffered too. In 1761 the *Parlement* of Paris had taken an opportunity of declaring the Jesuit Order financially bankrupt. Its colleges were suppressed, and many Jesuits were expelled from the country. This move had serious effects upon the educational system of the country, and was, in fact, a stupid and reactionary move, made out of spite by the Gallican-dominated *Parlement*. This kind of deliberate reaction, and opposition to reform, was paralleled by the obstruction faced by the Controller-General, Silhouette, when he put forward proposals for financial changes in 1759. All that remains to us of his ideas is the name of the fashionable form of portrait introduced to show how poor the rich would become under his reforms. At any rate, without any reforms, the fiscal situation went on deteriorating. And it was not a period which lacked ideas on the subject. Gournay and his "economists", with their *laissez-faire* theories, and Quesnay with his "physiocrats", and their ideas that only the land, as the source of all wealth, should be taxed, were becoming influential in some quarters, despite the satirical attacks of Voltaire.

In only one field were there significant changes. In the army, Choiseul was able to introduce some valuable reforms. He was aided by Gribeauval, an expert in artillery matters. There was a considerable building programme of ships, indicating that the lessons of the last war had been learned. Indeed, these ships were to play a significant part in the defeat of England in the War of American Independence. But France had little to be grateful for, to Choiseul, in the matter of foreign policy. He was determined to maintain the friendship with Austria which had done nothing, as yet, to promote the success of France. To strengthen this alliance, he negotiated the marriage of the future Louis XVI with the Emperor's sister, Marie Antoinette, in 1770. There seems to be little doubt that Marie was part of an Austrian scheme to keep Choiseul in the dark about Austrian plans to participate, with Russia and Prussia, in the partition of Poland. However, Choiseul's period of power was approaching its end. He seemed to be doing well, with Corsica being purchased by France, and with Lorraine reverting to France under the terms of the treaty of 1738. But he was the victim of the intriguing of other ministers, Terray, the new Controller, Maupeon, the Chancellor, and d'Aiguillon, a leader of the extreme Catholics. They used the growing tendency of the *Parlement* to obstruct governmental business, and trouble with the *Parlements* of Rennes and Paris, to persuade Louis to dismiss Choiseul from office.

The three "plotters" took office in what came to be known as the triumvirate, a government which took firm action over the *Parlement*, sending its members into exile, and setting up a *Grand Conseil* of seventy-five members. The powers of the *Parlements* were passed to a new *Conseil d'Etat*, and this new system, whatever the motives for its establishment, might have altered the administration of France for the best, had the new King, Louis XVI, allowed it to continue. As it was, the storm of protest from the vested interests scared him into revoking this reform of the triumvirs. The three ministers found their powers waning, however, even before the accession of the new King. They seemed to wane as the life of Louis XV came to an end. The King's last months were marked by Terray's failure to solve the financial problem except by reducing the interest payable on the national debt, and by the diplomatic snub administered to France when Austria announced the partition of Poland as a *fait accompli*. However, when Louis died in 1774, events in America were about to take a turn which would enable France, at last, to inflict a defeat upon her old enemy, England.

Despite all that has been said about the corruption of France under the *ancien régime*, the country was still great on the death of Louis XV—possibly still greater than England. France had by far the larger population, but her opportunity to excel in wealth and trade, as she did in culture, was made almost impossible by the antiquated inefficiency of the machinery of despotism. Not that despotism was inevitably inefficient; but it seemed to be so to the influential French philosophical writers, who did so much to prepare the ground for the revolution. Among them were Voltaire and Montesquieu. The latter had a great influence on political thinkers, in France and abroad. His earliest significant work was seen in *Les Lettres persanes* of 1721, in which he satirized Paris as seen through the eyes of Persian visitors, and discussed Christianity, among other topics. Montesquieu travelled extensively, and his visit to England persuaded him that the English had the best political system in contemporary Europe. He discussed some of his political theories in his *Les Considérations sur les causes de la grandeur des Romains et de leur décadence* in 1734, but his most important work appeared in 1748. This was *L'Esprit des lois*, which pointed out how England benefited from a constitutional monarchy, and in which he argued for a separation of the legislative and judicial functions of the machinery of the state, as in the "enlightened" English constitution. In fact, some of his ideas on the English system were incorrect; but his ideas did much for the reformers, who were beginning to demand inquiry and reason in the affairs of state.

Voltaire (1694–1778) was probably the most powerful philosopher of the "Enlightenment". The son of a lawyer, he had considerable abilities as a playwright and poet, and would have made a good businessman. But he was an even greater prose writer and wit. After a period of imprisonment in the Bastille for daring to quarrel on equal terms with a member of the nobility, he spent some time in England, and was considerably impressed by the way of life he saw there under Walpole's Prime Ministership. His *Lettres philosophiques*, or *Lettres sur les Anglais*, appeared in 1734, and foreshadowed his future campaigns against injustice and privilege—especially if the privilege was associated with the Church. His attacks became so bitter that, eventually, Voltaire had to leave Paris. He studied the latest work on scientific subjects, and produced a sound narrative of the events of the previous reign, *Le Siècle de Louis XIV*, in 1751. In 1759 he published a survey of human history to show the development from barbarian superstition to the age of enlightenment; this was *L'Essai sur les mœurs*. After his return to Paris, where he became something of a favourite, incongruously enough, of Madame de Pompadour, he went to visit Frederick of Prussia; but eventually, he settled on the borders of France and Switzerland, where he felt himself in less danger for his political and anti-clerical opinions. In 1763 there appeared a *Traité sur la tolérance*, followed rapidly by a *Dictionnaire philosophique*. Perhaps today he is best remembered for his brilliant satire, *Candide*, although there is as much amusement in his *L'Ingénu*, the story of the "noble savage" in the polite society of the eighteenth-century aristocracy. His vast output did much to spread criticism of the establishment, and to make such criticism fashionable. He did his best to laugh out of existence the absurdities of the survivals of feudalism in France.

Similar important work was produced by Diderot (1713–84) in the *Encyclopédie*, the first volumes of which appeared from 1751. Subsequent volumes were produced, sometimes clandestinely, until 1765. There was much propaganda to be discovered among the articles, some of it brilliantly written, not only by Diderot but also by men like d'Alembert. Diderot was a journalist first and foremost, but he had considerable abilities as a philosopher, novelist and writer on the theatre. He contributed to the *Correspondance littéraire*, and spent some time in Russia with the friendship and patronage of Catherine the Great. There is some possibility that Diderot helped Jean-Jacques Rousseau with the latter's *Discours sur les sciences et les arts*. Rousseau (1712–78) was a Genevan composer, largely self-educated, who moved to Paris and became well known because of such writings as his *Discours sur l'inégalité* (1754). He published his very popular novel, *La Nouvelle Héloïse*, in 1761, but his most famous and influential work was *Le Contrat Social*, published in the same year, while his progressive theories on education appeared in *Émile* shortly afterwards. His denial of some of the unquestioned Christian dogmas led to a rapid departure from Paris—he feared arrest. He spent a year in England, but even there he feared arrest and persecution; in fact, he never recovered from this fear until his death. Some of his important writings such as *Les Dialogues* and *Les Confessions* were published posthumously. His bold words in *Le Contrat Social* summarize many of his ideas: "Man is born free, yet he is everywhere in chains." Rousseau was probably the most dangerous of all the philosophers, from the point of view of the defenders of the *ancien régime*. He was more of a prophet than a philosopher. His precepts were put into practice first by the revolutionaries who were to create the United States of America. He owed a debt, himself, to the English philosopher, John Locke.

It cannot be said that the other literary figures of the eighteenth century were as important as those discussed above. However, Lesage wrote some interesting *picaresque* novels, like those of Defoe and Smollett. His *Gil Blas de Santillane* and *Le Bachelier de Salamanque* (1736) were examples, and Lesage also wrote many farces for the theatre. The *abbé* Prévost was also a novelist, as well as historian. He is chiefly remembered for his sentimental *L'histoire du chevalier Des Grieux et de Manon*, which is set partly in the Louisiana of the days of the financier, Law. Prévost also translated some of the novels of Richardson from English into French. For the theatre, the best tragic writer was probably

Voltaire, whose *Zaïre*, *Mérope* and *La Mort de César* were the most important in the period. Voltaire should also be remembered for his successful campaign to persuade theatre managers to remove spectators from their traditional seats on the stage. One result was to make it possible for scene changing to be introduced into the theatre. Other dramatists of the time were Lemierre (1723–93) and de Belloy. A new kind of tragedy emerged with d'Arnaud's gruesome play, *Euphémie*, and in the field of comedy one must notice Marivaux (1688–1763), whose *Arlequin poli par l'amour* and *Le Jeu de l'amour et du hasard* were produced for the court of Versailles, and written well, with a delicate, if affected, style.

The reign of Louis XV saw the development of the *opéra-comique*, the work of men like Favart and Sedaine. Much greater than these was, of course, the writer Beaumarchais, businessman, music teacher and editor, and creator of *Le Barbier de Séville* and *Le Mariage de Figaro*, which were to achieve such fame when used as operas by Rossini and Mozart. *Le Mariage*, with its epigrams of a somewhat democratic nature, was banned for six years; but *Le Barbier* was produced at Versailles with Marie Antoinette in the cast. There was little important poetry in Louis's reign, except there is some amusement to be gained from the reading of Jean-Baptiste Rousseau and Lebrun. The last of the epic poems came with Voltaire's *La Henriade*, and the other poets of the period were as artificial as one might imagine in the unreal atmosphere of the century of Versailles. Vigorous prose from the philosophers of the "Enlightenment" was to go far to produce an atmosphere of revolution, and a new kind of French attitude to literature once the revolution had arrived.

## RECOMMENDED READING

*Europe in the Eighteenth Century*. M. S. ANDERSON. Longmans, 1961.
*Histoire de France*. Ed. MARCEL REINHARD. Larousse. (Vol. II. R. MOUSNIER, *La France de Louis XV*.)
*Madame de Pompadour*. NANCY MITFORD. Hamish Hamilton, 1954.

*New Cambridge Modern History*, Vol. VII. *The Old Régime 1713–63.*
  Chapter X—The Decline of Divine Right Monarchy in France, A. Cobban.
  Chapter XX—The Seven Years War, E. Robson.
*The Regency of Philip of Orleans.* J. H. M. SALMON. *History Today*, Vol. XI,
  No. 1, p. 28 (January 1961).
*The Origins of Modern Europe, 1660–1789.* J. L. WHITE. Murray, 1964.
Writings of Voltaire, Montesquieu, Diderot, etc.

## CHAPTER 12

# *The Coming of Revolution*

Louis XVI came to the throne in 1774, determined—so far as such a man could be determined—to pursue a policy of conciliation. He was, so far as one may judge, well-meaning and devout, but idle. Perhaps it would be fairer to say that he was emotionally and intellectually retarded; and this made him maddeningly indecisive. He was unfortunate in his marriage to Marie Antoinette of Austria, whose political allegiance and failure to help her husband pursue a wise and determined course, made her the worst of queens, under the particular circumstances of the time. Neither of them could foresee that, unless there was a drastic reform, France might erupt into a tragic revolution. Admittedly, few could have foretold the course of events; but, as they occurred, Louis and his Queen did little but deplore this course, and to hope for the best. They did not realize that the absolute despotism of the eighteenth century might well give way to revolutionary republicanism. Constitutional, social and financial reforms were now so necessary that only disaster could ensue if no strongly determined action were taken. The nagging evil of national bankruptcy, which was largely the result of privilege among the richest classes in France, was calling for immediate surgery. That no surgeon was able to deal with the disease— mostly because of the patient's refusal to accept the operation— was to end in the death of the monarchy and the *ancien régime*.

The *Parlements* wanted no sweeping financial reforms; nor did the nobility. Few realized the significance of creating financial stability. Certainly Louis seemed unwilling or unable to support such of his ministers as seemed able to tackle the problem. However, there were undoubted changes for the better in the fifteen years of Louis's reign before the onset of the Revolution. French pride was salved in a successful war against England, the army was reorganized, and there were some hopeful signs of commercial and economic progress. The former *intendant*, Turgot, who was competent if not brilliant as a minister, realized the need for economies, and might have done much for France if his proposed attack upon financial privileges had not caused Louis to bow to demands for his dismissal. Vergennes and Necker were not without talent, and might have saved France had Louis shown a real understanding of the necessity to support his servants. Saint-Germain, for example, did much to improve the French army, bringing in new tactics, a reorganized artillery, founding military colleges, and doing something to abolish the purchase of commissions. His work was to have its value for the French army in the revolutionary and Napoleonic periods. Similar work was done for the navy by Sartine.

In foreign affairs early in Louis's reign, Vergennes was concerned to hold France aloof from the difficulties imposed upon her by the extremely unpopular alliance with Austria, which had been increased by the King's marriage. Vergennes was determined, for example, to prevent France from being involved in Austrian wars with Bavaria. However, in the American War of Independence, which began in 1775, Vergennes was willing to support unofficial aid to the rebels who were causing such acute embarrassment to the British. When Benjamin Franklin visited France in 1776, active intervention in the war became a possibility, and, when the news of the American victory over Burgoyne at Saratoga reached Paris, it was decided to make a treaty with the Americans and to engage openly in the war. Even then, Vergennes was concerned with the possibility of the outbreak of war between Austria and Prussia, and made it his business to negotiate a peace between the two so that French attention could be concentrated on events across the Atlantic. It was with French military and naval assistance led by Rochambeau and de Grasse, that Washington was able to defeat the British at

Yorktown in 1781. French forces also helped the Spaniards to take Minorca and to besiege Gibraltar—without success. When Britain agreed to make terms at the Treaty of Versailles in 1783, the American colonists won their independence and France received Senegal, Tobago and Saint-Pierre with Miquelon. But none of these were so important to France as the gain of prestige in a successful war against the old enemy. Vergennes, too, was conscious of the cost of war, and he again turned to an attempt to keep the peace between Austria and the Ottoman Empire, and between Austria and Holland. He did his best to maintain the peace, knowing that France could not afford the cost of glory— even going to the lengths of signing the commercial treaty with Pitt's England in 1786. Vergennes died in 1787. His successor, Montmorin, continued in office until 1791. Generally speaking, Montmorin followed in the same lines, although, with the difficulties France was facing at home, this is scarcely surprising. He even followed a policy of neutrality when the Prussians invaded Holland.

In these pre-revolutionary years, there could have been hopes of an economic revival, if only the question of taxation could have been satisfactorily dealt with. The free trade treaty with England (the so-called "Eden" Treaty) was a sign that commercial policies could be changed, and that protectionism might be abandoned. But unemployment was widespread, and nothing was done to alleviate the miseries of those who could find no work. Determined action could scarcely be expected of a king, who, on his accession, re-established the *Parlements* and their privileges. Louis did, however, appoint Turgot as Controller-General, and Turgot did his best to introduce some honesty into a corrupt system. In fact, Turgot was more of an honest administrator than a reformer, but he did try to abolish the hated *corvée* and to reduce indirect taxation. Unfortunately, the opposition of commercial vested interests, combined with a bad harvest in 1774, caused sufficiently vocal opposition for the timid King to be concerned when Turgot proposed certain reforms in industry and in the system of local government. Eventually, the

*Parlements*, the clergy and nobility united in opposition to the Controller, and Turgot was dismissed, to be replaced eventually by Necker, a Protestant banker, who attempted to raise sufficient funds for the war against England by raising loans and re-introducing protectionist legislation. Even Necker, however, saw the impossibility of solving the financial problem without dealing with the iniquitously corrupt and unjust taxation system. Lacking Turgot's courage, however, Necker did little to attack the privileged ones, and even presented a budget in 1781, the *Compte rendu au Roi*, which largely concealed the true state of the national debt. However, Necker, too, was dismissed in 1781, and nothing practical was done until the appointment of another *intendant*, Calonne, after the end of the American Revolutionary War. Calonne tried to introduce a land tax (*foncière*), and a stamp duty, which he hoped would raise revenue from those whose privileges normally enabled them to evade paying taxes. He also tried to abolish the *taille*, and internal customs duties, and to do something to reform the local government system. To create allies whom he might set against the *Parlements*, he persuaded the King to call an Assembly of Notables; but although there were some sympathetic reformers among them, like Lafayette, even here he found too many attached to the cause of privilege. Although Calonne had come nearer than the other ministers to finding possible solutions to the problems, he too was dismissed, and was replaced by one of his opponents, Archbishop Brienne. The Archbishop found, upon investigation, that Calonne had been perfectly correct in his arguments, and tried to reintroduce his ideas. He also found that the Assembly of Notables would give him no support, and that the *Parlements* were not to be persuaded to support a new land tax. It was this determination to resist reform that persuaded Louis to regret recalling the *Parlements* on his accession, and to try the expedient of exiling the members of the *Parlement* of Paris to Troyes. But even this show of determination on the King's part did not last. Before long, the *Parlement* was back, and being asked to agree that the *vingtième* should be extended; however, the *Parlement* was just as determined to prevent any reform and to refuse to register any new edicts, such as the one calling for a degree of religious toleration.

At last, Brienne decided to attempt to get rid of the *Parlement*. A replacement was to be provided in a *Cour plénière*; and the May Edicts of 1788 provided for this, as well as certain other judicial reforms. There were the expected protests against this coup in Paris; but also some unexpected ones, as in Dauphiné, where the local Estates met and sent in a call for the election of a States-General. Other people had been making such a suggestion for some time—Lafayette was one of them—and it had also been proposed that, to avoid an automatic majority for the privileged classes, the representation of the third estate should be doubled. The government therefore decided to call a meeting of the States-General for May of 1789, and the first step was taken towards forming a new constitution. As it happened, the first step had also been taken towards starting the French Revolution.

Brienne was replaced by Necker, which was, perhaps, an unfortunate move, for Necker was a financier but no reformer of constitutions. He was even foolish enough to ignore what Brienne had seen to be necessary. He recalled the *Parlement*, which immediately demanded that the States-General should be so constituted as to preserve the privileges of those who possessed them. This determined defence of the *status quo* decided the government to get rid of the *Parlements* for good, and also to dissolve the Assembly of Notables, so that the ground was prepared for the election of a States–General in which the Commons were to have the proposed double representation, but not *vôte par tête*. This, of course, immediately cut their numerical advantage over the other estates, who would combine two to one against them. Apart from this, no plans were made to give the new assembly a lead. It was as though Parliament were to be called in England without a government in office. Nothing was done to show that the King was aware that the States-General was being called at a time of acute crisis, to rebuild the constitution and to decide upon a revision of the old taxation privileges. Nothing was said to show the members of the States-General that their help was needed to get rid of the conservatives who were standing in the way of essential reform. By doing and saying nothing, Louis ensured that his despotic powers were to be limited, that a new constitution would be made whether he liked it or not, and that there might well be a growth of democratic, and possibly even republican, sentiment which he would be powerless to control. Louis's amiable lack of political persecution had permitted the spread of the powerful critical force of "philosophy", which had won over such liberal nobles as Lafayette.

It was decided that all taxpayers should vote in the primary elections. This alone ensured that there would be a far more democratic franchise in France than was known in the vast majority of constituencies in England at that time. The chosen candidates would then vote for electors who would choose deputies to represent them in the States-General. This body eventually consisted of 285 nobles, 308 clergy and 621 commoners—although, in fact, the latter included nobles like Mirabeau, a marquis, who actually bought a shop in order to qualify; and a great proportion of lawyers. Each deputy had a *cahier* of suggestions for reform and of local grievances. Every one of them was aware of the widespread demands for reform, for liberty, for a new constitution, and for the end of financial privileges. All the deputies knew that much legislation was required, and that no plan of reform was available for debate. No leader was in sight— least of all, Necker. The weaknesses of Louis were fairly obvious. Any tendency to forget the problems at issue would be prevented by the proximity of the unemployed rabble of Paris, so near to Versailles. The more radically inclined deputies were determined to demand *vôte par tête*, but even they were determined to do what they thought was best for the King, and there could have been few convinced republicans present when the States-General was formally opened on 5 May 1789. It was not surprising, however, when the commoners asked for a joint meeting of the Estates, and finally invited the others to join them. Before June was out, they were illegally calling themselves the National Assembly—and this began to approximate more to the truth when many of the clergy decided to join with them (19 June 1789).

One of the possible reasons for the King's inactivity during this period, apart from his habitual unwillingness to take decisions, was the death of the Dauphin; but when the King called for a *Séance Royale*, a full council meeting, the members of the so called Assembly not unnaturally feared a *coup d'état*, and so took the famous decision to adjourn to the nearby tennis court, to take an oath, as Mirabeau suggested, never to dissolve themselves until they had achieved their ambitions. Although Louis, two days later, offered to end such abuses as privilege in taxation, the commoners were of the opinion that such conciliatory moves were inadequate and too late. Faced by a determined body, which wanted far more radical legislation, Louis agreed at last to a union of the three orders in an assembly which was now determined to give France a new constitution. Had Louis been a more forceful character, he would have realized that he must get rid of the States-General, or choose to dominate the constitution-making, forcing it into acceptable channels. But by this time the government was as nerveless as the King. Paris was rapidly falling into a state of anarchy, many of the troops were in a mutinous state, and even the Assembly did not want to see troops used to restore order in the capital in case the troops were then to be used to disperse the deputies. Casting around for a possible move, Louis dismissed Necker; but this did nothing to solve the problem of disorder in the streets of the capital. Eventually the bourgeoisie in the city, frightened of the threat to property and life, appointed a committee which was to make arrangements for a civic guard. Their fears were justified. The mob was so out of hand that the Bastille, a state prison, was seized and destroyed, and its governor murdered. Much has been made of the event, but its significance was more symbolic than real. By this time, some of the aristocrats were leaving Versailles, and some were leaving France altogether, until, as they hoped, the troubles blew over. The King, changing his mind, recalled Necker, who again failed to take the lead as he should. Matters were left to the Assembly, whose president persuaded the King to recognize the civic guard and to show himself in Paris, in the hopes of restoring order there. This was almost hopeless. Food was scarce in the city, and neither Bailly nor Lafayette, the reforming noble who so much admired constitutional rule, and who was the commander of the guard, could do much to restrain the activities of the mob. Psychologically, the fall of the Bastille was vastly important. It proved to the mob that it had power successfully to defy authority; and hence its anniversary is still celebrated as France's day of liberty.

Meanwhile, the Assembly appointed a committee of eight to draft a constitution which would depend upon a monarch with limited powers. It was decided to allow the Assembly to discuss and to promulgate the new constitution as it emerged, in parts, from the committee. But as this slow process went on, the peasants in the provinces were organizing their own revolutions, burning *châteaux* and destroying the documents which recorded their own servile status. It was plain that, by now, France had no government which could keep order. The crowd had tasted blood and had discovered an animal lust for disgusting revenges. Bloody, as distinct from violent, disorder had begun. The revolutionaries had a free hand, and even in the Assembly it was becoming plain that the moderates could not prevent the more radical members from demanding—and getting—revolutionary reforms. Mirabeau, who might have been a leader who could lead the more moderate section of the Assembly, was not trusted because of his profligacy and the wildness of his private life, either by the King or by the deputies, and Louis felt that all he could do was to agree to the constitutional decrees—which he hoped to be able to claim later as being made under duress—and hope for affairs to calm down. It was, however, becoming plain that this was a forlorn hope, and one that became more forlorn when the Parisian mob arrived in Versailles, broke into the palace, and forced him to move into Paris as a suspect under constant hostile observation (October 1789). So far, no strong leader had emerged, either to save the King or to save France.

Neither Necker nor Mirabeau was capable of such a task. Although the emigrations continued—there were many whose pessimism was the dominant emotion—some thought that the worst must now be over. The Assembly plucked up sufficient courage to proclaim martial law in an attempt to put a stop to the rioting.

Gradually, the terms of the new settlement emerged. Deputies were not to accept office as ministers, which meant the revolutionary leaders would not become part of the "Establishment"; the system of government by *intendants* was abolished; eighty-three new *départements* were created and divided into municipalities; and a system arranged whereby the *départements* were to elect members for future Assemblies. So far as the franchise was concerned, about one-third of the men were to be refused the vote because they paid insufficient in taxes. Although this was undemocratic, it was remarkably generous for the time. But there were immediate protests from the radicals in Paris, and especially from Marat, that bizarre and dedicated individual, who worshipped the poorest of the poor. *Parlements* were to be abolished, magistrates were to be elected to preside over new courts, and arrangements were made for the reorganization of the army. The King was not to have an absolute veto, but only a suspensive one. To remedy the financial difficulties of the state, the property of the Church was to be seized and sold, on the grounds that such property was really "owned" by the nation, and held on trust by the Church. A paper currency—*assignats*—was issued. Even more revolutionary decisions were to come. In 1790 the religious Orders were abolished in France, and it was decided that archbishoprics were to be suppressed and priests were to be elected and paid, which meant controlled, by the state. This step showed the importance of the Jansenist, anti-clerical members of the Assembly, as well as the increasing number of atheist philosophers. Along with the annexation of church property, it was a step which was bound to cause trouble, not only with the faithful members of the Church in France, but also with the Papacy. The situation was made worse when revolutionaries in the south demanded that the Papal territory of the Comtat Venaissin, which had been under Roman rule for centuries and included Avignon, should be united with France. The immediate result was, of course, that the priesthood became an actively counter-revolutionary force, but the Pope's reactions were, for the moment, carefully diplomatic. The lesser nobility, which had also been divided on the question of the new constitution, also came out against the revolution when primogeniture and the titles of nobility were declared to be abolished.

In 1790 new local elections caused a new outburst of revolutionary enthusiasm. Louis attended the celebrations organized in Paris on 14 July, but he must have realized that things had now gone so far that the relics of the *ancien régime* could not last much longer. The priests were ordered to take an oath of loyalty to the new constitution, which many, of course, could not bring themselves to do. The Pope, Pius VI, had to make his attitude known, and as soon as he condemned the new civil constitution of the clergy, all the moral pressure of the Church was brought to bear upon the Assembly. Once again, Mirabeau advised Louis that his only hope was to take action which would show himself to be the true leader of his people. He also tried to help by becoming President of the Jacobins and of the National Assembly, both of which organizations he privately hoped to ruin. He did his best to keep France at peace with her neighbours, believing that war would be fatal to Louis's best interests. But these plans were too involved for the poor bemused King, who could only assume that the sly Mirabeau could never be trusted. But the religious troubles did force Louis to take some action at last. Although he had accepted the demands of the Assembly so far, he decided that the condemnation by the Pope had left him only one solution. He sent a representative to Switzerland, to negotiate for foreign aid, and secretly made plans to leave France. While he did so, the unfortunate Mirabeau was continuing his plans to persuade the revolutionary forces to go so far that they would forfeit all public sympathy, so that Louis, in restoring order, would gain all the credit for saving France. Fortunately for himself, perhaps, Mirabeau died in April 1791.

While, outside France, there had been considerable enthusiasm for the Revolution in its early stages, especially in England, where the belief existed that France was getting rid of despotism in order to institute a system based upon the English constitution, many of the rulers of Europe were beginning to be frightened in case revolutionary ideas should spread. The possibilities of intervention by foreign powers were lessened, however, at this stage, because Austria was involved in a war with the Turks, and Spain and England were engaged in a crisis over the Nootka Sound claims. However, in 1791 Leopold, Marie Antoinette's brother, the new Emperor in Austria, made peace with Turkey. Catherine of Russia tried to persuade him to intervene in France. But Leopold, like other rulers, was also conscious of the benefit for Europe of having France so tied up in her own problems that, for the moment, she could be discounted in foreign affairs. In fact, he felt no urgent wish to intervene, despite the urgent pleas of nobles who had emigrated from France. This attitude was shared, of course, by England and Prussia, but the fact was not known in France, where, in an atmosphere of fear and revolutionary exhilaration, foreign intervention was expected daily. The atmosphere of tension was exploited by Marat, who, in his journal, *Ami du Peuple*, poured out a torrent of anti-royal and anti-clerical propaganda, interspersing warnings of foreign reaction with demands for the death of those whom he saw as traitors to the cause of revolution in France. Gradually, more notice was taken of his warnings, and public disturbances began to grow more serious again. Lafayette's National Guard seemed to be unwilling to do much to keep order, and Desmoulins and the Cordeliers, with other revolutionaries, began to work on the feelings of the Paris mob. For the first time, there were signs of a growth in republican ideas. There were demands for a universal franchise, led by the lawyer, Robespierre. Although few members of the Assembly had much regard for him, Marat thought highly of this new star in the revolutionary sky. Even though republican propaganda grew in strength, though, there were few attacks at this stage on private property.

But there were signs that the moderates had had enough, and were thinking of making a stand against the extremists. Once again, there would have been a chance for Louis to emerge as the saviour of France, if he had been prepared to take a strong line. As it was, the King was still plotting an escape, even though he had been prevented from leaving Paris for St. Cloud by those who saw him as a useful hostage. Marie Antoinette, moreover, was still convinced that it might be still possible to command a successful counter-revolution from outside Paris. For the moment, extremism seemed to be giving way to moderation, but, as it was to appear, the Jacobins were not weakening. In fact, this revolutionary minority was building its strength—winning political power because of the willingness of its members to be active in political matters, and the efficiency of its cellular organization, comparable to modern communist techniques for spreading information, keeping discipline, and preparing political action before open meetings.

Then came the opportunity for the extremists. On 20 June 1791 Louis and his family escaped from the Tuileries in disguise, and set out for Varennes and the frontier, aided by the devoted Comte de Fersen. The arrangements went wrong because of some unnecessary delays, and the royal party was recognized, arrested, and sent back to Paris theoretically under escort, but in fact surrounded by a howling mob, demanding immediate vengeance. This was a serious blow to the moderates, although a pretence was kept up that Louis had left Paris unwillingly, and because he had received bad advice. But the King was now under guard in the Tuileries, and suspended from office while revisions were made in the constitution. He was no longer a deluded suspect monarch, but a fat pig Bourbon, a prisoner in his own palace. The republicans, not unnaturally, stepped up their demands for the deposition of the King. The moderates, of course, hoped that this would be unnecessary—such a step would endanger the new constitution, and probably ensure foreign intervention. For the moment, France remained officially a monarchy, and Louis remained nominally a king. For one thing, there was no obvious candidate to replace him on the throne. The atmosphere, however, continued to be tense, especially when some National Guards fired on a mob of people signing a petition for Louis's deposition on the Champ de Mars. For the moment, however, the moderates still held firm, although republicanism had increased, as the attempted escape had discredited the monarchists. Marat and Robespierre went into hiding. And then, incredibly, the royalist deputies decided that the moment had come for them to demand a restoration of the King, and broke away from the other moderates in the Assembly. Of course, the sole beneficiaries were the republicans. However, the moderates, the Feuillants in particular, decided to go ahead with the publication of the new revised constitution, which, if it had been accepted loyally by Louis, would have established a reasonably conservative new régime in France. The King, still suspended from office, was persuaded to swear an oath to maintain the new constitution, although he could not conceal his horror when the deputies remained seated in his presence. The Assembly, feeling that progress could now be made, went on to set up a much more humane penal code, to establish trial by jury, and to announce the official annexation of Avignon.

The next step was to hold new elections. The Feuillants—mostly former Jacobins who wished to retain the monarchy—and the Jacobins were candidates, but there were also many independents. As it had been decided that deputies in the old Assembly were ineligible for election, most of the Feuillants were new and inexperienced politicians. It was not surprising, therefore, that the new Assembly contained a majority of independents. There were few who had any idea which path France would take, and whether the new constitution and a limited monarchy would suffice to prevent the republicans from having their way. The bourgeois Feuillants found themselves opposed in the Assembly by a group of radicals from the Gironde, led by the conspicuous republican, Roland, and helped by Siéyès and

Brissot. But neither party was to be as powerful as the mob, the *sans-culottes*, who were uncontrollable in Paris. Everyone was conscious that a counter-revolutionary force of *emigrés* was being assembled at Coblenz; and all Frenchmen were determined to prevent any successful invasion by such an army. Nothing could have done more to make men even more suspicious of Louis than the presence of this force on the frontiers. Brissot wanted the *emigrés* publicly condemned as traitors, and the extremist forces began to rally their strength. A Girondin, Pétion, became *maire* of Paris, and Danton, a leader of the Cordeliers, became a procurator-general in the city. Lafayette, once so popular, was no longer in control.

Paris began to regard the National Guard as of little account, and, with the Girondins increasing their power, war with Austria became more and more probable. Although Leopold was still anxious to keep the peace, the rather vaguely worded Declaration of Pillnitz of August 1791 seemed to indicate that he might take some definite action to try to restore Louis's full rights as King in France. Marie Antoinette was still convinced that a declaration of war could save the monarchy—it would mean inevitably successful foreign intervention. Marat, of course, was all in favour of what amounted to a civil war, to destroy traitors to France before there was any attempt to fight foreign powers. On the whole, the Girondin leaders favoured the idea of war because it would make them appear to be the defenders of the Revolution against all comers. With good fortune, war might mean the spread of revolutionary ideas in other parts of Europe, where it was thought that the common people were in sympathy. But it was difficult to make war on an unwilling enemy. Leopold, even when he received an appeal for aid from the Bishop of Trèves, merely reminded the French government of the consequences if they provoked the powers to go to war. But war, obviously, could not be avoided eventually. The Girondins made speeches attacking Austria in the Assembly, and the Feuillants could do little, for their influence was shrinking as the weeks went by. The attacks did not cease when Leopold died. Even the men like Dumouriez were reconciled to the idea of war, for they thought that a victorious struggle against a foreign power could restore national respect for the monarchy. But it was the death of Leopold that changed the circumstances. The new Emperor, Francis II, was far from averse to making war on the revolutionaries, and his provocative messages caused the Assembly to decide openly in favour of a declaration of war on 20 April 1792.

The private feelings of Frenchmen on this new development varied considerably. Some hoped for a victory for the Revolution; others hoped that the monarchy might be saved, either through victory or defeat. But when hostilities opened, the weaknesses of the French infantry were revealed, and some regiments, according to Lafayette, their commander, would be willing to march on Paris and attack the revolutionary government in an attempt to restore the monarchy. The Austrians were also reluctant to engage immediately in full-scale war, when they saw that Catherine of Russia was prepared to use the opportunity to invade Poland. The Austrian allies, the Prussians, were just as concerned, and, in fact, there was no full-scale attack on France for several months. The delay, until August 1792, enabled the French government to do something to restore the morale of the army. Reliable revolutionaries were enlisted as officers—some, like Masséna, to become famous in after years as Napoleon's generals. But even with this breathing space, France's situation seemed desperate. There was hunger still, in Paris; and unemployment and rioting were still going on. There was loud controversy in the Assembly between the Feuillants, the Girondins and a new independent Jacobin group led by Robespierre. It seemed that the forces of the Revolution were divided. So they were, in the Assembly; but outside it, the common people were determined to preserve what they had already won, and all the leading radical forces were beginning to agree that the King and his supporters among the priesthood and the property-owning classes were likely to be traitors to the new régime. Emergency measures were decided upon.

F

Volunteers were to be recruited for a new armed force in Paris. Priests who opposed the constitution were to be arrested in readiness for deportation. When Louis decided to veto these decisions, and to dismiss some of his revolutionary ministers, public feelings were roused. There were violent demonstrations in Paris, which the National Guard could do little to prevent, and a mob went to the Tuileries to "petition" the King, and ended by breaking into the palace and threatening to dethrone him. Although there was considerable sympathy for the degraded monarch among the more moderate sections of the community, Louis still refused to take any outright action. He refused offers of assistance from Lafayette, and put all his hopes on the chances of rescue by foreign intervention. The Girondins were therefore left free to continue the enrolment of volunteers for the defence of Paris and the Revolution, and to take measures against the National Guard. The Jacobin leaders were given a bodyguard, and Robespierre put a formal motion to depose the King and to elect a new Assembly on the basis of universal suffrage.

The Duke of Brunswick, in command of the invading forces, made it known that he was to attempt the suppression of anarchy in France and the restoration of the royal authority. The Assembly was still in a dilemma. A majority still opposed formal deposition of Louis. On the other hand, they were afraid, now, of the mob violence which some of the members had done so much to encourage in the past. For the time being, it was decided to do nothing and to await the outcome of events, but this only gave a new opportunity to the more violent revolutionaries. The Hôtel de Ville was taken over, and the Municipal Council began to accept orders from the Jacobins. Mandat was dismissed from office as commander of the National Guard, which was removed from its duties at the Tuileries. Huguenin, one of the revolutionary leaders, took over the Council within a few days, ordered Mandat to be killed, and the stage was set for the attack on the Tuileries. Louis, beginning to realize at last how serious the situation was, decided to take refuge with the Assembly, but by this time, even this had little authority and prestige left.

The mob invaded the Tuileries, and there was considerable bloodshed in the street fighting. The Swiss Guards fought bravely to save the King. The members of the Assembly decided that they had only one choice left. They declared Louis to be suspended from his office, called for elections to be held for a national convention, and nominated members of a provisional executive committee to rule France in the absence of a monarch. The next move, for which all France was now waiting, was the dethronement of the King. Lafayette's attempt to use part of the army to save Louis came to nothing, and so the famous army commander fled, only to fall into the hands of the invading Austrians. Kellermann and Dumouriez were appointed as the new commanders of the army, in his place. Meantime, in Paris, the situation was becoming rapidly more and more chaotic. The Assembly, with such few powers as it had, was controlled by the Girondins, and the Commune, the government of revolutionary Paris, becoming daily more important, was in the hands of the Jacobins. The council of the Commune was joined by Robespierre, and the Commune's Vigilance Committee began to take actions upon all sorts of matters which were properly the business of the Assembly; but the latter dared do nothing about it. Marat emerged from hiding, and Danton's power, as the darling of the mob, was undefined but vast.

At length, on 19 August Brunswick's army invaded French territory. Danton, now officially Minister of Justice, made innumerable speeches, demanding *toujours l'audace*, in which he told the Parisians that unity in the face of the enemy was of greater importance than inter-party rivalry. Even so, the struggle for power went on, even when Verdun, on the road to Paris, was being besieged. The hour of the Terror had now come. Priests and other "traitors" were executed in their hundreds, Girondin deputies were arrested, as being too moderate, and all the real power fell, at last, into the hands of Marat, Danton and the Commune. The Assembly gave way to the Convention, and France, for so long the bastion of monarchy, became a republic.

Louis was declared to be deposed on 21 September; the final act of the tragedy was about to be played.

That the years of Louis XVI's reign are of little importance in literary history is scarcely surprising. It was not to be expected that France in turmoil would produce great writers and poets. The Revolution, indeed, was the cause of a break in French literature, as well as being the reason for a completely new attitude to life and letters in after years. However, one may notice Laclos (1741–1803), who died as an army officer serving under Napoleon, but whose great novel, *Les Liaisons dangereuses*, was published in 1782. The notorious Marquis de Sade, who eventually died in a lunatic asylum, published a novel, *Justine*, in 1791. His name gives us the term, sadism. But these years of the Revolution only produced minor poets like Parny and André Chénier (1762–94). The latter is often regarded as the earliest of the Romantics. He was guillotined during the Terror, despite an enthusiasm for the Revolution which had brought him back from the safety of London. Perhaps the literary world was as much in need of the Revolution as was the state of France. Certainly the sterility of the *ancien régime* could not be expected to do more than to produce a literature of revolt, or a theatre which, accepting the conventions of Versailles, might produce wit, but never initiate new ideas.

## RECOMMENDED READING

*A History of Modern France*. Vol. 1. *Old Régime and Revolution, 1715–99*. A. COBBAN. Penguin, 1957.

*Historians and the Causes of the French Revolution*. A. COBBAN. Historical Association, 1958.

*Interpretations of the French Revolution*. G. RUDÉ. Historical Association, 1961.

*Louis XVI at Bay: the Tuileries, June 20th, 1792*. M. J. SYDENHAM. *History Today*, Vol. XI, No. 8, p. 564 (August 1961).

*Robespierre and the French Revolution*. J. M. THOMPSON. English Universities Press, 1952.

*The Coming of the French Revolution*. G. LEFEBVRE. (Translated by R. R. PALMER.) Princeton, 1949.

*The Fall of the Bastille.* GEORGE E. RUDÉ. *History Today,* Vol. IV, No. 7, p. 448 (July 1954).

*The French Revolution, 1788–92.* GAETANO SALVEMINI. (Translated by I. M. RAWSON.) Jonathan Cape, 1954. (Published in Italy, 1905.)

*The Girondins.* M. J. SYDENHAM. Athlone Press, 1961.

*The French Revolution.* J. M. THOMPSON. Oxford, 1943.

CHAPTER 13

# The Revolutionary Republic and the Napoleonic Empire

BETWEEN the Cannonade of Valmy and the battle of Waterloo, from 1792 to 1815, the history of France is largely a history of war. It was the first great war of modern times, and it produced a man of genius who became the first of the modern dictators. It began as a war to make the Revolution safe, and ended as a war to make France the chief state in a Europe ruled by one man, Napoleon Bonaparte. The Convention, which ruled France in 1792, was to give way to the Directory, and that, in its turn, gave way to the Consulate and then to the Empire. In 1814 there was to be the first restoration of the Bourbons, and a second restoration followed Napoleon's final defeat at Waterloo. But in 1792 France was still in the chaos of the Revolution, with a government still conscious of the danger of foreign intervention in favour of the King. The Convention consisted of Jacobin deputies who were in favour of the execution of Louis XVI, Girondins as their chief opponents, and in between them a majority of moderate republicans, who were prepared to be reasonable so long as the rights of property were to be protected. The Jacobins were known as the Mountain, because they sat on the high seats, and the moderates as the Plain. As the Jacobins grouped themselves on the Left, and the Girondins on the Right, so it has become customary ever since to describe political parties of radical and conservative persuasions.

The foreign situation in 1792 was dangerous; but the artillery duel at Valmy, as good as a victory for the French when the

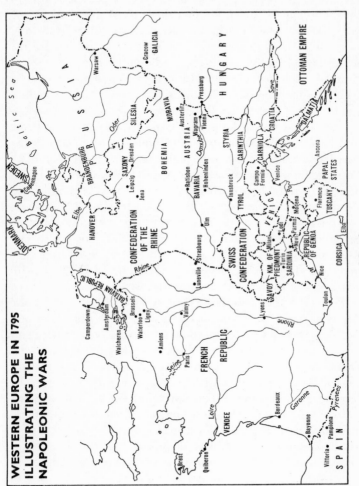

WESTERN EUROPE IN 1795
ILLUSTRATING THE
NAPOLEONIC WARS

MAP 6

invaders withdrew, was followed by a genuine victory, for Dumouriez at Jemappes in November, which made the situation much more comfortable. The *élan* and zeal of the heroic revolutionary troops did much for French *moral*. Worms and Mainz were taken by the French, and Belgium was "liberated" from Austrian rule. But these victories were accompanied by the September Massacres, when Danton began his reign of terror in Paris. Drunken men were hired to kill the victims indiscriminately. Danton's success meant a decline in the power of the Girondins, and it was not long before Robespierre's Jacobins were demanding that Louis should be put on trial. This was done, and the trial began on 26 December. After much debate, he was declared to be guilty, and was guillotined on 21 January 1793. The execution of the King was a victory for the extreme revolutionaries, but the horror which the event evoked in Europe, and the war which it made inevitable, meant that the Republic was to gain nothing from it. The unfortunate declaration by the government, in accordance with its idealistic desire to end economic barriers, that the River Scheldt was to be opened to trade to all countries, despite a treaty to the contrary with England, was the last step towards war, which was duly declared on Britain and Holland on 1 February. Not long afterwards, the Republic was at war with Spain as well. Once again, the new Republic was in a dangerous position, especially as the Belgians were turning against their liberators, despite the symbolic French gesture of returning the keys to their towns. The government ordered conscription, partly to reinforce Dumouriez, who was under orders to invade Holland; but the situation in Belgium, and the failure of Custine, in command of another army, to do more than retreat from Mainz, meant that Dumouriez had to withdraw from Holland. In the process, he was defeated at Neerwinden. This was the last straw for the French commander, who blamed ineptitude in Paris for the disaster. He tried to persuade some of his regiments to march on Paris to support the Girondins, and, having failed, decided to desert to the Austrians.

The cries of treachery in Paris were reinforced, and became louder when the peasants of La Vendée joined in a royalist rising which proved to be difficult to suppress. These peasants were Celtic Catholics with a traditional devotion to their *curés*. They had good leaders in their reforming nobles, who led resourceful guerilla campaigns. It was therefore easy for the Jacobins to persuade the Convention to establish a Revolutionary Tribunal and a Committee of Public Safety, the main weapons in the tyranny now being established by Danton. On these bodies, about thirty fanatics exercised power in the name of the people. This situation is classical, of course, in most revolutions. The struggle between the Girondins, who believed that the provinces were at least as important as Paris, and the Jacobins, who, controlling the capital as they did, thought that it was the birthplace and the shrine of the Revolution, and should be the saviour of the country, was unremitting. Danton tried, for a time, to rally the moderates, whom he thought could provide the money and the power to save the nation and the Revolution. He had little sympathy with the idea that the revolutionaries should try to spread their ideas into Europe as a whole. Unfortunately, perhaps, the Girondins had no great leader of the quality of Danton or Robespierre; and this may explain their lack of success even when they tried to take the initiative and show themselves worthy of governing France, or summoned up sufficient courage to denounce Marat and to appoint a commission which would deal with the Commune. Their determination was too late. The Jacobins, supported by the Parisian mob, voted for the suspension of the leading Girondins; and power passed to the Commune and to Danton's Committee of Public Safety.

The period of Jacobin rule, from June of 1793 to July of 1794, was of considerable importance. Although Danton began by producing a very democratic constitution, which could not be put into operation while matters were so critical, it was useless to attempt to disguise the tyranny which the Revolution had produced. There were counter-revolutionary movements in Marseilles and Lyons as well as in La Vendée, and foreign armies under Coburg and Brunswick preparing to invade from the Rhine. Mainz and Valenciennes were being besieged, but Danton was convinced that a united France could win through. He considered that unity could only be achieved by dealing fairly with the Girondins and their supporters, but the extremists would not have it. Danton lost his seat on the Committee, and the new one, which contained Robespierre, voted for a revival of the Terror. It was just at this moment when the most unsavoury character produced by the Revolution, Marat, was stabbed in his bath by Charlotte Corday (13 July 1793). Vainly, she hoped to end the Terror by killing its most fanatical leader, in the hope that others would follow her example. None did so. During this renewed Terror, the Queen, Philippe "Egalité", the unsavoury Duke of Orléans, Louis's over-ambitious cousin, a number of Girondins, and "suspects" by the hundred went to their deaths. It is difficult for us to feel any sympathy with the members of the Committee, because of the horror of these weeks; but there have been régimes with a similar record in the twentieth century, and it is perhaps easier for us to realize that there were men of considerable ability in a government responsible for such crimes, than it would have been in the nineteenth century. Robespierre, Saint-Just, Varennes and Carnot did a great deal to make the achievements of the Revolution permanent, and to prepare the way for the period of greatness under Bonaparte.

The armies were successful in regaining Toulon from royalist control (with the aid of Bonaparte, then a young artillery officer); in taking Lyons; and in suppressing the insurrection in La Vendée. Inspired by Carnot, they began to win victories as at Hondschoote and Wattignies. A new kind of military enthusiasm made good the deficiencies of these, by eighteenth-century standards, unschooled armies. Generals like Houchard, who allowed the Duke of York to retreat comparatively unscathed, were guillotined for inefficiency. Carnot's successful conscription of the *levée en masse* won him the title of Organizer of Victory. In his armies, military ability could win promotion and commissions, for the first time in French history. Carnot, with Jourdan, used the new military machine to win at Fleurus, thus regaining Belgium; and, indeed, the only setback for the Republic came at sea, where the French were defeated by Howe on 1 June 1794. In other spheres, the Committee had less success; for although plans were made for the revival of commerce, agriculture and education, there was too much corruption and fear of the Terror for the new schemes to be anything more than ideals on paper. Indeed, the extremists had control to such an extent that the supporters of the atheist, Hébert, pushed a measure through for the closure of the churches and the "reconsecration" of Notre Dame cathedral for the "worship" of Reason. This caused so much dissension that Robespierre and Danton sent Hébert and his chief supporters to the guillotine in March 1794. Now that Robespierre had got rid of so many of his rivals, he turned against Danton, too. After some preliminary manœuvring, Danton and his leading disciples were arrested and executed. Robespierre was left as sole master of France, and, for a very short period, used the weapon of the Terror to silence all opposition while he attempted to establish his own "Government of Virtue" in Paris. This government had some peculiar ideas. Robespierre believed that children should belong to the state, and have a Spartan upbringing: on the other hand, there was a sincere concern for the poor, who were to be given land and living space cheaply.

But the extremist had gone too far. The Convention turned against him, especially as the victories of the French army made his plea of military necessity for all his actions an absurdity; he was placed under arrest, and immediate action was taken against the Commune, which might have rallied to his support. His brief career was over; but his tremendous character was not to be forgotten by later revolutionaries. He followed Danton to the guillotine on 28 July, in what was called the crisis of Thermidor, from the name of the summer month provided by Romme for the Republican calendar, which replaced the Christian calendar in France between 1792 and 1805. With Robespierre gone, the moderate Plainsmen were determined to establish a settled, peaceful Republic, and to end the Terror. They controlled the Convention now, and the dreaded Committee of Public Safety was made harmless by being split up into smaller bodies, while the Terror was declared officially to be at an end (August 1794). Catholicism was to be tolerated again, and the Jacobin Club, along with other revolutionary societies, was closed. The weakness of the Jacobins in economic affairs—in printing too many *assignats* (money bills), in food shortages and in chaos over land values—was being felt. Their removal meant that trade began to revive a little, and the moderates gained confidence in their own ability when the National Guard put down a riot in Paris in April of 1795. The surviving Girondins were reinstated, and there was a strong move to try to end the war. Robespierre had gone, but the memory was to linger. Later, even Karl Marx was to study Louis Blanc's "Life" of the great revolutionary.

Holland being now entirely in French control, the government could negotiate from a position of strength. The Treaty of Basle was made with Prussia, and peace terms were agreed with Spain. There were even voices heard suggesting the restoration of the monarchy, but, although these were comparatively loud in the south of France, the leaders were not prepared to surrender the Republican ideal. They were prepared to withstand the Jacobins, even when the latter attempted a coup in May of 1795; but they were not ready to restore the Bourbons. The Revolutionary Tribunal was abolished, and some extremists were arrested, but there had been too much blood shed for any hope of a restoration. In any case, the Dauphin, recognized by the royalists as Louis XVII, died in June of 1795, probably as a result of the ill treatment he had received in the days of the Terror. With his death, the safety of the Republic seemed to be assured, and the Convention went on to prepare and issue a new constitution, which established a five-man Directory as the government of France. With the Directory there was to be a bicameral legislature, elected on a reasonably democratic franchise, and it was seen that the Revolution was at an end, or at least in its tyrannical phase.

However, the members of the Convention were still too frightened of the future to be willing to see the new constitution operate without their guidance, and announced, in the Decrees of Fructidor, that two-thirds of their members must be guaranteed seats in the new assembly. This roused considerable resentment in some quarters, and street fighting broke out in Paris. However, Barras and his protégé Bonaparte had little difficulty in dispersing the rebels with the famous "whiff of grapeshot". So the members of the Convention were left in power, and in October 1795 the five Directors took office. Any chance that there might have been that the new constitution would succeed and take root had been prevented, though; the Decrees of Fructidor had made certain that the new régime was as unsteady as any of the previous experiments in revolutionary government. The members of the Directory were Rewbell, Barras, Larévellière-Lépeaux, Letourneur and Carnot. All were regicides, but only two had much ability—Barras and Carnot. Siéyès, the builder of the new constitution, refused to take office as one of the Directors. These men might have been determined, when they came to power, to establish a strong state, but they were defeated, partly because of their own internal rivalry, partly because of the jobbery, bribery and corruption which developed under their oligarchic rule, and partly because of the problems of the war in which France was involved. The new *jeunesse dorée* began, by its corruptly gained wealth, to make a mockery of revolutionary ideals and virtue.

It was true that war was no longer necessary to save the Revolution, but the army was growing into a rapidly more professional organization, and conquest had its temptations. The year 1795 saw a victory against the Austrians at Loano, and there might have been another in the Rhineland had not Pichegru turned traitor and made peace with the Austrians there. A rather desultory war against Spain on the area of the Pyrenees was brought to an end by negotiation. Then, in March 1796, the command of the French forces in northern Italy was given to the Corsican artillery commander, Bonaparte. He had spent the previous winter planning what should be done in an Italian campaign, and, on taking over, he put his plans into immediate operation. He had almost instantaneous success, reaching Mantua, forcing the Pope to come to terms, and defeating the Austrians at Montenotte and the Sardinians at Mondovi. The Sardinians withdrew from the fighting immediately, and Napoleon went on to defeat the Austrians at Lodi, and to drive them out of Milan, where a Lombard state was set up. The victorious French forces began to loot northern Italy. Bologna, Parma and Modena were taken, and Naples and Venice had to pay heavily to escape conquest. The Austrians were defeated yet again at Bassano, Arcola and Rivoli, and further French victories in 1797 eventually forced the Austrians to come to terms and to negotiate the Treaty of Campo-Formio, by which they lost the Netherlands to France, recognized the new Lombard Republic, and gained only Venice, which lost its independence for the first time since the days of the Roman decline. Arcola remains, even now, an evocative term. After this battle, his men would follow *le petit caporal* anywhere. In other areas, the French were not so startlingly successful. In fact, Jourdan's army was beaten by the Archduke Charles in Germany, and France's new ally, Spain, was defeated at sea in the Battle of Cape St. Vincent.

Things were not particularly happy in Paris, either. The Directory was facing national bankruptcy, trouble over the lack of genuine religious toleration, and even a plot, led by Babeuf, to overthrow the régime. In the elections of 1797, the former members of the Convention lost their majority, and the new Assembly wanted peace. This was awkward, for three of the five Directors wanted war, and the only solution was a *coup d'état*, in which some of the new deputies were arrested, and the renewal of the persecutions. A number of returned *émigrés* and some priests were deported to Cayenne, and the government then attempted to try to solve the financial problems by declaring the state bankrupt. Matters seemed to be improving, however, when, within three weeks, the treaty was made with Austria. France was now at war only with Britain, and that power was also willing to negotiate peace terms. But the Directory still had a majority for war, and in 1798 hostilities were renewed against the Papacy, and in Holland and Switzerland. Preparations were set on foot for a projected invasion of England, but, as the military advisers reported that this was an impossible proposition owing to the lack of French sea power, the government agreed to a plan to attack Egypt, which was then to serve as a base for an attack on the British power in India. The Directory was delighted to let Napoleon become engulfed in his dream of "Glory from the East". It removed him from Paris.

In May 1798 Bonaparte sailed for Egypt. He seized Malta *en route*, landed in Egypt, and won the battle of the Pyramids before entering Cairo. The train of victories was then halted by Nelson, who attacked the French fleet under Brueys as it lay at anchor at Aboukir Bay, and this defeat left the French army stranded, without hope of reaching France again except by a long march overland. By this time, Austria, Naples and Russia had decided to join in the war against France, and the Directory reintroduced conscription to deal with this threat. Before long, Championnet had defeated the Neapolitans, and Naples had become a French satellite. Piedmont was also taken, and the French turned to face a coalition of Britain, Austria, Russia, Portugal and Turkey. At first, the allies had some success. The Russian Suvorov defeated the French at the Trebbia; and when he repeated this at Novi, French power in Italy had fallen as fast as it had been created. But the tale of allied success was not to last. Partly owing to the Austrian unwillingness to co-operate with the Russians, Masséna defeated the latter at Zürich, while a British and Russian expedition to Holland was defeated by Brune and left the Netherlands. Even so, the French defeats in Italy had done nothing for the reputation and prestige of the Directory which now included Siéyès, and who, by this time, was secretly campaigning for the restoration of a constitutional monarchy.

The Directory was so unpopular, indeed, that it only held on to power by passing tyrannical edicts which were reminiscent

of the days of Jacobin control. One such law was the Law of
Hostages, authorizing the imprisonment of the relations of
royalists, and it was becoming increasingly obvious that the
only hope of reviving French patriotism was the establishment of
a strong government, headed by a man like Bonaparte, who was
still in Egypt, having failed to get his army past Acre, held by
Smith, in an attempt to get his force back to France by the
overland route. In Egypt, Napoleon had made his mark. His
archaeological, scientific and exploratory achievements are
shown in the birth of Egyptology, the deciphering of hierogly-
phics and even in the popular fashions in furniture and design
after this time. Now Bonaparte, probably knowing how matters
stood in Paris, deserted his army, which eventually capitulated
to a British force commanded by Abercrombie in 1801; and
returned to France. He could see that the Directory commanded
little loyalty, joined forces with Siéyès, and, in a swift coup, got
rid of Barras, and had himself nominated as one of three consuls.
Having made himself joint master of France, he made a bid for
popular support, promising moderation, the end of corruption in
government, protection for property and military glory. The
French knew already that his promises of the latter would
probably be genuine enough, and, shortly afterwards, a new
constitution was issued, by which Bonaparte became First Consul,
with two completely insignificant colleagues. Bonaparte had
emerged as the ruler of France, and, as Foreign Secretary, he
appointed Talleyrand, acceptable as a negotiator because of his
links with the *ancien régime*. Dealing swiftly with immediate
problems, Bonaparte suppressed another rebellion in the western
provinces, introduced a censorship, and then turned to military
affairs.

The undistinguished commander, Moreau, gave way to
Bonaparte, who took an army across the Alps towards Milan,
refusing to turn aside to help Masséna who was being besieged
in Genoa, and who therefore had to surrender, and went on to
defeat the Austrians in a brilliantly organized battle at Marengo.
The victory not only restored French power in Italy, but

completely vindicated Bonaparte's coup in France. From then onwards, he was secure in the affections of France. The war continued. The Austrian forces were pushed back, defeated again at Hochstädt, and again at Hohenlinden in December 1800. The Austrians had no choice but to come to terms again, and peace was made by the Treaty of Lunéville, 1801, by which France gained the Rhine frontier and most of Italy. Austria was now out of the second coalition, and it was not long before the Czar, Paul I, decided to come to terms with Bonaparte. Indeed, he went further, actually joining in the League of Armed Neutrality of Sweden, Denmark and Prussia, which was deliberately aimed at British maritime supremacy. This state of affairs did not last, either. The Czar was soon murdered, and a British victory at Copenhagen, where Nelson disobeyed the orders of Hyde Parker to gain the day, ended the League. Once again, Bonaparte, so successful in land war, had come up against British sea power, which thwarted his ambitions so often; and the new Czar, Alexander, renewed the alliance with Britain.

For the moment, Bonaparte saw the advantages of peace, or, at least, of a truce, and negotiations were set on foot which resulted in the Peace of Amiens of 1802, by which Britain gained Ceylon and Trinidad, while the French promised to evacuate Naples and the Papal States. From the beginning, the peace was unpopular in France and in England, and it was unlikely to last for more than a few months. However, Bonaparte used the time as valuably as he could, both to build up French naval strength and to try to solve some of France's problems, both in domestic and in foreign affairs. Already, in 1800, he had introduced a new system of local government, with *préfets* ruling departments. He ordered a repudiation of part of the national debt, as had been done in 1798 by the Directory, but this time there was a thorough reorganization of the taxation system, so that public confidence began to return. Public works were begun, such as the building of roads and canals, and the codification of French law, which had been initiated by the Convention, was continued under Bonaparte's personal control. By 1804 civil law was codified, and by 1808, criminal law. After negotiations with Cardinal Consalvi, a Concordat was made with the Papacy by which catholicism was restored in France, with safeguards to ensure that the Church was subject to the state except in purely spiritual matters.

The universities, which had been destroyed during the Revolution, returned in the form of a new University in Paris which was to be the apex of a national educational system; and a system of "honours" suitable to a revolutionary Republic, based upon the new Legion of Honour. An amnesty was granted to *émigrés*, and a plebiscite was held, by which Bonaparte became Consul for life. All these were, no doubt, great achievements, but the renewal of war was now inevitable. Bonaparte had not kept the terms of the Treaty of Lunéville with the Austrians, and his apparently insatiable ambitions in Italy provided Britain, anxious for her power in the Mediterranean, with an excuse for not giving up Malta. Holland and Switzerland were only too obviously still under French control, and it was not surprising, therefore, that Britain declared war again in May 1803. Bonaparte promptly imprisoned all the British visitors and residents in Paris, and ordered the invasion of Naples and Hanover. He had just sold Louisiana, which Spain had surrendered to France in 1800, to the United States for 80 million francs. But at this stage, although war had been renewed, there was no coalition against France, and Bonaparte himself was not yet prepared for full-scale military activities. He announced the closure of the ports of Europe which were under his control to trade with Britain, and took vigorous action over a plot to overthrow his régime. Among others, Moreau, Cadoudal and Pichegru were executed, and, the crisis over, Bonaparte emerged, no longer as First Consul, but as Emperor. He had made an amoral and Machiavellian use of his enemies' plots, to further his own designs. He used Vendéan plots as an excuse to execute innocent Jacobins, who might have opposed his becoming Emperor. In December 1804 he was crowned by Pius VII—and France returned to the use of the Gregorian calendar. Napoleon, it seemed, was as indispensable to the Republic as was Pitt to England; and the "Jacobin Emperor" began to make plans for the invasion of that country.

At the time, one French fleet, commanded by Ganteaume, was blockaded in Brest; Villeneuve's was similarly at anchor in Toulon, while the Spanish fleet was in Cadiz. Villeneuve managed to get his ships out of the Mediterranean and across the Atlantic to the West Indies, pursued by Nelson; and then returned to fight an indecisive battle in fog against Calder before getting into Corunna harbour. He then moved along the coast to Cadiz to join forces with the Spaniards, and the British blockade was then renewed. Alarmed by Bonaparte's taunts of cowardice and the knowledge that he was to be replaced as commander, he then sailed out to defeat at Trafalgar on 21 October 1805. Nelson was killed, after having made a calculated destruction of enough of Villeneuve's ships to make invasion virtually impossible, and Villeneuve committed suicide after the battle. The engagement completely destroyed Bonaparte's hopes of gaining sufficient power at sea to make it possible to invade England. By this time, too, Austria was, perhaps rather reluctantly, joining yet another anti-French coalition with England, Sweden and Russia. To deal with this, Napoleon withdrew his armies from Boulogne, attacked the Austrians, and defeated General Mack in another great battle, at Ulm in October. The French then continued their advance, reached Vienna, and went on to the triumph of Austerlitz. The Austrians made peace, losing many provinces to France, at Pressburg, while the Prussians, who had joined in because of Napoleon's violation of the neutrality of Ansbach before the battle of Ulm, made terms by the Treaty of Schönbrunn. These great victories were followed by the formal end of the Holy Roman Empire, when Francis II gave up the title in August 1806, and the establishment of Napoleon's brothers, Joseph and Louis, on the thrones of Sicily and Holland.

Napoleon, by now, had decided to make sure that the power of Prussia should not be used against him again. He forced a war against the Prussians, despite their determination to adhere to their policy of neutrality, and crushed them at Jena. Berlin was seized, and it was while he was in the Prussian capital, dictating terms to the defeated, that he issued the Berlin decree, which banned all trade with Britain. Britain, as promptly, issued Orders-in-Council on the subject of trade with France and her conquered territories in Europe; these ordered a blockade which ruined European trade, and caused vital shortages of food and equipment. Frederick William III had retired with what was left of his army to Königsberg, and asked for Russian help; but Russia could do little while Austria was prostrate, and, in any case, she was involved with a war against the Turks. Napoleon seized his opportunity. He advanced into Poland and reached the Vistula, and began the siege of Danzig. This was sufficient to provoke the Russians to take determined action, and while the siege was in progress, Napoleon had to fight a battle at Eylau against the Russians which cost him large numbers of men, and nearly ended in defeat. However, as was usual with Napoleon, he made an extremely rapid recovery. He realized that the eastern allies were now determined to continue the struggle, and decided that a quick defeat of the Russians, followed by some adept diplomatic manoeuvring, might solve the difficulty. His victory he obtained against Bennigsen's army at Friedland— Bennigsen being the man who had come so near to defeating him at Eylau—and then offered terms and an alliance to the Czar, Alexander.

These were accepted; and Napoleon's "continental system" was all but complete. The alliance with Russia was forged in a series of treaties made after a meeting between the two rulers on a raft on the River Niemen at Tilsit, and, while Prussia regained some of the territory she had lost, the significant result was that Alexander and Napoleon signed a secret offensive and defensive alliance. Napoleon had, at this moment, a complete personal domination of the Russian ruler. This may well be the highest point of Napoleon's power. Never again was Europe to be so obviously at his feet. He saw that if he could force Sweden, Portugal and Denmark into his Empire, it would remain only for him to defeat England. In particular, the Danish fleet was to be the nucleus of a naval force which might make an invasion of England a possibility again. This was, of course, foreseen by the British government as well; and the order was given for an immediate attack on Copenhagen, as a result of which the Danish fleet was towed out of Danish waters. Yet again, English sea power had thwarted Napoleon's schemes, and this action by the enemy navy had made the agreement at Tilsit of far less value than it might have been. British naval action was to be just as annoying when Napoleon sent an army through Spain to attack Portugal, and the Portuguese royal family sailed for Brazil in British ships.

But Napoleon's schemes were not yet at an end. Although the alliance with Russia was already wearing a little thin, as it was difficult for the two powers to agree on the subjects of Prussia and the fate of the Turkish Empire, Napoleon felt that, at least, he had no need to worry any more about Austria. This country had signed an alliance with him, so he decided that he could now complete the subservience of all Italy to his power, and add Spain to the Napoleonic Empire. After that, it might be possible for him to launch an attack on Turkey. For a start, he invaded Spain. With complete indifference to the Spanish feelings, he forced Charles IV and his equally incapable heir, Ferdinand, to abdicate, and placed Joseph Bonaparte on the Spanish throne. This was a great error—within days, the Spaniards rose in rebellion against the French, as godless invaders, and began a guerilla warfare against the occupying army. Indeed, they even managed to defeat a French force at Baylen, and to hold on to Saragossa for eight weeks. While they were doing so, a British force, led by Arthur Wellesley, landed at Mondego Bay in Portugal. This invading force soon managed to defeat Junot at Vimiero, and although Hew Dalrymple, the commander sent out to replace Wellesley, was foolish enough to make the Convention of Cintra, by which the French were allowed to leave Portugal, it had been shown that the French forces in the Iberian peninsula could be defeated.

In fact, the reputation of Napoleonic France was declining. Alexander of Russia was alarmed by the fate of the royal families of Portugal and Spain, and he was also made aware that Napoleon was in difficulties, if only temporarily, when the French evacuated Prussia. Also, Austrian strength was beginning to recover, and Napoleon invited Alexander to a meeting at Erfurt to renew the alliance made at Tilsit, and to try to persuade the Russians to threaten Austria with war if they showed any signs of making an attack upon him while he was occupied elsewhere. Napoleon found the Russian replies somewhat unsatisfactory, and he had no choice but to return to dealing with affairs in Spain and Portugal. He entered the peninsula, defeated the Spaniards at Burgos and Tudela, and took Madrid, only to discover that his lines of supply and communication were being attacked by the British and their Spanish guerilla allies. There was no alternative but to try to drive the English out, and he began to do this before leaving Soult to complete the operation while he returned to Paris. Soult was successful; the British conducted a heroic rearguard action, but eventually were forced to withdraw by sea from Corunna, where their commander, Moore, was killed in action.

What had caused Napoleon to leave for Paris was the news that yet another war with Austria was imminent. He dismissed Talleyrand, whom he suspected of treachery, and heard that the Austrians, commanded by the Archduke Charles, were, in fact, preparing to renew the struggle. War was actually declared in April 1809 and, within days, Napoleon had won yet another victory at Eggmühl, near Ratisbon. He took Vienna, but the Austrians went on fighting and even came near to victory again at Aspern. However, Napoleon was also tenacious, and won a great battle at Wagram. Yet again, this time by the Peace of Schönbrunn, the Austrians came to terms, and lost a good deal of their territory. Once again, Austria was an unwilling satellite of France. Napoleon, once again, was convinced that final victory was not far off. He divorced Josephine, and planned to strengthen the Russian alliance by a marriage with the Archduchess, Anne. It was no easy matter for him to get the Pope's approval to such a measure, even though the Pontiff was a virtual prisoner; but Napoleon was not to be dissuaded, and, even though the marriage to Anne came to nothing, he did go on to marry the unwilling sacrificial victim, the Archduchess Marie-Louise of Austria, gaining, as he thought, vast prestige from a marriage to the Hapsburg princess. By this time, Napoleon had probably decided that he could never rule Europe in peace until he had made war on, and defeated, Russia; and this was what he was making plans for in the years 1810 and 1811.

The only serious fighting in these years was in Spain and Portugal. Another British force, commanded by Wellesley again, had landed and won victories at Oporto and Talavera. Then, in 1810, after a victory at Busaco, they had retired behind the lines of Torres Vedras, which Wellesley had ordered to be built to protect his base camp at Lisbon. As the British commander had also arranged for a "scorched-earth" policy to be adopted before he retired behind the lines, Masséna was unable to penetrate to follow the enemy. In 1811 there was serious fighting at Badajoz and Ciudad Rodrigo, and the French were unable to inflict any serious defeat against the British forces. The Czar, seeing that little profit was coming of his alliance with Napoleon, decided to change sides again, even though Prussia and Austria were still the unwilling allies of the French Empire. He prepared for war, conscious of the fact that Napoleon's armies could no longer be as great as they had been, and hoping that his rival's military genius was waning. These hopes were not to prove false, even though Napoleon managed to recruit 600,000 men to march into Lithuania and on into Russia. Alexander's policy was to avoid a pitched battle for as long as he could, enticing the French far into Russian territory. Napoleon discovered that the geography of this campaign, besides the state of the Russian roads, made it impossible for him to use his usual speedy methods on the road from Smolensk to Moscow. He lost many men at Borodino, and, by the time he reached Moscow in September of 1812, he found the city largely deserted and in flames. Hoping, perhaps, that the Russians would ask for peace, he remained encamped there for over a month. At the end of that time, with the approach of winter, there was no alternative but retreat. The French were then attacked continuously by Russian forces, while they were at their weakest through lack of provisions and through their exertions on the long march. In fact, the retreat became a massacre, and thousands were killed at the crossing of the Beresina alone.

Finally, Napoleon left the remnant of the *Grande Armée* and went on to Paris. At last, he had lost an army because he had attempted something beyond his powers. He had been defeated by over-ambition, and the defeat meant the end of his power, whatever the great events which were to follow. There was an immediate reaction in western Europe. In the Peninsula, Wellesley had taken Ciudad Rodrigo, and, on 6 April 1812, Badajoz. Spain was open to attack by the routes which these fortresses had guarded. In August the British took Madrid, and King Joseph Bonaparte fled. Admittedly, the withdrawal of French troops for the march on Moscow had made things easier for the British, but the successes of Wellesley infuriated the Emperor. However, he proceeded to attempt the rebuilding of his shattered armies, which were now needed to face a rebuilt Prussian force, commanded by men who wanted their revenge. Napoleon came to terms with Pius VII in the Concordat of Fontainebleau, and then, with the renewal of hostilities in 1813, took his raw levies to Erfurt. Many were teenage conscripts, levied in desperation. He began an attack on Leipzig and Dresden, defeated his enemies at Bautzen—although at considerable cost to himself—and then, perhaps foolishly, made an armistice. Admittedly this was of value to him, but it was even more valuable to the Prussians, and to the Austrians, who, under Metternich, decided to intervene yet again. Within two months, hostilities were resumed.

Even larger armies now faced the French. However, Napoleon won a victory at Dresden, and then moved on to Leipzig, where, in the great Battle of the Nations, so called because so many were involved, Napoleon was defeated at last in a large set battle. Only a small part of his forces escaped from Blücher, Bernadotte and Bennigsen, to reach France. At the same time, Wellesley was in pursuit of Soult, and invading French territory by way of the Pyrenees. However, despite her state of exhaustion in men and money, France remained loyal to the Emperor. For this reason, perhaps, Napoleon refused to accept the terms which were offered him at a conference at Frankfort. On his refusal, the allies invaded. He was defeated at La Rothière in February 1814 and despite a victory over Blücher and the withdrawal of Schwarzenberg from Troyes, Napoleon found that his forces were insufficient to inflict a serious enough defeat on the enemy. The allies began the march down the Marne towards Paris, and eventually entered the capital on 31 March. At last, Napoleon's marshals deserted him, and, on 13 April 1814, Napoleon agreed to the Treaty of Fontainebleau, by which he lost France and was exiled to Elba, of which island he was to be sovereign ruler.

For the first time since the execution of Louis XVI, the Bourbons ruled again in France. Louis XVIII, the aged, invalid brother of the guillotined monarch, refused to accept the constitution drawn up by the Senate, but issued one of his own in June, which established a constitutional monarchy in France, almost as though the Napoleonic era had never occurred. The unpopularity of Louis was heightened by the terms of the Treaty of Paris, by which France lost all that she had gained since the Revolution. The new government, in fact, infuriated the people, who saw the restored dynasty as one which had "learned nothing and forgotten nothing". The only minister of real ability was Talleyrand, and he was concerned almost exclusively with foreign affairs. It was not long before an opposition began to grow, led by Constant; and meanwhile, in Vienna, an international congress was debating the settlement of the Europe which Napoleon had disturbed so much. The unpopularity of the restored dynasty was so great that it was scarcely surprising that Napoleon decided to leave Elba and to see how great were his remaining powers.

He landed in France on 1 March 1815. The army deserted the royal service *en masse* to join him. Ney, sent to capture Napoleon, went over to his old commander on seeing him again. In twenty days, Louis XVIII had fled to Belgium, and Napoleon was back in Paris. He established a new government, issued a revised constitution, and proclaimed his desire to rule France in peace. But the allies were determined not to accept this. They announced that they intended to remove Napoleon by force, and massed their armies to invade again, while Napoleon recruited 200,000 men, many of them veterans released from captivity, to defend his régime. This was a strong army, even if some of Napoleon's best generals were not there to weld it into a great fighting machine. Napoleon decided to attack in Belgium, aiming to defeat the Prussian army first. Despite his success at Ligny, the last of his victories, and his brilliant attack on Wellington at Quatre Bras, Ney let Napoleon down by failing to break the British commander's lines, and the Emperor was forced to fight, at Waterloo, a battle which, with the arrival of the Prussians imminent, he could not hope to win. He lost the battle on 18 June; on 21 June he reached Paris. The following day he abdicated, and on 15 July took refuge on board H.M.S. *Bellerophon*. The great drama of the Revolution and of the Napoleonic Empire was over.

Napoleon's achievements were vast, of course, especially in the military sphere; but he left an impression upon France which has never been eradicated, despite the loss of his Empire. One cannot help but notice the importance that he gave to Paris, a city of 600,000 which had an influence altogether out of proportion to a country with a population of 26,000,000. The "imperial" return to classical forms in art and architecture is to be seen in the triumphal arches like the Étoile, and the temples like those of the Bourse and the Madeleine. Similarly, Napoleon's idea that *Ce qui est grand est toujours beau* may be seen in the paintings of "great moments in History" by David. Although these may not suit the taste of the mid-twentieth century, they remain as significant a monument to the man of destiny as his foundation of a French bureaucracy, which, in his time, was under the direction of his Council of State. The secularization and centralization of the educational system, the foundation of *lycées*, and the establishment of a new pattern of local administration, all trace their origins to him. It was not to be expected that this would be a great period in French literature, but one may notice, among the journalism and propaganda of the time, the beginning of romanticism in the work of Chateaubriand (1768–1848), whose *Atala* and *René* appeared in 1801 and 1802. Also, Constant wrote his *Adolphe* in 1807, although it was not published until after the Bourbon restoration. Mme de Staël was another significant writer on important literary and social themes. Her *De l'Allemagne* appeared in 1810, and she also produced *Delphine* and *Corinne*. Perhaps the artistic achievements of the imperial period may best be understood if we conclude that Mme Tussaud's immortal waxworks date from this era. But, if the arts declined, it was a time of great interest to the historians of science. Men like Lamarck, Laplace, Monge the mathematician, Cuvier, Ampère, who worked on electromagnetism, and Lavoisier, the chemist, were adding lustre to the reputation of France when Napoleon was making it, perhaps for the last time, one of the greatest of world powers.

## RECOMMENDED READING

*A History of Modern France.* Vol. 2: 1799–1945. A. COBBAN. Penguin, 1961.

*Could Napoleon have won?* C. S. FORESTER. *History Today*, Vol. III, No. 1, p. 13 (1953).

*Daily Life in France under Napoleon.* J. ROBIQUET. Allen, 1962.

*Napoleon and the Awakening of Europe.* F. M. H. MARKHAM. English Universities Press, 1954.

*Napoleon Bonaparte; his Rise and Fall.* J. M. THOMPSON. Blackwell, 1952.

CHAPTER 14

## From Waterloo to the Revolution of 1848

LOUIS XVIII, naturally enough, was viewed by most Frenchmen
with mistrust and suspicion. Although Napoleon was to be in-
carcerated on the island of St. Helena until his death some years
later, and although the last years of the Emperor had shown that
his powers had been declining, the legend of Bonaparte was a
reality to the French, and was not to lose any of its glory over the
years. The new King was getting old; he was more alert, perhaps,
than some of his Bourbon predecessors, but he was no genius.
Anyone who succeeded Napoleon was bound to suffer from the
comparison, and Louis, who had returned "on the bayonets of
the allies", was bound to be regarded as a symbol of defeat,
except by the *émigrés*, who formed such an insignificant part of the
population, and who were foreigners to the new France, but who
were bound to play an important part in affairs from now on.
The King did his best to realize that the ideas of the Revolution,
and its achievements, had to be taken into account by his new
constitutional monarchy; but he failed to see that the achievements of the Empire had to be recognized as well.

On 8 July 1815 Louis entered Paris. A government, which
contained Talleyrand, Fouché and Pasquier, was established—a
government which, from its composition, seemed likely to accept
the facts of the events of the previous twenty-five years. An
election was held, which resulted in the accession to power of a
reactionary ministry, led by the Duke of Richelieu. Talleyrand
and Fouché were dismissed, some Bonapartists who had shown
their opinions in the Hundred Days, like Marshal Ney, were
shot, and in the south there was an outbreak of royalist vengeance

on leading Republicans. The Chamber of Deputies—the equivalent of the British House of Commons—was full of reactionaries, and is known to History as the *chambre introuvable*. Richelieu had been employed, during the Napoleonic period, in the service of the Czar, Alexander; he offered posts in the administration to Decazes, Vaublanc and Corvetto, and the government held office until December 1818, in those difficult years of the occupation of France by foreign troops, and with a King on the throne who wished to be moderate and accommodating, while the majority of the Deputies were Ultra-Royalists, and the heir to the throne was a known reactionary who had learned nothing during his exile.

Richelieu's policy was to hold on to office and to govern the country by paying a proper regard to all political groups, without going too far to the support of the reactionary Ultras. By the terms of the Treaty of Paris, the new government had to accept that France should be occupied for the time being, with a supervising committee of the allies in Paris; and that France should pay a war indemnity. Further humilation for the country was the establishment of a Congress system, from which she was omitted. While these were being settled, the right wing extremists in the Chamber were making demands concerning taxation and the franchise which were so likely to cause trouble that even Wellington condemned them as unreasonable. Like the Restoration Parliament in England in 1660, the Chamber was *plus royaliste que le roi*, full of returned *émigrés* planning vengeance. Decazes saw that the only answer was a dissolution; and new elections returned a Chamber that was rather more moderate, and more likely to support the government. The franchise was then limited by a new law, passed by a group of moderate constitutionalists called *Doctrinaires*, among whom was Guizot. The army was reorganized, the allies decided to remove the costly armies of occupation in 1818, and when, in the annual elections for a part of the Chamber, the Ultras began to lose some of their predominance to the Moderates, Richelieu was dismissed.

A moderate, liberal government, which contained Decazes

still, but was headed by Dessoles, took office. Dessoles was considerably more moderate than Decazes, who wished to continue the policy of trying to satisfy Ultras and Radicals. In fact, he occupied a position midway between Richelieu and Dessoles, so his role in the new government was different from what it had been in the last one. But the elections, of course, did nothing to alter the political complexion of the Chamber of Peers, which was still full of Ultras. The King, in order to enable some of Dessoles's moderate legislation to be passed, created about sixty new peers. In the elections of 1819 there was a clear tendency for even more Ultras to lose their seats to the left wingers, and the debates became fierce over a motion to change the electoral law yet again. It was while this discussion was in progress that the heir to the throne, the Duke of Berry, lost his life; and the Ultras, looking for a scapegoat, put the blame on Decazes. To quieten them, Louis offered to let Richelieu return to the government; and as the Duke would not serve with Decazes, the latter resigned and became Ambassador to London.

Richelieu, in fact, was in a difficult situation, for his new government could hardly expect much support from the Radicals. This became even plainer when legislation to weaken the freedom of the press and to make the franchise less democratic caused the left wing to launch scathing attacks on his government. The comparatively moderate *Doctrinaires* decided to give their support to the opposition, and the political situation was so tense that there were several conspiracies, including one against the dynasty itself. However, the next elections, owing to the restrictions in the franchise, saw a return to power of the Ultras in the Chamber of Deputies, and, with Louis rapidly becoming more and more senile, and thus the Ultra, Charles, ruling in all but name, even Richelieu found himself being forced to adopt policies which he did not approve of. This was particularly so in foreign affairs, where the right wingers were anxious to intervene in Spain. In December 1821, therefore, the Duke resigned, and the government passed to Villèle, a reactionary of considerable ability who set himself to tighten the restrictions on the moderates and left wingers. He found that France, in spite of the changes in government and the backwash of defeat, had been making considerable progress, and was in a prosperous state, financially. His government determined to use this prosperity, and the newly reconstructed army, to cut a dash in foreign affairs; he also wanted to do something to restore the power of the Roman Church. Like Walpole, he knew that it was possible to strengthen his hold on affairs by inventing or exaggerating conspiracies against the régime. But he was particularly concerned, like his Ultra supporters, to "strengthen" France by making her a force again in foreign affairs.

The Quadruple Alliance, created by Castlereagh and Metternich in 1815, was created to preserve the peace treaties, and its signatories were Britain, Russia, Austria and Prussia. These powers agreed to consult upon their common interests, and had so begun the Congress System, which prevailed until England decided to co-operate no longer, in 1822. Alexander I had also founded the Holy Alliance, which Castlereagh called a "piece of sublime mysticism and nonsense", and Metternich, "mere verbiage". However, it turned out to be a reactionary association for the prevention of revolutions in Europe, once Alexander's liberal sympathies had cooled a little. France had been permitted to join the Concert of the great powers at the time of the Congress of Aix-la-Chapelle in 1818, and 1820 had brought the first signs of revolution, especially in Spain, Naples and Portugal. In Spain, Ferdinand VII had established a brutal tyranny, and the army showed that it was willing to mutiny. When the powers met at Troppau, a protocol was issued, stating that any state which changed its constitution as a result of internal revolution ceased to be a member of the Concert, and that the other powers would consider it their duty to intervene. Britain objected to this decision, but Villèle wanted to give assistance to the Bourbon absolutism in Spain, massed an army of 100,000 on the Pyrenean frontier as a *cordon sanitaire* (for yellow fever had broken out in the Peninsula), and, despite Britain's stand against intervention at the Congress of Laibach, and the change in atmosphere when the

Greeks rebelled against the Turks, the army invaded Spain in April 1823 to restore Ferdinand's authority. In fact, French troops were not withdrawn until 1826. Austria, Prussia and Russia gave their tacit support when the French force, commanded by the Duke of Angoulême, invaded Spain—but the action did more than any other to break up the Congress system.

The success was exhilarating to the Ultras. In fact, their enthusiasm was too much even for Villèle, who dismissed Chateaubriand, the chief advocate of an "active" foreign policy. Having done so, he proceeded with his plans for France's domestic policy. New peers were to be created to strengthen the right wing in the Chamber of Peers, "packed" elections were to be held to strengthen the reactionaries in the lower Chamber, a Septennial Act was to reinforce his own power, steps were to be taken to help the Roman Church, and the interest on the National Debt was to be reduced, and the surplus money used to provide compensation for those who had been *émigrés*. However, these plans were defeated by the reactionaries themselves. They were rejected in the Chamber of Peers, for Chateaubriand was determined to get rid of Villèle, who had dismissed him so summarily, and introduce a more vigorous foreign policy. And then Louis XVIII died. Charles X (1824–30), an *émigré* in England from 1795 to 1815, but who had learned nothing from his exile, came to the throne, with all his frankly reactionary ideas. His sole interest, it seemed, was to restore the *ancien régime* completely. Villèle's plans went ahead, and, in addition to the policies he had already introduced, primogeniture was restored, the Jesuits allowed to return to France, and the rules of censorship made more rigorous. Chateaubriand, however, was still determined to oust Villèle, and, when the elections went against the latter, he resigned (December 1827). There was no alternative, in Charles X's mind, to a ministry of extreme Ultras. Martignac formed a ministry, and, although he made some slight attempt to persuade the moderates that he was willing to make some concessions, there was absolute deadlock on the question of a reform of the electoral law that the moderates knew they must have if they were ever to attain power again. With Martignac unable to make progress, Charles asked the completely incompetent politician Polignac, an Ultra of Ultras, a member of the family of Marie-Antoinette's close friend, to form a government. He was a full-blooded reactionary, and his only idea of a policy seemed to be to stir up trouble in Algiers and to ignore trouble at home. In fact, an expedition was sent to Africa in May 1830, which resulted in the colonization of North Africa, and provided some resurgence of *la gloire* in its Algerian conquests, to divert criticism from the loss of internal liberties, but the moderates had had enough.

They sent a protest to Charles X, and, when new elections resulted in an anti-Polignac majority, the King dissolved the Chamber. At this sign of the King's complete lack of comprehension of the feelings of France, street fighting broke out in Paris. The barricades went up, and it was soon evident that the government could not control the citizens, for the troops had no enthusiasm for the resurrected Bourbon régime. Charles X, realizing that he could do nothing, withdrew, and sailed for England. The idea of the Divine Right of the Bourbons sailed with him. The leaders of the late opposition, Thiers, Lafitte, Guizot, the aged Lafayette and Talleyrand, came into the open, and, not wishing to instigate foreign intervention, nor to encourage the Left too much, offered the crown to Louis Philippe, the Duke of Orléans, the son of Philippe "Egalité". This, the July Revolution of 1830, was a middle-class insurrection—it was, in no sense of the word, democratic. Louis Philippe was 57 years old, and very much a bourgeois. He had lived in exile for many years, and now his sole aim was the quiet enjoyment of prosperity. As it happened, he turned out to be quite adept, politically, and used all the weapons he could to maintain himself on the throne— which was quite an achievement, for his only supporters were the middle classes, and they were scarcely enthusiastic about the monarch they had created. He was essentially a man of peace, who wanted no involvement in European affairs; he thought they could well be dangerous. He had no desire for glory, and was

G

quite content to let France be governed quietly by the moderate *Doctrinaires*, and by the middle classes. He was even prepared to allow the new government to put on a democratic attitude—but there was nothing genuine about this.

In religious matters, Louis Philippe was much more tolerant than his predecessors. The royal powers were circumscribed in a new constitution, conscription was abandoned and the Roman Church lost its privileged position. But, although the new régime was conciliatory, its real autocracy was always apparent. As the years went by, France began to suffer from a national *ennui*. At the outset of his reign, there was trouble over the Belgian Revolution. Here was an opportunity for France to gain influence in the Low Countries, which Polignac would have seized, without thought of the consequences. Palmerston was quite determined that no French aggression could be tolerated, and made this very clear to Talleyrand, who hoped to obtain Luxemburg, or, at least, Philippeville and Marienburg. In the end, however, the French had to accept the establishment of an independent, neutral Belgian state, of which Louis Philippe's son, the Duke of Nemours, was not permitted to accept the crown. Even when the dissatisfied Dutch refused to accept the decision, and sent troops into Belgium, whereat the French sent forces to occupy Brussels, the new government had to withdraw in the face of determined opposition from Palmerston and the Czar. Eventually, the French army was used merely to force the Dutch out of Belgium in order to enforce the terms of the Treaty of 1831. De Broglie and Guizot were dismissed, and Louis Philippe decided that, to counteract the obvious hostility of Russia to this new, upstart, régime in France, he would be well advised to get on friendly terms with England. This was not always easy, and the policy had to be dropped, eventually, over the controversy concerning the Spanish marriages. The short-lived ministry of Casimir Périer (1831–2) ended with that minister's death, and, although the King was under considerable pressure to offer the government to Guizot, and trouble was brewing from the extremists on both wings, he finally managed to introduce a government under Soult, which included Guizot as Minister of Education and Thiers as Minister of the Interior. These two men of letters were considerable rivals —the former a bourgeois Protestant whose motto, *enrichessez-vous*, has long been remembered.

A number of problems faced Soult's ministry, but the industrial and economic changes of the time were faced in a determined way. A large programme of public works was initiated by Thiers, and a new educational system was begun by Guizot. Strikes were firmly dealt with, and so was an insurrection in Paris. In fact, the government was sufficiently successful for Louis Philippe to attempt to interfere in its programme, and particularly in foreign policy. The result of this was that Talleyrand, with the King's support, was angling for friendship with Austria at a time when de Broglie, the Foreign Minister, was building up an *entente* with England. The government resigned in 1836, and Thiers, a shrewd and able journalist from Marseilles, took office; but his foreign policy seemed to be likely to embroil France with both Spain and England, and the King persuaded him to resign in favour of Guizot and Molé, in the same year. From then onwards, Thiers's opposition to the government was strong and fierce. Although the new ministry was prepared to be reasonable, and to make concessions to Republicans and Legitimists, nothing it could do was popular. France was becoming prosperous as the months passed, and the colonization of Algeria was going steadily ahead; but the opposition to the corruption of the Orléanists was growing even more rapidly. The Republicans, led by Lamartine, the socialists led by Louis Blanc, and Thiers himself, were becoming determined to end this rather sordid period. The growth of the Napoleonic legend and the propaganda of Victor Hugo and Béranger were having an effect—and this at a time when Louis Philippe, in the eyes of many Frenchmen, was allowing Palmerston to insult France over the matter of Egypt. Here, where the French were inclined to support Mehemet Ali against the Sultan, his legal suzerain, Britain and the other powers ignored France in an international agreement to support the power of the "sick man of Europe".

While Thiers and Guizot were indulging their political rivalry, nothing was done for the poorer people. The insubstantial nature of the new monarchy became even clearer in 1842, when the heir to the throne, the Duke of Orléans, died, and a Regency Bill had to be passed. Eventually, it was a piece of mean trickery which brought the new monarchy down. Louis Philippe was ambitious for his sons, the Dukes of Aumâle and Montpensier, to marry Isabella, Queen of Spain, and her sister. Britain made it clear that any such attempt to revive the old days of the Family Compact could not be accepted; and, although Louis Philippe abandoned the scheme, Guizot went on with a plan, which came to fruition in 1846. Isabella was to marry the Duke of Cadiz, reputed to be incapable of having children, while her sister Luisa Fernanda was to marry Montpensier after all, which meant that the throne of Spain would, one day, revert to Louis Philippe's dynasty. The immediate result was the break up of the *entente* with England, just when the king needed all the support he could get if his rule were to survive. Guizot had lost most of the popularity he had once possessed. His failures to annex Morocco and Tahiti when the opportunity occurred annoyed imperialists, while Barrot and his Radicals campaigned loudly for a more democratic franchise. When the opposition decided to hold a banquet, at which speeches were to be made against Guizot, it was decided to ban the meeting. But the opposition stood firm, Louis Philippe dismissed Guizot, and asked Molé to form a government. The outbreak of fighting in the streets was the sign of pent-up dissatisfaction with the monarchy and the government, and, although Louis Philippe sent for Thiers instead, this constant shuffling of the pack proved to be useless. When the National Guard showed its unwillingness to protect the King or to keep order, Louis Philippe decided on abdication. He and his family escaped to England, and by March 1848 the discredited Bourbon monarchy had passed into history.

As the middle classes came to power, politically speaking, in the first half of the nineteenth century, so there was a great change in the literary atmosphere. Literature came to life after 1815, but it was a new kind of life. Novelists began to usurp the place which had been held by poets and philosophers. The great names of the period include Stendhal (1783–1842), who, after some experience in Napoleon's armies and a period of residence in Milan, wrote *De l'Amour* (1822); but he made his name with the rather melodramatic *Le Rouge et le Noir* in 1831 and *La Chartreuse de Parme* in 1839. Although a romantic writer, some of his work shows signs of looking back to the classical writing of the eighteenth century. Honoré de Balzac owed a good deal of his reputation to his vast output, and to the characterization in his novels. This was, to say the least, colourful. Although he made a claim that all his work was part of a survey of the *Comédie humaine*, there is no obvious systematic plan or order in his work. Some of his novels were philosophic, but the majority were meant to be scenes of life in Paris or in the provinces. Among his best-known works were *Le Père Goriot*, *Eugénie Grandet* and *La Peau de chagrin*. The Romantic writing of the period to the end of the July Monarchy included a good deal that was sentimental—like the work of George Sand (Aurore Dupin) (1804–76). She produced *Lélia* in 1833 in the style of a romantic emotionalism, as well as the rather different *Le Péché de Monsieur Antoine* in 1847.

A new development came with a growth of writing on travel, and also a good deal of romantic historical fiction. Examples of the latter include Vigny's *Cinq-Mars* in 1826, Hugo's *Notre-Dame de Paris* (described by Professor Cobban as "that astonishing, ridiculous and wonderful source-book of romantic clichés") in 1831, and Dumas père's enormously popular *Les Trois Mousquetaires* in 1844. This and its successors were serialized in the press—a sign of the times and of the appeal of the style to a new audience. Other historical novels were also written by Prosper Mérimée, who had been appointed as Inspector of Ancient Monuments; but he is as well known for his *nouvelles* and his translations from Russian authors. Alongside this new genre, there came a renewal of French poetry. Although Lamartine won acclaim for his *Histoire des Girondins* (1847), his poetry was of great importance, especially, perhaps, his *Les Harmonies poétiques et religieuses* of 1830. Victor Hugo (1802–85) was the most significant of the Romantic school. His historical fiction has already been mentioned, but his long life and his conversion to Republicanism, added to his enormous quantities of plays, ballads, love poems, and almost any kind of literature one can name, made him one of the great figures of the nineteenth century. His *Hernani*, the first "modern" play, caused a great critical storm when it was first produced. He had a great influence on poets as diverse as Sainte-Beuve, Barbier, Gautier, Musset and de Vigny. The last two produced work which still has a considerable appeal today. The poetry of ideas, which de Vigny (1797–1863) claimed to have written, was full of a romantic despair and pessimism. Suffering was one of his main themes. Musset (1810–57) had a self-mocking, ironical wit, which, in the poems published from 1830 onwards, was shown in a poetry of personal emotion which was typical of the romanticism of the era.

Hugo produced, as might be expected, some plays of significance, particularly *Ruy Blas* (1838) and *Le Roi s'amuse;* Musset was also responsible for some rather sentimental comedies. But a new style began with the work of the incredibly productive Eugène Scribe (1791–1861). The "historical" romanticism of the age can be viewed in the work of the painter, Delacroix, and, most incredibly of all, in the tragic architectural "preservations" of Viollet-le-Duc, who did more than most to destroy the heritage of the past in the buildings of France. But there were signs that, with the end of the Bourbon monarchy, a new age was dawning in literature and ideas. As Proudhon, the socialist printer, writing at a time of *bourgeois* supremacy (1840) said, "Qu'est-ce que la propriété?" His answer became famous: "C'est le vol", and there were other socialist writers who followed his lead.

## RECOMMENDED READING

*A History of Modern France.* Vol. 2: *1799–1945.* A. Cobban. Penguin, 1961.
*A Poet in Politics: Lamartine and the Revolution of 1848.* G. Wright. *History Today,* Vol. VIII, p. 616 (September 1958).

*Between Two Empires: a History of French Politicians and People between 1814 and 1848.* M. D. R. LEYS. Longmans, 1955.

*France, 1814–1940.* J. P. T. BURY. Methuen, 1951.

*Histoire de France contemporaine.* Ed. LAVISSE. Volume by P. DE LA GORCE, *Louis-Philippe, 1830–48.* Paris, 1931.

*Talleyrand.* H. KURTZ. *History Today,* Vol. VIII, pp. 741 and 847 (November and December 1958).

*The Art of Viollet-le-Duc.* T. EDWARDS. *History Today,* Vol. XIII, p. 459 (July 1963).

*The French Restoration, 1814–30.* D. W. BROGAN. *History Today,* Vol. VI, pp. 28 and 104 (January and February 1956).

# CHAPTER 15

## *The Second Empire and its Collapse*

THE accidental revolution of 1848, brought about by the weakness of the constitutional monarchy of Louis-Philippe, was one more event in French history, the responsibility for which can be placed on the people and politicians in Paris. There is no other country in Europe in which the capital city is so influential, possibly because of the concentration of power and authority there, for which Napoleon I was partly responsible. Once Guizot's unpopular government had fallen, and the barricades had gone up in the streets of Paris, it was inevitable that a provisional government should emerge, largely at the behest of the mob. For a few hours, there was a slight possibility of a Regency for Louis-Philippe's grandson, but, as this was being debated by the Chamber of Deputies, the people broke in and demanded a Republic. Almost immediately, a provisional government was nominated, quite illegally, and among its members were Ledru-Rollin, Marie, and that incredible political figure, the writer Lamartine. These men, in a frenzy of democratic goodwill, announced the introduction of universal male suffrage, the right of all men to be employed and the establishment of a Labour commission under Louis Blanc, which would establish *ateliers*, or national workshops, to put this dream into operation. The workshops failed owing to insufficient economic knowledge; but the idea carried the germ of the modern labour exchange. With the political machinery and economic expertise of the time, it could never have amounted to anything. Although, for a time, some men drew money for performing largely useless public works, and others were paid what amounted to unemployment benefit, the scheme had no planners or public determination behind it, and began to cost the government a considerable amount of money which it could ill afford. New taxation was introduced, which immediately robbed the new administration of much of its popularity; and other measures were seen by the extreme Radicals as being purely reactionary. But the government was not so much reactionary as unable to get its policies obeyed, especially in the provinces. In Paris, it was not long before the dissatisfaction of the people was being shown by a riotous demonstration (17 March 1848) and by street fighting in what came to be known as the revolt of the June Days.

The government was saved, perhaps, by the fact that the Radicals had also nominated a provisional government, which joined forces with the one which emerged from the Chamber, and so put Blanc and Marrast in the administration. In those early days, however, the most interesting—and perhaps most persuasive—member of the government was Lamartine. But the most important was Ledru-Rollin, who organized the election for a new Assembly, and appointed new local prefects to make sure that the peasants were not bullied into voting for the candidates nominated by the priests and landowners. This was the beginning of the situation, so common in France since then, when there is a constant battle for influence between the village priest and the local schoolmaster. However, when the election results were known, the Radicals had not done well. Although the Republic was safe, many of the former deputies were returned, and among them were many known Legitimists and Orléanists. There was rioting in Limoges and Lyons, but, in general, the elections were quiet, and there was a moderate Republican majority in the Constituent Assembly of 900 members. When it met, it was decided that a ministry, responsible to an executive committee of the Assembly, should govern until a new Constitution had been written.

Meantime, it was clearly the wish of the deputies that the *ateliers* should go, and that the government should pay no more *soldes d'inactivité*. The news of this was the spark that led to the insurrection of the June Days, put down by the National Guard and by army units after a harsh struggle, in which 10,000 may have died. Afterwards, there was an even harsher reaction. Many prisoners were sent out to Algeria, and many died of the inhuman cruelty of the prison guards. The War Minister, who had put the insurrection down, was Cavaignac, and he was now entrusted with forming a government. France was under martial law, and there could easily have been a military dictatorship if Cavaignac had desired it. As it was, constitution making went on, until, in November, it was decided to introduce a document by which France was to have government by a single Chamber, of 750 members, of Deputies who were to be elected for three years, and were to be paid for their services. There was fierce controversy about this, and even fiercer debate over the plan to elect a President, who was to be the chief executive power in the state, by a system of universal suffrage. The danger of this was realized by Ledru-Rollin, who could foresee a tyranny—a tyranny, perhaps, set up by Louis Napoleon Bonaparte, son of the Louis Bonaparte who had been King of Holland and of Hortense Beauharnais, Napoleon's stepdaughter. This nephew of Napoleon I, who had spent part of his life in prison and another part in exile, was now a Deputy, and was determined to take advantage of his name and of the influence of the Napoleonic legend. His sole chance of attaining power was on an open, popular vote for the Presidency; and this he might never have had, but for Lamartine, who spoke up for direct election for this office, instead of the scheme, favoured by Ledru-Rollin, for election of a President by the members of the Assembly.

The election was held in December, and the result was that Louis Napoleon won easily, by 5,434,226 votes to Cavaignac's 1,448,107. Ledru-Rollin and Lamartine gained an insignificant percentage of the poll. Merely because his name was Napoleon, a mediocre President, without vision or much ability, had been elected to supreme power. The only ability he possessed was that of making plots. A. J. P. Taylor has described him as a procrastinating revolutionary. Certainly he believed in his Napoleonic destiny, and liked to see himself as an enigma; the truth seems to be that he had ambition but no policy save that of courting popularity—and few political principles save that of doing something, rather vaguely, to improve conditions for the workers. His first idea, on being elected, was to approach Cavaignac and Lamartine, his opponents in the election, to form a government; when the impossibility of this was made obvious, he turned to Barrot and the Legitimist, de Falloux. Finally, a ministry emerged which was predominantly one of royalists, and this was plainly one which would not get on well with the Assembly. The government was soon forced to take strong measures in view of the union of the moderate Republicans with the more extreme supporters of Blanc, and sufficient pressure was exerted to force the Assembly to dissolve itself in 1849. Popular rioting in the capital and provinces caused the President to reshuffle the government, and d'Hautpol and Rouher formed a ministry which was more amenable to him, although it did pass an act for free education, introduced by Falloux in the previous administration. One of Napoleon's reasons for dismissing his first government was that there was dissension on foreign policy. The European situation had been fluid for some time. Before Napoleon had been elected President, there had been revolts in Italy and in Austria, where, as a result, Metternich had fallen from power. Charles Albert, the ruler of Piedmont, had thought that Italian independence might well emerge from this welter of insurrection, until the Austrian, Radetzky, had taken firm action to hold back the advancing tide in northern Italy. The Pope, Pius IX, fearing the establishment of a republic in the Papal States, had made an appeal to France, which had been ignored until Napoleon had come to power. The President then decided to intervene, partly to show hostility to Austria, and partly to aid the Pope. A French expedition was pushed back from Rome by Garibaldi, and de Lesseps was sent to make terms with the revolutionaries; but while he was engaged in this, the elections in France had returned a more conservative Assembly, and Napoleon decided to try again. This time, Rome surrendered to the French, and the

President invited Pius to return to his capital. Unfortunately, when it became clear that there was to be repression of the revolutionaries, Napoleon made it clear that he believed in toleration, and wanted to see a much more liberal policy. This was unacceptable to the Papacy, and, when the crisis had passed, the *status quo* was restored, and the French intervention seemed to have achieved nothing in particular.

At home in France, it appeared that the left wing was growing in power. The government therefore introduced an amendment to the new constitution, by which 3 million voters were disfranchised, and this step was seen, by Thiers among others, as a step on the path which would lead, inevitably, to a dictatorship. Despite the safeguards of the 1848 Constitution, it appeared that a *coup d'état* was being planned, which would result in Napoleon's Presidency being renewed. France did not have to wait long. On 2 December 1851 the Assembly was declared to be dissolved, the universal suffrage restored (this, an obvious vote-catching manœuvre), and a plebiscite announced. There was some protest, but only slight; very few died on the barricades. But to make it clear that there was to be no trouble from the opposition, tribunals were set up which sentenced so-called traitors to prison or to terms of exile in Algeria. Men suffered midnight arrests. Key posts like arsenals and printing presses were seized. A new Constitution—yet another—was promulgated, by which Napoleon was to be President for ten years, with the title of Consul. Associated with him was a new government, including Saint-Arnaud, Morny (Louis Napoleon's half-brother), Rouher and Fould. A Senate and *Corps Législatif* were established, which set about the introduction of policies which were, it must be admitted, fairly sensible and liberal. Eventually, yet another plebiscite resulted in the election of Napoleon as Emperor, on 2 December 1852. Napoleon III took the throne of France on the anniversary, not only of his previous coup, but on that of Austerlitz. The Second Empire, with all its bungling tyranny, its opportunism, and its stupidly aggressive foreign policy, was established. The Emperor and his Council of State decided what was to be done, while the *Corps Législatif* meekly obeyed orders. The régime seemed to be secure, and was made more so after the birth of a son to Napoleon III and his consort, Eugénie, in 1853. The Republicans, the Legitimists, the Orléanists—all lost power to the incompetent dictator. However, economically, France was doing well. New banks were founded, railways were being built, the coal and iron industries flourished, and foreign trade grew. Public works were developed, and contemporary France owes much to Napoleon. In particular, Paris as it now exists is the creation of Napoleon and his *préfet* of the Seine, Haussmann, who opened up the Bois de Boulogne, the Bois de Vincennes and Longchamps; and who tore down the old city to build one of wide boulevards. Much that was of historical interest disappeared, but considerable beauty was created, even if one of the reasons for the wide avenues was to make it more difficult for Parisians in the future to man the barricades.

It was not long before the Empire became involved, rather reluctantly, in a war. The Crimean War was undoubtedly the most useless of the wars of the modern period, and could easily have been avoided. It was, perhaps, inevitable that Russia should be involved in a war with Turkey, under some pretext or other, and that the western powers should be concerned to see that Russian power should not grow too much; but the quarrel itself, over the protectorate of the Christian Holy Places under Turkish rule, was ridiculously unnecessary. When the Russians invaded Moldavia and Wallachia, the British and French intervened, and, when the Russians withdrew from these Principalities, the Anglo–French force was sent to the Crimea to teach the Russians a lesson by taking Sebastopol. A siege was commenced when it was decided not to attack the Russian fortress immediately, and all the armies involved suffered as a result, more from disease and inadequate equipment than from the battles, such as Balaclava and Inkerman. The French commanders, in turn St. Arnaud, Canrobert, whom the English unkindly dubbed "Robert can't", and Pélissier, did not get on well with the incompetent British commanders; and when the French took the Malakov and Sebastopol was taken, the Czar also being dead, it was with considerable relief that the powers made the Treaty of Paris in 1856, by which the Black Sea was made neutral, the Danube opened to shipping of all countries, the frontiers returned to their former state, and no one lost face. Much more important, for France, was to be the next war. At the conference which made the Treaty of Paris was Cavour, the chief minister of the ruler of Piedmont, who, in order to create allied indebtedness to his cause, had sent troops to participate in the struggle in the Crimea.

What Cavour wanted was a promise from Napoleon III that French support would be available in case of a war against the Austrians. There was nothing for which the Emperor had more sympathy than the cause of Italian independence, although he was aware that this might mean alienating the Papacy, and, of course, French Roman Catholics, if it came to the point when the Italian revolutionaries tried to rob the Pope of the territories around Rome. Napoleon, however, was determined to help the Italians, and even used the famous Orsini bomb plot of January 1858 to show the world that he was a supporter of the cause of Italian liberation. In fact, the plot caused more inconvenience to Palmerston in England than it did to the Emperor. The machinery for war was established in July 1858, as a result of a meeting between Napoleon and Cavour at Plombières; a verbal promise was given to the Italian, and it was arranged that Napoleon's cousin should marry Victor Emmanuel's daughter—none of this with the agreement of Walewski, the French foreign minister, because the Emperor liked to keep foreign policy in his own hands. Cavour went ahead with the plans for war, although there is some possibility that Napoleon hoped for gains without recourse to fighting. If so, his "brinkmanship" came to nothing. The Austrians began to make war, as Cavour had foreseen, and the French were dragged, once again, into a struggle in which the greater part of the people had no interest. Napoleon went to Genoa to take command of the French forces, but he had none of the military ability of his namesake, and it was more to the slowness and incompetence of the Austrians than to the genius of MacMahon that the French won victories at Magenta, which gave them control of Milan, and at Solferino. The Emperor's luck may have lasted, if the war had gone on. But these victories were sufficient. It is said that Napoleon was horrified by the sights of carnage on the battlefield of Solferino—it is true that the more modern distaste for the cruelty of war caused that battle to be the reason for the foundation of the Red Cross organization.

The Emperor, at any rate, was willing to make peace. Negotiations were begun with the Austrians, which resulted in the Peace of Villafranca, by which France was given Lombardy on the understanding that she, in turn, would pass it on to Piedmont. The contracting parties made terms without reference to Victor Emmanuel, and this slight caused Cavour to resign; so did Walewski, who objected to Napoleon's attitude to the Papacy, which was now revealed. Tuscany and other Italian states joined in a union with Piedmont, now that the Austrian threat had been removed, and the Emperor decided that he would support the people of the Papal States if they joined in, too. The Pope, he claimed, needed only the city of Rome itself. He hoped that, as a result of this decision, Italian unification would go far enough to completion for him to be able to claim Nice and Savoy for France, as had been arranged at Plombières. This, indeed, he did, and, after carefully managed plebiscites, these territories were united to France. In some sense, the intervention in Italy brought credit to Napoleon, but the Italians, whom he had done much to help, did not look to France with overmuch gratitude. Instead, Palmerston and Russell were to be credited with a great part of the achievement. At this time, Napoleon was on reasonably good terms with England; he even moved against the economic traditions of France, to enable Cobden to arrange a Free Trade Treaty between the two powers in 1860. This may partly have been an insurance policy. It was becoming clearer that a policy of peace was what France wanted; and popular feeling was something that a democratically elected emperor must always be aware of. The opposition could not be kept pent up for ever, and the economic and financial state of France seemed to be weakening after a decade of prosperity. Napoleon was beginning to take a new interest in French colonial policy. He intervened in Algeria on behalf of the natives, sent an expedition to Syria in 1860, encouraged de Lesseps who had begun the building of the Suez canal in 1859, supported the successful colonization of Senegal, and was responsible for the annexation of Cochin-China and Cambodia, besides joining with England in an action to open China itself to foreign trade.

The Emperor was aware that much of what he had achieved was a matter of luck. There was serious opposition to him amongst the Catholics, and also amongst those Frenchmen who objected to his neutrality in the matter of the Polish revolutionaries who were treated so brutally by the Czar. Men like Thiers were becoming influential among the Republican ranks, of whom little had been heard since the coup, and the Emperor's answer was to take Rouher into the government and to announce a more liberal policy. But his determination to avoid being entangled in dangerous foreign policies was stillborn. When, as a result of a civil war in Mexico, a new President, Juarez, refused to acknowledge liabilities incurred by his predecessors, Britain, Spain and France intervened. The French force, defeated at Vera Cruz, remained in Mexico, set up a provisional government there, and offered the throne to the Archduke Maximilian, a brother of the Austrian Emperor. The expedition, popular at first with the Catholics, eventually cost France so much that, with the end of the American Civil War, when the United States reminded Napoleon of the Monroe Doctrine, he was only too glad to withdraw. Almost immediately, his protégé, Maximilian, was defeated, tried and shot, and the whole episode had merely discredited the Empire.

One reason for Napoleon's wish to cease being involved in Mexico was the development of Prussian power in Europe. When Denmark tried to get Schleswig and Holstein in her orbit, Prussia and Austria had intervened, and had taken the territories while France had remained a spectator. By the Treaty of Gastein,

Prussia swallowed Schleswig; Napoleon protested, but was talked into accepting the *fait accompli*. Conscious as he was of the history of France in the previous century, and of the Napoleonic Wars, he still thought of Austria as the chief enemy of France. He was even willing to act as a broker, to arrange a treaty between Prussia and Victor Emmanuel's new kingdom. It was not until the outbreak of war between Prussia and Austria in 1866, when the Austrian weakness was shown up at Königgrätz, that the Emperor began to realize that he could not afford to show friendship for a power rapidly developing into the greatest threat to France. However, by the 1860's, his Empire was recognized as a great European power again, and he thought that it might be possible to gain some territory by a gentle form of blackmail. Prussia became the ruler of a unified north German state by the Treaty of Prague—Napoleon's request for a Rhine frontier was rebuffed by the triumphant Bismarck, and the imperial prestige was weakened once again. It was becoming increasingly obvious that a policy of peace was the one thing that the French Empire could not afford; and equally plain, that a vigorous foreign policy was beyond Napoleon's ability. His failure to annex Belgium, the neutrality of which was guaranteed by the European powers in the Treaty of London, 1839, was yet another blow to his pride.

The year 1867, despite the publicity of another French Exhibition, brought no respite. The opposition was growing in strength, as it had been since 1863. The power of the Roman Church was greater than it had been for a very long time; pilgrims had begun to flock to Lourdes after the miraculous events there in 1858. On the other hand, there were bitter disputes between the Catholics and the intelligentsia, especially concerning the control of education. Republicanism and anti-clericalism began to be synonymous. The quarrel might have been even fiercer if the press had been free from government control, but, until 1868, when the law was relaxed, fines, warnings and suspensions were used to keep the journalists in order. Economically, the Empire was weakening. The spread of phylloxera ruined the vineyards, and the bankruptcy of the financial house, the Crédit Mobilier, in 1867 was a sign of the times. Rouher, Napoleon's chief minister, found it difficult to raise sufficient money to finance the administration, or to pay for the rearmament and reorganization of the army, which were so badly needed. Haussmann also became unpopular when it was realized how much the replanning of Paris was costing. In the elections of 1869, the opposition vote went up to over 3 million, out of nearly 8 million. This was the end of the road for Rouher, who gave way to Ollivier. Inevitably, Napoleon shared some of the unpopularity of his minister. Those who sympathized with the Italian revolutionaries were furious when French troops were used to defeat Garibaldi, campaigning for the inclusion of Rome in a united Italy. Few seemed to think more of the Emperor for attempting to liberalize the régime. It might have been possible for Ollivier to win support for a reforming ministry. The new minister was willing to appeal for support to the leaders of all groups of opinion; but war was now very near, and the committees set up to discuss the government of Paris, local government in the provinces, and the future of the educational system were not to get very far. It was a difficult period for any government. Pius IX's declaration at the Oecumenical Council of 1869 for the doctrine of Papal Infallibility caused an outright split between the Ultramontanes and the liberal Catholics. The Emperor was frantically trying to find allies for the imminent struggle with Prussia—in fact, he was negotiating with Austria, until Daru, the Foreign Minister, objected to Napoleon carrying on negotiations unofficially.

However, in April 1870, there was a plebiscite on the suggested revision of the constitution, by which France was to be given an upper Chamber with genuine power, and, as a result of the voting, a new government was installed, in which Daru was replaced by de Gramont. The latter was in favour of an Austrian alliance, but, although an unofficial agreement was made, its value was of no account. When the time came, no aid from Austria was forthcoming. Nothing could be expected from Italy, either. The Italian government would not consider joining in a French alliance unless Napoleon promised support for the annexation of Rome, and this, owing to the need to keep on friendly terms with the French Catholics, he could not give. And so France entered on the year of war with Prussia, without firm allies, economically weakened, and with an army which did not compare with the Prussian forces, created and sustained by a compulsory system of military service. Admittedly, the French had a machine-gun, the *mitrailleuse*, and the new *chassepôt* rifle, but these were to be of no avail in the hands of half-trained soldiers led by incompetent generals.

The excuse for war was found in the situation in Spain. The Spanish Queen, Isabella, was deposed, and the provisional government offered the throne to Leopold of Hohenzollern, who accepted it. The prospect of a Prussian prince on the throne of Spain caused immediate protests in Paris, and the French ambassador asked William of Prussia to promise that he would not support Leopold's candidature. William refused to make any such promise, but did so in a friendly and diplomatic way, to the dismay of Bismarck, who saw an excuse for conflict being thrown away. He had been informed of the discussion by a telegram from the King, who was at Ems; and decided, by a discreet "cutting" of the telegram, to make it appear that William had been insulting and abrupt to the French ambassador. This revised version of the Ems telegram was then published, to the fury of the French government, and Bismarck's aim was achieved when the French declared war on 19 July. Both sides mobilized, and, although it was generally considered that the French would win, the war went almost completely according to the Prussian plan. On 6 August 1870 MacMahon, in command of the French armies in Alsace, was defeated at Wörth, while the other French commander, Bazaine, came to grief at Spicheren. Already, signs of French disunity and chaotic preparation for war were visible, while Moltke's Prussians were superior in most of the military arts. In Paris, Ollivier's ministry fell, to give way to one led by Count Polikao, and, although there had been ideas that the

French forces should retreat towards Paris, the shame of this was considered to be too great. It was concluded that Metz should be defended, but this only led to another defeat—that of Gravelotte, after which Napoleon gave the command to MacMahon. The latter then wished to retreat towards Paris, but was ordered to attempt the rescue of Bazaine, who was surrounded near Metz. He did so, and the French were led to the last catastrophe, on 1 September, at Sedan. At the end of the day, the French army surrendered, and Napoleon was a prisoner.

The news caused a revolt in Paris against the Assembly. The mob crowded into the Chamber, and then adjourned to the Hôtel de Ville, to declare the Empire at an end. A Government of National Defence was set up, which included Favre, Gambetta and Trochu. The Empress Eugénie departed for exile in England, and the question then arose, for which all Europe was awaiting the answer, whether Bismarck would make peace with the new Republic—for this it was, in fact, if not in name. Although the Germans were beginning to find that the French population was prepared to resist, Bismarck was determined to take Alsace and Lorraine. Without these, he was not prepared to discuss terms of peace, and he said so, to Favre, at Ferrières, near Paris. Trochu and Favre were not prepared to agree to these harsh terms, and so the war continued. The Germans proceeded to invest Paris; a state of siege began on 19 September. The people of Paris defended their city with enthusiasm, if not much discipline, and the heroism of the time was symbolized by Gambetta, who escaped from the city in a balloon to join the delegates who were organizing a renewal of the war at Tours. His efforts failed, but they were incredibly heroic. He organized an army which defeated the Germans at Coulmiers, near Orléans, but any further triumph was prevented by the premature surrender of Bazaine at Metz on 27 October. Gambetta claimed that Bazaine had betrayed France; and, after the war, he was sentenced to death—a sentence which was later commuted to imprisonment for twenty years. The other French forces failed to make any impression on the German armies; and, with their failure, and that of the Parisians to break out, Favre capitulated on 28 January 1871. An armistice was signed at Versailles, and it was agreed that there should be elections for a new Assembly, which would be able, legally, to sign a peace treaty. Already, Bismarck had achieved a great triumph at Versailles, where, on 18 January, William of Prussia was proclaimed as German Emperor. The new French Assembly met at Bordeaux, and promptly elected Thiers as Chief of the Executive and Favre as Foreign Minister. Thiers, back in power after the years in the wilderness—during part of which time he had written his *History of the Consulate and Empire*—was now to make history himself.

Bismarck wanted to annex Alsace and Lorraine, besides Belfort, and to claim a large cash indemnity from the French government. Thiers was able to persuade him to reduce the amount of the indemnity and not to take Belfort, but otherwise the Prussian minister was immovable. The Assembly ratified the terms, under considerable protest, on 1 March—but Victor Hugo made his point. He said: "Henceforth there are in Europe two nations which will be formidable—the one because it is victorious, the other because it is vanquished." With peace forced upon an unhappy France, the Assembly now turned to the other problems which faced her. Foremost among these were the events which were taking place in Paris. Here the people had established a Commune, which refused to accept the order, given by Thiers, to withdraw some guns from Montmartre. The government therefore withdrew its troops from the city, and Thiers and MacMahon then ordered the French army to besiege it, and to restore order there by force. Paris was governed, for a few weeks, by Pyat and Delescluze, leaders of a Committee of Public Safety. The worst week for the citizens came in May, at the end of which much of central Paris, including the Tuileries and the Hôtel de Ville, was destroyed by fire. The fighting was over by 28 May, in the same month that the government of France had signed the Treaty of Frankfort, by which it was agreed to pass over to Germany the fruits of war: Alsace, Lorraine, Strasbourg, Metz and the indemnity. Meantime, Russia had seized her chance to tear up the Treaty of Paris, which had made the Black Sea neutral at the end of the Crimean War. The Italians had taken Rome, and the Pope had retired into the Vatican. Thiers was trying to establish the Third Republic, in a Europe where the dominating figure was now Bismarck. Louis Napoleon, released from imprisonment, had gone to live in England, in exile, where he eventually died in January 1873. Monarchy was dead in France. The Republic, which was born in the shame of defeat, was to die in similar shame, in its turn. Karl Marx's study of the Commune was read by Lenin, who used its lessons to avoid similar mistakes in 1917 in Russia. There was much bitterness, and a sense of betrayal among the extreme Left, at this second defeat.

Just as a visitor to Paris, who studies the city around him, is still conscious of the achievements of the Second Empire, so the student of literature must be conscious of the importance of that period, also. In the theatre, Emile Augier was producing plays which exalted the *bourgeois* virtues, like *Les Affrontés* (1861). More popular than these were the works of Dumas *fils*, whose sentimental *La Dame aux camélias* was first performed in 1852, and is revived occasionally to this day. Later, Dumas was to emerge as a campaigner for moral reform. A more light-hearted and occasionally satirical writer for the stage was Labiche, among whose works appear *Le Voyage de M. Perrichon*, and farces like *Un Chapeau de paille d'Italie* and libretti for the music of Offenbach and Bizet. For example, he wrote the libretto for *Carmen*. Among the novelists of the period are Gustave Flaubert (1821–80), whose work began a fashion for realism, of a kind to be seen in *Madame Bovary* (1857) and *L'Éducation sentimentale*, the latter written against a Parisian background and published in 1869. Other writers about contemporary Paris were the brothers Edmond and Jules Goncourt—the first left funds to institute the Prix Goncourt, a literary prize which still retains considerable importance. Towards the end of the Napoleonic régime, Alphonse Daudet was beginning to achieve fame. His *Lettres de mon moulin*, with a Provençal background, came out in 1869. It is not surprising that some of the writing of the period should have been on historical and political topics—among it the socialist work of Louis Blanc, whose *Life of Robespierre* was to be studied by Marx and other communists; besides the more scholarly work of Thiers and Guizot. Marx lived in Paris for some time, and much of his general socialist theory was derived from the early French political writers. Greater than any of these was de Tocqueville, who published his *L'Ancien Régime et la Révolution* in 1856, some years after his famous *La Démocratie en Amérique*. The most important critics writing during the Empire were Sainte-Beuve (1804–69) and Taine.

Victor Hugo was continuing to make his name, although for much of the period he was living in exile in the Channel Isles. His chief work to be produced there was *La Légende des siècles;* but he earned more popular fame with *Les Misérables* (1862), soon to be translated into several other languages. There was some distinguished poetry from the pen of Gérard de Nerval, whose sonnets, *Les Chimères*, were to be surpassed only by the poems of Baudelaire (1821–67), whose *Les Fleurs du mal*, despite their obsession with death, were to become extremely influential. On a far less important level was Mistral, who attempted, with other *Félibres*, so called, to attempt a revival of the Provençal language and literature, without a great deal of success. At the same level, perhaps, was the work of the school of the Parnassians, named after a contemporary periodical, *Le Parnasse Contemporain*. Mallarmé was at work, although his famous *L'Après-midi d'un faune* did not appear in its final form until 1876. Finally, the roll of distinguished writers of this mid-nineteenth-century era must include the names of de Lisle (1818–94), who wrote on religious themes; and Verlaine, who published two collections of poems before 1870, including the well-known *Fêtes galantes*. The Empire may have been a time when a rather shabby ruler set France on the road to disaster; but there was nothing of disaster in the cultural and literary achievements of the bourgeois régime.

## RECOMMENDED READING

*A History of Modern France.* Vol. 2: *1799–1945.* A. COBBAN. Penguin, 1961.

*Europe, 1815–1945.* ANTHONY WOOD. Longmans, 1964.

*Gambetta and the National Defence.* J. P. T. BURY. Longmans, 1936.

*Louis Napoleon and the Recovery of France, 1848–56.* F. A. SIMPSON. Longmans, 1956.

*Louis Napoleon and the Second Empire.* J. M. THOMPSON. Blackwell, 1954.

*Napoleon III and the Rebuilding of Paris.* D. H. PINKNEY. Oxford, 1958.

## CHAPTER 16

# The Third Republic, 1870–1914

THE Assembly, which was elected by the people of France while the German troops besieged Paris, was largely royalist in its sympathies, and opinion generally seemed to be in favour of a Restoration. Yet from it there emerged a republic which was to last until the mid-twentieth century, and this may be because the republican ideal was far more popular in France than the election of royalists to the Assembly might have led one to believe. It is true that the elections were held in most unhappy circumstances, and probably the instincts of the electors led them to vote for local dignitaries, men who were well known to them, who could be relied upon to make peace, and not to attempt the continuation of a patriotic war of resistance. France was frightened: she had been beaten easily in the war, her middle classes thought that a revolution might break out at any time, the peasants feared that the crisis would result in financial ruin for them, and the new working classes in the industrial areas thought that the time was ripe for them to seize power—as their leaders did, in Paris. The bitter struggle between the Communards of Paris, and the government forces, the Versaillais, left marks which were not to be obliterated for a long time. The Republicans hoped that the defeat would lead to a reorganization in France which would restore the democracy of the 1793 constitution.

For a time, the conservative majority in the Assembly thought that it might be possible to restore the Legitimist, de Chambord, to the throne, under the title of Henri V. But his obstinacy, his outright refusal to grant any concessions in view of the events of the previous century, his belief in Divine Right and not in election to the royal office, all ruined any chance he might have had. Indeed, the royalists gradually lost faith in him, and began to weigh up the possibilities of the Orléanist Comte de Paris, to whom Chambord's claims would pass one day. Meantime, the Republic went on existing, and, with the peace terms made with Germany, and the indemnity inflicted upon France paid off by an intense concentration of patriotic effort within three years, the radical politicians began to make a come-back, and the strength of the opposition began to grow. The unwillingness of Thiers to grant everything the conservatives wanted, or to throw his weight behind the royalists, or even to take the steps to deal with the radicals that the moderates thought were necessary, led to a vote of no confidence in him, and to his resignation. He was replaced, as President, by General MacMahon. Under his rule, the new Constitution of the Third Republic was accepted—but only by a majority of one vote. The new system provided a President, whose responsibility it was to choose the ministers and to initiate legislation, and to preside over a lower Chamber and an upper house called the Senate. Such a system might well have developed to give the President the same kind of authority that the President enjoys in the United States, but events took it in an opposite direction. Eventually, the President retained very few powers. His position became like that of a constitutional monarch, except that his term of office was limited to seven years—perhaps because the men responsible for designing the new constitution were conscious that they might have to fit a monarch into the scheme of things.

Politically, there was still much bitterness in France. The association between catholicism and the reactionary policies of the right wing was a factor which the Republicans never played down. By the time of the elections of 1876, a new situation had developed—a Chamber with a majority of Republicans of various kinds, with a right wing Senate and President, which made the day to day work of governing the state almost an impossibility. The new constitution had been created by compromise, and could easily be altered. Few politicians wanted to see the election of a President by plebiscite, of a kind which had given France Napoleon III in 1851. The conservatives did not want to see a weakening of the Senate, which was elected, not by the public, but by the communes, or municipal councils. MacMahon, faced by an impossible position, and unwilling to relinquish his powers, dissolved the Chamber and called for a new election. He was fighting for the independence of the President against the power of the Chamber; and he failed. The electors returned a republican Chamber, and the President was faced with the inevitability of Republican ministries in office. He continued to fight this, until, at last, in 1879 he resigned, to give way to the more moderate Jules Grévy. Grévy's election meant that the Third Republic was well established, and that all hope of a royal restoration was gone. So was the possibility of a President controlling the executive, or, as MacMahon had wished, the chance of the Church taking a leading part in the affairs of state. What was established was the state of affairs that came to be particularly associated with the Third Republic—a state of numerous political interests and parties, all represented in the Chamber, all dividing and combining to present rapid changes in government, the rise and fall of ministries, a lack of the rigid party loyalty which grew up in England, and a lack of stability which meant that the Chamber itself and the ministerial officials had far more power than the ministers themselves.

Economically, France made a surprisingly rapid recovery after the war, but phylloxera was still the curse of the vineyards, until, under Grévy, rewards were given to farmers to encourage them to burn their land and grow new stock. In other fields, an economic decline was on its way. The silk industry began to feel the cold wind of competition from other textiles, luxury trades suffered generally, as did all the industries which depended upon the well-to-do who could afford to pay for quality and craftsmanship. This was the age of power derived from coal, a commodity scarce in France, except in a few areas where its production was costly, owing to the depth of the seams or to the distance from the cities where it was needed. At a time when ferrous metal production was becoming a basic industry in other countries, France could not compete. The economic decline of the last two decades of the nineteenth century was accompanied by an insufficient population growth, and an exodus of people from the countryside to the towns, where, unable to find industrial employment, many tried to set themselves up as shopkeepers. As a result, France has had too many small business men ever since. They are the urban equivalents of the peasant proprietors, who were taking over the land from the large landowners during the same period. While Britain was benefiting from a free-trade economy, and Germany and the United States were entering on a highly successful time of industrial growth, France was an industrial backwater, trying to overcome her difficulties by a protectionist policy, as symbolized by the Méline general tariff of 1892. French shipping declined, and the country was very conscious of the loss to Germany of the minerals of Lorraine.

There was, however, some successful colonization at this stage. The European powers were all concerned with the acquisition of colonies, particularly in Africa, and France took Tunis in 1881, Madagascar in 1884, and Tonkin in 1885. Thirty-six million people were added to the population of France, for the colonies were governed, wherever possible, as though they were French *départements*. A joint Anglo–French commission undertook the administration of Egypt, and there was serious rivalry between the two powers until 1904, when Egypt was recognized at last as being a British sphere of influence. At home, education was a burning issue, for the Republicans wished to ensure that their rivals, the right wing Catholics, should not exert their old control over the schools. It was Jules Ferry, chief minister from 1883 to 1885, who took strong action in the matter. Despite the objections of the Catholics, he established *lycées* for girls, alongside those that existed already for boys; set up primary schools, attendance at which was compulsory; and even expelled from France members of teaching orders, like the Jesuits. Schoolmasters were already the deadly rivals of the village priests— this new system made them even more so. Ferry was also responsible for abolishing the system whereby members of the Senate were elected for life, and for doing something to extend the freedom of the press. The growth of democracy was also the growth of lay control of institutions in France. Ferry himself was not as popular as Gambetta, who, until his death in 1882, was the leader of Republican radicalism. Both were, however, comparatively moderate in their views, and always aware of the importance of not being too far ahead of public opinion. They were what came to be called Opportunists, who believed in empirical progress, as opposed to the Intransigents, the radicals who wanted the government to set a lead to the people. A typical Intransigent was the socialist, Louis Blanc, whose political importance had grown up during the days of the Empire. On the whole, the Opportunists believed in supporting the constitution, and in attempting to provide prosperity rather than in reform for the sake of reform. Admittedly, Gambetta was a radical, but he was no socialist, either of the old Louis Blanc school or of the newer, Marxist variety. But his influence was great, even though, when given an opportunity to form a ministry in 1881, he failed to make any real impression. His appeal to the French may be judged, however, from the fact that his heart is preserved beneath the *Arc de Triomphe*.

In the elections of 1885, the lack of unity among the various types of Republican led to a growth of the more conservative elements in the Chamber. Perhaps the peasants were voting against the economic depression which was beginning to be felt, and against some of the Ferry legislation for secular education and the increase in the powers of the elected *maires* in 1884; whatever the cause, the elections caused a situation which led to the Boulanger crisis. There was a good deal of frustrated national feeling in a France which had been so crushingly defeated in 1870. The army had been reformed, but there was considerable debate on the terms of conscription. The left wing supported a short term of military service, in order to prevent the emergence of soldiers with political ambition. By the system then operating, service with the army was for a period of five years, but exemption was available for intending priests and schoolmasters. The officers, fairly naturally, tended to be politically conservative and often downright royalist in their sympathies. Grévy having resigned as the result of a financial scandal (his son-in-law had been selling "honours"), Sadi Carnot had been elected President. Among other ministers, he inherited General Boulanger at the War Office, the friend of the radical, Clemenceau. Boulanger looked the part of a distinguished soldier, and was extremely popular as a speaker, and, as a result of his attacks on Grévy for not supporting sufficiently strongly one Schnaebele (arrested illegally by the Germans), became so popular that he initiated a demand for the revision of the constitution. At first, the army officers had disliked Boulanger cordially, mainly because he tried to improve conditions for the troops, and had tried to get rid of him because of his "socialist" sympathies. He was dismissed from the government, which soon found that he was a more embarrassing figure in opposition than he had been while he held office. The extreme left wingers supported him already, with all their knowledge of crowd tactics, as used by revolutionaries before and since; and the monarchists then changed their minds and rallied to him as well, thinking his popularity might be sufficient to overthrow the Republic. The government was determined that he should be shown up for what he was, and dismissed him from the army. This made him a martyr, and everyone who disliked the ministry flocked to his support. He stood as a candidate in several by-elections, including one in the Seine *département* in 1889, and won resoundingly. There were constitutional perils in this. A *coup d'état* was the obvious next step, but he perhaps realized that the royalists who were supporting him were doing so for their own ends, and would never work in harness with his left-wing friends. Lacking the confidence that he needed to seize dictatorial power, he decided to leave the country when the government preferred charges against him. The crisis blew over almost at once, his friends were discredited, and two years later he committed suicide in Brussels.

It was a victory for the Opportunists, and the radicals, who had stupidly supported Boulanger, lost a good deal of support from the workers, who turned to the new socialist parties instead. The moderate Republicans were to have it all their own way for the rest of the century, and, under their rule, some valuable progress was made, in social legislation, colonial expansion and the breaking down of isolation for France in the matter of foreign alliances. Something was done to give more freedom to the trade unions, and there was legislation on the limitation of hours of work for women and children, as well as safety in mines and factories. The conservatives, having learned a lesson from the failure of Boulangism, began to be more moderate, and the Roman Catholics, under the influence of Leo XIII, began a *ralliement*, a rallying of support to a Republic which they realized they could not destroy. The election of about fifty socialists to the Chamber in the polls of 1893 showed that a new kind of political attitude was growing up in the industrial areas. Guesde's *Parti Ouvrier Français*, founded in 1879, and the parties led by Brousse and Blanqui, beside the growing significance of syndicalism, showed that the traditional parties had begun to lose their appeal. Republicans like Jaurès realized that it was necessary for the old-fashioned radicals to come to terms with the socialists and to work with the unions, which were doing something practical to benefit the workers by setting up *Bourses de travail* in the towns.

But the politicians in Paris were concerned with other problems than these. Carnot, who had held power during the Boulanger crisis, and is also remembered for the Paris Exhibition of 1889, which gave the Eiffel Tower to the Parisian skyline, remained in office during the Panama Canal crisis. A company, founded by de Lesseps after his Suez success, to put a canal through the Panama isthmus, had lost money, and, despite various schemes to attract more capital, was finally declared bankrupt. Accusations of bribery and corruption were inquired into, while the newspapers had a field day. Over a hundred deputies were accused of taking bribes, and several political figures went down in the

storm, including Clemenceau, the famous radical *maire* of Montmartre. Even so, when the crisis was over, little change in the
political scene was visible. The Republican moderates remained
in power, even when President Carnot was assassinated in 1894.
This was one of the most tragic events in a period of anarchist
violence. He was succeeded by Casimir-Périer, but, finding that
the President's powers were few, he resigned to make way for
Félix Faure. The murder of Carnot had led to the passage of
some repressive laws, to which the left wingers objected; and
they were joined by some of the more radical Republicans, who
were beginning to think seriously of joining forces with the
socialists. One of the themes they took up was the revision of the
tax laws. French taxation was still based on the indirect purchase
tax and on the direct tax on land and movables. Plainly this was
not equitable, and it was to the credit of the radical minister,
Léon Bourgeois, who formed a government in 1895, that he
introduced the idea of an income-tax. However, the independent
French shopkeepers and peasants, often in a small way of
business, had rooted objections to accountants and officials, and
there was considerable opposition and obstruction to the introduction of the new idea. Bourgeois's ministry did not last.
Méline took over in April 1896, and there was little political
excitement until a new passion arose in 1898 with the Dreyfus
affair, which burst upon the public with Zola's letter, *J'accuse*.
By the end of the century, the old royalist parties were in permanent eclipse, and the Republic had lasted longer than any
régime since 1793. Even if it aroused little enthusiasm, and had
gained for itself a corrupt reputation, the third Republic seemed
to have come to stay.

Its worst moment, apart from the Boulanger crisis, came with
the Dreyfus affair. This incredible business began when a
memorandum, or *bordereau*, was discovered which indicated that a
spy in the French army had been passing information to the
Germans. One of the members of the army's counter-espionage
section was a certain Alsatian officer, Major Henry, who saw
fit to accuse Captain Alfred Dreyfus, an Alsatian Jew, of the

crime. Undoubtedly, one of Henry's motives was a blind anti-semitism, of the kind that had been aroused in France by Drumont, in his journal, *La Libre Parole*. Urged on by the press, which demanded a scapegoat, a court martial found Dreyfus guilty, despite the total lack of evidence that he knew anything at all about the matter, and sentenced him to dismissal from the army and to deportation. He was sent to Devil's Island—and while he was there, another Intelligence officer discovered some fresh evidence that pointed to the implication of another man, named Esterhazy. Astoundingly, the War Office permitted Henry to forge further evidence of Dreyfus's guilt, declared Esterhazy innocent, and refused to grant a retrial when asked to do so. The story was passed on to certain politicians by the officer who had discovered the evidence against Esterhazy—and had been posted to Tunisia for his pains—and the public got to know what was going on when Zola's open letter appeared in the journal, *L'Aurore*. But the government would not retreat. Zola fled to England. Although it would have liked nothing better than to see the whole affair hushed up, the government now saw all its enemies coalesce, and the country was split into factions, pro- and anti-Dreyfus.

Apart from Henry's anti-semitism, it is difficult to know what other motives impelled him to act as he did; similarly, the action of the authorities in defending him seems to have had only the motive of saving the face of an important government department. Sides were taken in the dispute in some rather unexpected ways. Among the *Dreyfusards* were Waldeck-Rousseau, Poincaré, Jaurès, most of the anti-militarists, and the right-wing paper, *Figaro*, as well as the left-wing *Aurore*. Their opponents included the radical Cavaignac, as well as the army leaders and the right-wing Catholics. The Catholic journal *La Croix* supported the anti-*Dreyfusard* Prime Minister, Méline, and its virulent campaigning undoubtedly caused a good deal of anti-Jewish rioting. There may have been another spy at work, who was determined to keep suspicion riveted on Dreyfus; but, in any case, when it was decided to bring Picquart, the officer who had started the investigation, for trial before a magistrate, the game was over for Major Henry, who committed suicide. Although all kinds of delaying tactics were used to prevent Dreyfus from getting justice, and another court martial, held at Rennes, declared him guilty of treachery again, a pardon was issued at last. But it was not until 1906 that the Appeal Court finally cleared Dreyfus's name.

The whole affair nearly brought the Republic down. *A coup d'état* was attempted in 1899 on the occasion of the funeral of the President, Faure, but fortunately it came to nothing. It was the work of Déroulède's *Ligue des Patriotes*, but their influence and power were too slight. In the end, the possibility of civil war was overcome when the moderate but determined Waldeck-Rousseau formed a government, with Galliffet at the War Office, which was prepared to take determined action to quell disorder and trouble-makers. He was supported in this by the new President, Loubet. The compromised Méline had resigned ministerial office in 1898. Waldeck-Rousseau began by introducing legislation against those extremists who had exacerbated the situation for their own ends, and particularly the Assumptionist Order, which, in the journal *La Croix*, had attacked the Jews and also the Republican régime. Laws were passed against the unauthorized "religious congregations", forbidding their members to engage in teaching, and forcing them to obtain legal recognition or authorization. These measures were disliked by the Catholics, but their record during the Dreyfus affair made some punitive legislation of this kind inevitable. The 1902 elections were fought fiercely, and among the workers there was a clear anti-clerical feeling. The catholicism of the upper classes was yet another reason for the anti-clericalism of the proletariat. The middle classes, many of whom were Freemasons, and therefore inevitably (in France) anti-clerical, gave their votes to the more liberal candidates, and, after their victory in the elections, one could see that the end of the road had come for the old right-wing parties. The royalists, the imperialists, and even those who wanted the Church to intervene in political matters, were important forces no longer.

Waldeck-Rousseau retired in 1902, and the anti-clerical Combes formed a government which was, perhaps, unnecessarily severe towards the clerical interests and the congregations, most of which were refused recognition. He even engineered a diplomatic crisis with the Vatican, ordering the French ambassador to be recalled from the court of Pius X. Consideration was given to the separation of state and Church, and, under the next ministry, in 1905, legislation to this end was passed, with surprisingly little protest. Combes was also responsible for the appointment of General André to the War Office, and this minister took steps to remove the power of the old supporters of the Catholic right wing, promoting instead officers who were known to be Republican and anti-clerical. Unfortunately, André used informers to get information about the sympathies of the officers, and when this became known, he was forced to resign. Combes followed him, and it was Briand, in the next government, who was responsible for the Act of Separation. The state was to permit complete religious freedom, but there was to be no official recognition of any particular faith. Church property could be retained by legally responsible associations, who first had to register themselves for approval, with the state authorities. Despite the protests of the Catholics and the Pope, the law was put into effect—fortunately, with good sense and moderation. Although the Papal power in the matter of the choice of bishops was inevitably increased as a result, and the parish priests lost a large part of their stipends, becoming poorer than the teachers, the new law did a good deal to end the old rivalry between the Church and the Republic, and to remove Catholic obstructionism.

Briand, Picquart at the head of the War Office which had once posted him to Tunis as an objectionable nuisance, and Clemenceau formed the next government in 1906. Although this was a strongly radical administration, it did very little to pass reforming legislation. One of the reasons for this was the rise of syndicalism, the latest fashion among the socialists. It reflected a considerable dissatisfaction with parliamentary institutions and methods of government, and its importance shows that socialism and trade unionism were growing features of French political life. The attempt to form one united socialist party in 1905, and the growth in the power and wealth of the Conféderation Générale de Travail, showed which way the wind was blowing. The right wing suffered a severe defeat in the 1906 elections, and the majority of the deputies were left wing or socialist in their views; but there was little co-operation between the parliamentary socialists, led by Jaurès, and the syndicalists outside, who thought that the workers would only achieve their ambitions through strikes and outright violence. Even postmen and teachers were prepared to go on strike in the violent and troublesome period of syndicalism, from 1907 to 1910. Eventually, Clemenceau had to resort to severe measures, and Briand found a weapon to deal with the strikers when he issued orders calling them up for military service. Part of the trouble was, of course, that the industrial workers found themselves to be in a minority in a state which was still predominantly ruled by the *bourgeoisie* and the officials, and where so many citizens were small business men and independent peasant proprietors. France was still, primarily, an agricultural state, despite the steady growth of heavy industry in the north. Partly because of this emphasis on agriculture, and the consequent backwardness of France, she was falling behind Britain and Germany, not only in economic strength but also in population.

With syndicalism overcome, a new government took office in 1912—that of Poincaré. Within a year, Poincaré had become President, and was doing his best to make the presidential office considerably more important than it had been under Loubet, or, indeed, under anyone since Carnot. By the time Poincaré achieved power, all Europe was buzzing with rumours of war. For years, France had taken little share in foreign affairs—she had been far too concerned with her own domestic crises and problems, and the majority of Frenchmen were too convinced of the blessings of peace to want any further rivalry with the Germans. Even the bitterness occasioned by the loss of Alsace and Lorraine had died down over the years. There had been some attempt to keep up with the Germans over armaments in the last decade of the nineteenth century, but that seems to have come to an end while France was occupied with the Dreyfus affair. Although Delcassé had worked hard to end France's political isolation—and with some success—by making relations good with Italy and Britain (the *entente cordiale* was produced by Edward VII's state visit to Paris in 1904), and although there had been an alliance with Russia since 1894, strengthened by much French investment in that country, it was generally true that France was much more concerned with colonization in Africa than in rivalry with the powers in Europe.

There had been considerable colonial activity in the 1880's, which had been continued in the years following. There was even, very briefly, a crisis in 1898, when Marchand had come face to face with British troops, commanded by Kitchener, at Fashoda in the Sudan; but as neither France nor Britain was prepared to go to war for the sake of a piece of desert, the diplomats kept the peace, and France turned to Morocco instead. Here again, there might have been trouble, for Britain was unlikely to approve the development of a French administration so near Gibraltar, but this was one of the points settled by the *entente* of 1904, as was the recognition by France that Egypt was virtually under British rule. This new development was helped by the increasing nervousness felt by Britain about the rise of German naval strength—and Germany was undoubtedly provocative in the early years of the century, concerning French expansion in North Africa. For example, in March 1905 the Kaiser, William II, visited Tangier and made a forceful speech about the necessity for Germany to safeguard her interests, demanding an international conference. This could have led to war, but Delcassé resigned when the government took no notice of his advice to decline the invitation to confer. Germany had won an undoubted diplomatic triumph, and seemed to have done so again, when, at the Algeciras conference, France agreed to the maintenance of Moroccan integrity. However, supported by Britain and Russia, France was granted the power to control the

Moroccan police, and this was sufficient to enable France to penetrate Morocco fairly systematically within the next five years.

In 1911 the Agadir crisis occurred. Public disturbances in Fez caused the French to send an expedition to pacify the situation; this objective achieved, they withdrew, for the Sultan, although a usurper, still ruled the country in theory. Although the Germans had signed a Morocco pact with the French in 1909, which had admitted that the area was the special concern of France, they were annoyed that the terms which would have given Germany trading rights there had not been kept. A German gunboat, rather rashly sent to Agadir in southern Morocco, gave notice to the powers that the Algeciras conference agreement had been scrapped. There were angry diplomatic exchanges, which nearly came to an end when the Germans demanded the Congo, and there was an excellent chance that war would result. However, Lloyd George, in a speech at the Mansion House, made it clear that Britain would support France, especially if the Germans thought that international agreements could be flouted in this way. As a result, further negotiations took place, which resulted in France establishing a protectorate in Morocco, while Germany obtained some parts of the French Congo adjacent to the Cameroons. The Germans blamed Britain for this "defeat", and the French also considered the result of the negotiations unsatisfactory —so much so that the chief minister, Caillaux, resigned. The undoubtedly bellicose attitude of Germany had, at last, begun to persuade the peaceful French that another war was likely with the enemy of 1870.

It would not be possible, in the space available here, to give an account of all the events which caused the outbreak of the First World War. Suffice it to say that, when Poincaré became President of France in 1913, affairs in the Balkans had already shown that an international crisis might be caused by events there at any time. The independent Bulgaria, the ambitious Serbia, the expansionist Austria, all were concerned with events in this politically and economically primitive area of Europe.

The baneful influence of alliances, which formed vast power *blocs*, and of which any one member could precipitate a war involving others, appears plain to us today. Poincaré, realizing the dangers of the international situation, as a patriotic Republican, suggested that conscription should be extended to give all young Frenchmen three years of army service instead of two. This would necessitate higher taxes, and, in particular, the introduction of the detested income-tax, which was now proposed by Caillaux. As a result of the elections, there was a victory for the parties of the left and centre, and it was clear that most of the deputies mirrored the desire of France to be strong, and yet peaceful. The new Prime Minister, Viviani, a socialist, agreed to refrain from attacking the three-year conscription period, so long as income-tax, which the socialists thought was more equitable than the existing taxes, should be introduced. A good many Frenchmen were more interested in the murder of the editor of *Figaro* by Madame Caillaux, the wife of the Finance Minister, because of what she considered the persecution of her husband by that journal, than in the events in the Balkans. No one took a great deal of interest in the news that, on 28 June 1914, the Archduke Francis Ferdinand, heir to the Austrian throne, had been assassinated at the Bosnian capital, Sarajevo.

The French government failed to take any serious notice of the crisis between Serbia and Austria in July. In fact, Poincaré and Viviani visited Russia in that month, to discuss the betterment of Anglo–Russian relations rather than events in the Balkans. Even so, the good relationship with Russia which the French were establishing did much to encourage the Russians to stand firm against German intervention in Serbia. The Russian visit may therefore be considered as one of the many factors which caused the Serbian affair to be the spark in the European powder keg. The absence of the French leaders from Paris between 16 and 28 July 1914 also meant that the French Foreign Office could scarcely be expected to take decisive action during those weeks. Once the events which led to the declaration of war had been set on foot by the mobilization of Russian and German troops, the

Germans had also decided to prepare for the lightning attack on France which was known as the Schlieffen Plan. This meant attacking the French left flank by a march through neutral Belgium. A German note was sent, demanding French neutrality; if this had been agreed to, the Germans would have demanded the surrender of some fortresses on the frontier as a guarantee—it was an obvious attempt to force the French into declaring war.

The French were aware that there was no guarantee that Britain would go to war merely to support her; but they behaved wisely, doing their best not to provoke the Germans, even withdrawing their troops from the forward areas, and making no effort to invade enemy territory. On 2 August German troops crossed into French territory, which Joffre, the Commander-in-Chief, was at last ordered to defend—he had been threatening to resign unless some direct orders were given for mobilization and the defence of France—and on 3 August the Germans formally declared that a state of war existed. The British government agreed to enter the war as a result of the German refusal to respect Belgian neutrality, and France found herself at war again, but this time with powerful allies.

The first four decades of the Third Republic were of considerable importance in literature and the other arts. In poetry, one must notice Verlaine (1844–96), a Bohemian debauchee, the writer of *Romances sans paroles* (1874). The work of Rimbaud (1854–91) in his early years, before he gave up literature to become a merchant in Abyssinia, and Mallarmé, the teacher and intellectual whose skill in writing has few equals, brought glory to the closing years of the nineteenth century. Valéry published his first poems in the 1890's, but then produced no more until 1917. With the new century came new fashions—Laforgue's *vers libre* had pointed the way, and now there came the symbolists, led by the Belgian Verhaeren, the Greek Moréas and the French Régnier. They were accompanied by Claudel, whose *Cinq grandes odes* were published in 1910, Péguy and Jammes. Their writing just preceded that of the surrealists, who began to attract attention just before the outbreak of war. Among the novelists who were publishing work which built a reputation for them and for France in the first years of the Republic were de Maupassant, the greatest of all the short-story writers; Emile Zola (1840–1902), whose series of Rougon-Macquart novels, published between 1871 and 1893, provided a naturalistic and often sordid portrait of life in France during the Second Empire; Nuysmans, Barrès, Renard and Philippe, to mention a few.

It was also the period of Anatole France (1844–1924), the pen-name of Jacques-Anatole Thibault, the anti-clerical satirist who wrote *L'Île des pingouins*, *Les Dieux ont soif*, a novel on the Revolution of 1789, and *Le Crime de Sylvestre Bonnard*, all of them extremely popular in his day, if not regarded so highly since. The age was to see the publication of the first volume of Proust's *A la recherche du temps perdu* before the 1914 war began, and the first works of André Gide. The age was one of a minor Renaissance in music, with César Franck, Massenet, Debussy, Saint-Saens, Fauré, Ravel and Bizet all making their distinct contributions to it; while the impressionists, and especially Degas, Gauguin, Cézanne, Renoir, Matisse, Pissarro and Toulouse-Lautrec created an impression of France and of Paris in their art which has not faded yet. Finally, the theatre was influenced by Becque, whose *La Parisienne* had more importance later than it did when it was first produced; the farcical writer, Feydeau; the humorist, Courteline; the symbolist, Maeterlinck, whose *Pelléas et Mélisande* was produced in 1892 and *L'Oiseau Bleu* in 1909; and finally the romantic, Rostand, whose *Cyrano de Bergerac* began its incredible life in 1897.

## RECOMMENDED READING

*Clemenceau and the Third Republic*. J. HAMPDEN JACKSON. English Universities Press, 1946.

*Democracy in France*. D. THOMSON. Oxford, 1958.

*The Development of Modern France, 1870–1939*. D. W. BROGAN. Hamish Hamilton, 1940.

*The Dreyfus Case*. G. CHAPMAN. Hart-Davis, 1955.

*The New Cambridge Modern History*. Vol. XII. *The Era of Violence*. Ed. D. THOMSON. Chapter XI. International Relations 1900–12. J. P. T. BURY.
Chapter XII. The Approach of the War of 1914. J. M. K. VYVYAN.

CHAPTER 17

# The Last Fifty Years

FRANCE has always proved herself stronger than her enemies (and, often, her friends) have thought; but she has had more than her fair share of troubles in the last half-century, and she has not found that her systems of government have been able to cope at moments of crisis. Whether her new-found strength under the ageing de Gaulle will put her on the right path only the future will show. Since 1914, she has fought victoriously in a war which cost her nearly 2 million of her citizens; she has been defeated and occupied by her old enemy for five years; and she has rebuilt her strength in economic matters with outstanding success at a time when her governmental system was put to a severe test, and failed. The critical half-century began in 1914, when the expected German stategy almost succeeded in knocking France out of the reckoning in the first few weeks of war. There can be little doubt that the Germans expected that the Schlieffen plan would be entirely successful, and that France would have fallen before any British aid arrived, or before the Russian threat on the eastern front would have materialized. The plan, to invade France by way of Belgium, might well have come to fruition, had not Moltke weakened the German right wing in a way that Schlieffen would never have allowed. The gallant Belgian resistance, which many strategists think was vital in delaying the invasion, because it forced a modification of German long-range plans, was also stronger than the Germans expected. So the Germans sent their thrust to the north of Paris, instead of encircling it by going round to the south. The French and British

226

armies retreated from Mons, but then decided to make a stand on the Marne. French troops even arrived from Paris in taxis. As a result of this, the German attack failed, a French force under Gallieni made a counter-attack, and the enemy fell back to the Aisne. The first battle of the Marne, costly though it was, proved to be the salvation of France.

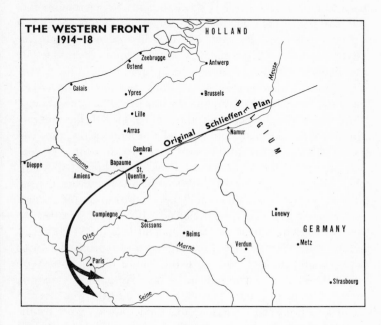

MAP 7

With the situation changing daily, there was no obvious move but for both sides to consolidate their strength where they stood, and so the trenches were built all the way to Nieuport in the north, and France and her allies set to work to defend a line which stretched from there right down to the Swiss border. Viviani's government, with Delcassé at the Foreign Office and Millerand as War Minister, left Paris for Bordeaux for three months in those early days, when it appeared that the German thrust was not to be held; but the administration returned after the German failure to get beyond the Marne, and a second German failure, in the first battle of Ypres, to penetrate further into France. As a result of this second failure, the pattern of the fighting for the greater part of the First World War was fixed—trench warfare, with artillery strength, and the determination of the infantry to hold on, the most important factors. After first Ypres, the war in the west, like that in the east, despite the German victory at Tannenberg, was a struggle to break the state of stalemate. All the participants had proved to be in the wrong. The French Commander-in-Chief, Joffre, an intelligent soldier, had thought, as had Moltke, that the war would be a short one.

Although the French and their allies lacked the military abilities of the Germans, and were inferior numerically, they had a great advantage in that they were besieging the central powers. The failure of the Germans to break through, added to the blockade which was the work of the British navy, meant that, in this war of attrition, they could never emerge as the victors. Other factors, of course, were not negligible. The defeat of the German fleet by Sturdee off the Falkland Isles in 1914, and the failure of the German fleet to emerge again from their harbours after Jutland in 1916, added to the failure of the U-boats to break the British convoy system, by however narrow a margin, meant that the war must be won or lost amidst the trenches and barbed wire on the western front. Numerous attempts by the allies to break the German line in 1915 failed—the French in Champagne, the British at Neuve Chapelle and at Loos, were as unsuccessful as the Germans at the second battle of Ypres, despite the use of poison gas in the latter. There was a change of government in October of 1915. There was still a coalition ministry, but Viviani gave place to Briand as its head.

The year 1916 was the year of the great tragedy of the loss of lives at Verdun. Once again, the Germans attempted to break through to end the war of attrition in the trenches, and they knew that the French would fight to the death to defend Verdun, the importance of which was symbolic rather than military. They were quite right, and the French defence of the town, in which Pétain made his heroic reputation, was successful, except that a quarter of a million French lives were sacrificed in the fighting. Pétain's brave "Ils ne passeront pas" was a heroic and costly cry. A British offensive on the Somme helped to relieve the pressure on the French, but unfortunately, although tanks were available to make a breakthrough a possibility, there were too few of them, and the senior officers regarded this new invention with too much suspicion for its potentialities to be realized. However, the Germans fell back to their newly prepared Hindenburg line, and, although this could be counted as a triumph for the allies, its cost in human misery caused so much disillusion in France that a war weariness set in, and a scapegoat was demanded. Joffre filled the role, and was succeeded as Commander by Nivelle. It was not a good year for the allies. The Russians suffered another crushing defeat, and the British attempt to open another front, from April to December of 1915, by the expedition to the Dardanelles, had left a bitter taste in the mouth of France's main ally. Almost more bitter were the consequences of the blockade of Britain by the U-boats, although the sinking of the *Lusitania* by the Germans off the Irish coast, and the continual bombardment of the Americans by propaganda, contributed to the gradual determination of the United States to enter the war.

In 1917 there was a mixture of good news and bad. There was another change in the French administration. In March, Briand gave way to Ribot, in whose ministry was a new War Minister, Painlevé. The latter badly wanted to dismiss Nivelle from the command of the army, but found this difficult, as he was supported, for different motives, by Poincaré and Haig. Nevertheless, he continued his efforts and, in May, Pétain became Commander-in-Chief. This was the year of the third battle of Ypres, and the first comparatively successful use of tanks, at Cambrai. In April, the United States entered the war, but it was to be some time before her weight could be brought to bear on the western front. The reason for Wilson's decision to declare war was the

German determination to try to end the war quickly by sinking all ships, including neutral vessels, in European waters. Germany now knew that it would be possible to send increased forces to fight in the west, for the Czar, Nicholas, had abdicated in March, and the Russians, now ruled by a provisional government and entering the decisive stage of what was to be the Communist Revolution, were incapable of fighting the Germans on the eastern front any longer. For the British, this was the time of the most bitter losses—culminating at Passchendaele in November. The reason for throwing British troops into the holocaust in this way was the possibility of French collapse. Thousands of Frenchmen deserted, and French morale was at its lowest ebb. A mutinous spirit was developing, as soldiers were hurriedly shot on the battlefield for alleged cowardice, and there might well have been a revolution. Such a possibility was prevented by Pétain, who did all he could to restore a patriotic spirit in the French army. The endlessly waterlogged trenches, the deadly monotony of the mud, the stench of death, the innumerable corpses, the perpetual artillery bombardment, and the Zeppelin raids on Paris, meant that total and mechanized war had finished the romantic conceptions of *la guerre*. Even the government was near collapse, and Ribot was replaced, very briefly, by Painlevé. The determination of the new Russian government to come to terms with the Germans, which they did at Brest-Litovsk in 1918, the vast losses of shipping in the north Atlantic, the suffering caused by the rationing of food, and an outbreak of strikes and violence by the workers, encouraged by the socialists, meant that France was very near to defeat. It was against this background that Ludendorff decided to make an attack which, he thought, would end the war. Fortunately for the allied cause, Clemenceau had assumed the office of chief minister late in 1917, as requested by Poincaré. Clemenceau, "le tigre", was determined to fight to the bitter end, and, having got rid of the potential defeatists, Briand, Caillaux and Malvy, he decided to get rid of the pessimistic Pétain, who had served his purpose, and to appoint instead Marshal Foch, with Weygand as his chief of staff. Foch was a far better commander than Pétain or Haig, but he was prepared to be coldly calculating, despite the enormous losses which might occur while he was waiting the right moment to attack.

This came after the Germans had pushed the British back in the Somme area, and then broke the line, at last, reaching the Marne again. Ludendorff then decided to attack the French near Reims, but this time he had come up against a cool and able commander. Foch ordered Mangin and Haig to counter-attack, and the allies began to win ground at the expense of the Germans. Gradually, in July, August and September they advanced, taking Cambrai and Lille. American reinforcements were pouring in, while news came through of allied victories against the Austrians, the Turks and the Bulgarians. Ludendorff gave up his command in October, when it was clear that there might well be revolution in a demoralized Germany. The new German Chancellor, Prince Max of Baden, requested an armistice. The German fleet mutinied, and, two days before an armistice was signed at Compiègne, the Kaiser abdicated and went to Holland. The war was over. France had lost nearly 2 million dead, and thousands of square miles of her territory had been devastated. She was near to collapse—but the Germans had collapsed first. The following months, until the Treaty of Versailles was signed on 28 June, 1919, were taken up in the debate over the terms of peace. Despite the wishes of Foch for complete disarming of the Germans, and those of Clemenceau for an insurance that Germany would never fight again, they were defeated by Wilson and Lloyd George, who were determined to exact reparations from Germany and to set up a League of Nations to preserve the peace in the future.

Clemenceau was as obstinate as he could be under the circumstances, but all that he could obtain for France, apart from the somewhat suspect power of the League to prevent war, was a treaty which passed the Saar to an international authority for fifteen years, after which a plebiscite was to decide its future; the control by France of the Rhine, the right bank of which was to be demilitarized; the return of Alsace and Lorraine; and a mandate to rule the Cameroons, Togoland and Syria. It was not a vast

return for a country which had suffered as much as France had—
but it had not yet dawned on some statesmen that war always
cost far more than it was worth, in an age of mass slaughter. To
try to strengthen her position in Europe, the French made
alliances with the new countries which emerged in eastern
Europe, like Czechoslovakia and Jugoslavia. Meantime, France
was hoping that German reparations might help to solve the
problem of her enormous national debt, and the ruin of her
north-eastern provinces. She was scarcely surprised—for France
has no lack of cynics—when the American Senate refused to
ratify the Treaty in 1920.

By 1919 the French, in common with many others, were
beginning to fear the continued existence of communist Russia.
This fear, combined with a rather jingoist patriotism, produced a
right-wing majority in the elections. Clemenceau's *Bloc National*,
as it was called, dominated the Chamber. The next five or six
years saw the departure of Poincaré and the appointment of
Millerand to the presidency. There was trouble between France
and Britain over the French administration of Syria, and also
some diplomatic ill-feeling when Britain made it clear that she
was willing to agree to a scaling down of the German reparations.
France began to suffer from a bad dose of inflation, and furious
that nothing seemed to be forthcoming from the German
Republic, joined Belgium in 1923 in an occupation of the Ruhr—
but this did not solve the problem, either. They withdrew the
following year, when the Dawes plan, to inflict some financial
controls on Germany, came into operation. In fact, France made
an astonishingly rapid economic recovery, in so far as industrial-
ization and production were concerned, but currency stability
did not result from this. The problem of the purchasing power of
the franc did not help the popularity of the socialists, who joined
the radicals in 1924 in a *Cartel des Gauches* which had a clear
majority in the Chamber after the elections of that year. Doumergue, the new President, appointed Herriot, a leading radical,
as chief minister, and reforms were begun, which might have
done much for France if only the radicals, representing the

peasants and small business men, could have worked together with the socialists, their nominal allies in the *Cartel*. As it was, the socialists, afraid of the growing power of the communists, especially in the trade unions, failed to co-operate with the government in the measures necessary to solve the financial crisis, or the problems of governing the colonial territories and applying the laws of France in religious matters to Alsace and Lorraine.

All through the 1920's there were colonial troubles. The greatest failure for the French was in Syria, where Arab nationalism was a growing force, and where the problems of government were never really solved. Elsewhere, French rule brought considerable prosperity to Tunisia and Algeria, to Indo-China, and to Morocco after a Riff invasion was suppressed with Spanish assistance. But it was finance which was to be the downfall of Herriot. The low value of the franc was not to be raised until, in 1926, Poincaré returned to form a government of deputies from the right and centre parties, which restored confidence and stabilized the currency. Although the left-wing parties were determined that they could do as well, and reorganized the *Cartel*, demanding the reintroduction of single-member constituencies in the hope that this would give them a clear majority in the elections, the right wing still triumphed in the elections of 1928. Instead of causing the left wingers to unite, this only led to a clash between the socialists, led by Léon Blum, and the communists, which went on until the formation of the Popular Front in 1936. Meantime, foreign affairs were the province of Briand, who did his best to make the League of Nations a worthwhile union, and to bring France and Germany together. After five years at the Foreign Ministry, he was able to look back at the entry of Germany into the League (1926), and the end of the interminable quarrel over reparations by the adoption of the Young plan in 1930. France showed her willingness to adopt a peaceful policy by withdrawing her troops from the Rhineland, but the future began to look bleak again, especially after the financial crash in the United States in 1929, which led to such bitter economic problems and unemployment, on both sides of the Atlantic. France did not suffer as much as the more industrial states, but nevertheless, by 1932, there were a million people there who were unemployed. Briand's achievements were considerable, and, but for the rise of Nazi power in Germany, might have been long-lasting. His hopes of succeeding Doumergue as President in 1932 came to nothing; his successor at the Foreign Ministry was Laval. The ingratitude of the politicians to Briand may have dated back to the days of defeatism. Clemenceau had severely "lashed" him in 1917.

In the 1932 elections, the communists received a severe setback, but the socialists gained considerable support, and a left-wing ministry came to power again. Their failure to deal with the financial crisis from 1924 onwards was to be repeated. With Lebrun as President and Herriot in office again, it seemed to be impossible for them to deal with the unemployment which was causing so much distress. Several ministries in turn tried to remedy the situation, and the political atmosphere became even more bitter in 1933, when the Stavisky scandal came to the fore. Stavisky, a financier whose activities were more frequently dishonest than otherwise, killed himself when he realized that his frauds were to become known. The right-wing journals claimed openly that his career had been known to various ministers, who had used their influence to protect him. Chautemps, never a strong chief minister, took the easy way out and resigned, giving place to Daladier, a radical, who attempted to take a strong line by dismissing Chiappe, head of the Paris police and so right wing as to be almost a Fascist. But taking such action was dangerous; the more extreme among the right wingers organized a demonstration which could have developed into a *coup d'état*, with members of organizations like the *Action Française* marching on the Chamber, so Daladier resigned in his turn, frightened of the "blackmail of the streets", and an emergency national government, excluding the socialists, was formed under Gaston Doumergue, the former President. The Stavisky affair blew over in time, but the demonstrations had thrown a light on the unpleasant nature of some of the extremists on both political wings.

Doumergue's administration resigned in 1934, and Flandin became chief minister, with Laval at the Foreign Office.

By this time, France was conscious of what was happening in Germany. Hitler's rise to power frightened all but the extreme right wingers. The communists decided to cease working in isolation, and, at their request, the socialists formed a Popular Front with them, to campaign for social reforms, disarmament, and friendship with the Soviet Union. The Front was rewarded in the 1936 elections, in which the socialists and communists did very well at the expense of the middle-of-the-road radicals. But the property-owning classes were still not prepared to allow the social reforms which might have saved France from the worst consequences of these years of unemployment, nor were the communists prepared to sink their differences with the socialists completely. As a result, Blum's efforts to ameliorate the conditions of the working classes, to persuade the employers to pay higher wages and to limit the hours of work, only roused the opposition of the conservatives. Once again, the value of the franc fell, and devaluation in the October of 1936 did little to halt the slump. Blum was not popular with the communists either. He steadily refused to send aid to the Spanish government, fighting for its life against Franco's rebels and their Fascist allies in Germany and Italy. With these difficulties facing him, Blum halted his programme of reform in 1937, and asked for more authority in his campaign against the Fascist leagues, and for the nationalization of the armament industry. Not surprisingly, the Senate stood out against his requests, and he had to resign. Chautemps achieved power again, and the *Rassemblement populaire* had failed. Eventually, in April 1938, a radical administration led by Daladier, with the conservative Reynaud to comfort the right wingers and capitalists, took over. The economic situation improved again, but by this time, another German war was looming over Europe.

Briand's successor at the Foreign Office, Laval, had been responsible for signing a pact with the Soviet Union, and had been in office when the plebiscite in the Saar had resulted in the return of that area to Germany (1935). In the following year he had lost his office, and France, in fact, had no strong government in power when Hitler had taken the decision to flout the terms of the Treaty of Versailles and march his troops into the Rhineland. Britain was extremely unwilling to take a strong line over this, and so Sarraut, the French Premier, decided to take no action. In any case, Pétain, for the army, favoured a policy of non-aggression, as did Flandin, the Foreign Minister. Too many Frenchmen had sympathy with the Nazi régime, too many were in favour of appeasement, too many thought that the new Maginot line of concrete fortifications would protect France in time of war, for there to be any real will to resist Hitler's aggression. But the remilitarization of the Rhineland with impunity only encouraged Germany to go ahead with her plans, and made France's allies conscious of her weakness. So were the allies of Britain, when, in September 1938, Chamberlain, the arch-appeaser, came to terms with Hitler at Munich, and allowed Germany to swallow Czechoslovakia. Daladier was concerned to strengthen the defences of France, but his efforts were too late, too slow, and too much concerned with the Maginot line. But the months after Munich made it clear that the policy of appeasement had failed, and, with a man like Hitler, could never have hoped to succeed. This was not the view, of course, of the strong French communist party, as soon as the German–Soviet Pact of August 1939 was signed.

On 1 September 1939 Hitler ordered the invasion of Poland, having already agreed to partition it with Stalin's Russia. On 3 September Britain, mindful of her guarantee to Poland, and of Hitler's failures to honour other agreements, declared war, and France followed her lead. Daladier was chief minister, and Bonnet was at the Foreign Office during those early months of the "phoney war", the *drôle de guerre*. War had been begun, but with a sense of anti-climax, as no serious fighting developed on the western front. No effort seemed to be needed, and the mood of France relaxed. But then came the Russian attack on Finland, as a prelude to the *Blitzkrieg* of April 1940. It led to the resignation of Daladier, who decided to serve as Minister of Defence under Reynaud. This was the last true government of the Third Republic, and it was to see Hitler send his armies through Holland and Belgium, defeat the French at Sedan, drive on to Abbeville and eventually towards Paris. The British forces escaped, miraculously, from Dunkirk by sea, the Belgians capitulated, Reynaud appointed Weygand to take command of the French armies in place of Gamelin, but it was too late. The only problem left was whether Weygand should surrender while the government escaped to North Africa, to continue the war from there, or whether, as Pétain suggested, the government should come to terms as soon as possible with the Germans. Hitler's troops entered Paris on 14 June 1940, Reynaud resigned two days later, the government having moved to Bordeaux, and Marshal Pétain formed a new administration which would ask for an armistice. Such an agreement was signed on 22 June, in the forest of Compiègne, in the railway carriage which had been used for a similar purpose in 1918. The choice of the carriage was a final humiliation for the French.

Conditions in France were chaotic. The roads were choked with refugees, Daladier had attempted flight to North Africa, and de Gaulle, a young Under-Secretary for War, had reached England and was moving heaven and earth to set up a Free French organization. But, for France, the war was over. Pétain agreed to let France pay the expenses of the German occupying forces, to allow the Germans to keep their French prisoners of war as hostages, and to pass French military stores over to German control. Any hope that the Germans might have had of seizing the French fleet was wrecked when the British sank much of it at Mers-el-Kebir. Eventually, the National Assembly met at Vichy, recognized Pétain as Chief of State and Chief Minister, and was declared to be adjourned. For the next few years, the Pétain administration kept a sort of semi-independence in existence, which never descended to being a puppet government of "quis-lings", and left most Frenchmen only with the hope that, one day, the war would be over, and that Laval and the other appeasers who were in Petain's government would get their deserts. But, for the moment, a defeat for Germany seemed to be an impossibility. Britain alone fought on, and her power seemed to be insufficient to hold up Hitler's dreams of world conquest. Meantime, a defeated France was being ruled by an 84-year-old pessimist, who had made his name nearly a quarter of a century previously, with the cry before Verdun, "They shall not pass". It was unfortunate that, in the months and years of occupation, many Frenchmen, particularly the radical socialists, were prepared to collaborate with the Germans. It would not be fair to call the years of the Vichy government part of the history of the Third Republic—this had come to an end in 1940, and the members of Pétain's administration were bound to feel that Germany would be eventually triumphant in the war, and that their duty was to begin the rebuilding of a new French state, one in which a certain amount of French independence was retained, and which would be more authoritarian in its nature than the old republic had been. Economic collaboration with the Germans was plainly inevitable in the occupied areas in the north; it became inevitable, also, in the south, for no raw materials were made available by the Germans unless work was being done in the factories on their behalf.

Some Frenchmen carried on a resistance, sometimes active and sometimes passive, in obedience to their patriotic duty and to the broadcast appeals from London of de Gaulle; but the resistance did not become serious until the Germans attacked the Soviet Union in 1941. This immediately brought the well-disciplined French communists into the resistance movement. But, possibly more important, the French were given a cause for which they could fight when, in November 1942, Anglo–American forces were landed in Morocco and Algeria. A French provisional government was established in Algiers, and the Germans, concerned with this threat to the Mediterranean "underbelly", promptly occupied the French territories which had been left to the Vichy government in the Treaty of 1940. Darlan, the admiral who had, so far, remained loyal to Pétain, ordered the French ships in Toulon to be scuttled, and fled to Algiers to join the allies there. His arrival was something of an embarrassment, for the allies, knowing that de Gaulle's Free French movement was not completely acceptable to the Vichy officials in North Africa, had already decided to acknowledge Guiraud as French leader. However, Guiraud gave place to Darlan, but the latter was assassinated in December 1942, and Guiraud took up the reins again until, in June of 1943, after much negotiation, de Gaulle's French Committee of National Liberation was acknowledged by the allied leaders. Resistance to the Germans continued inside occupied France, for few Frenchmen were prepared to follow Laval in his policy of collaboration, or to support men like Doriot and Déat who were trying to recruit volunteers to fight against the Soviet Union on the eastern front. Blum and Daladier had been tried for war guilt in 1942, but had never been sentenced—a sign, perhaps, that the collaborators knew that the real guilt for French defeat lay elsewhere. Laval took over from Pétain as head of government in April 1942; but his unpopularity increased as German demands for French workers to go to Germany increased, and as the amount of food available in the shops became less and less. The resistance forces grew daily, and both they and the Germans, with some of the anti-semitic allies of the latter, conducted horrifying campaigns of murder, assassination, arson and destruction.

This situation continued until, in June 1944, the allies landed in Normandy to begin the liberation of France and the attack on Germany. Within two months, the Germans were in retreat to the Seine, and an American army had been landed in the south to advance up the Rhône valley. The Germans sent Pétain and Laval into Germany under armed guard, and on 19 August street fighting against the occupying forces broke out in Paris. Four days later, the first invading army of liberation entered the city as the German troops withdrew. Although fighting continued on French soil for some months afterwards, not only against the Germans but also between the partisans and the ex-collaborators, de Gaulle had set up a government in Paris by 26 August, the authority of which grew so rapidly that the allies recognized it as the *de facto* régime in October. Within a month, a referendum was being held, in which it was decided to have a new constitution, to forget the 1871 Republic, and to begin a Fourth Republic. Women were enfranchised for the first time, partly as an acknowledgement of their gallant share in the resistance, and elections were held for a new Assembly. In the new Chamber, the communists, cashing in on their work for the resistance movement during the war years, became the largest single party, with 183 seats. Bidault's moderate Catholic *Mouvement Républicain Populaire* had 164 representatives, and the socialists came third, with just over a hundred. These three provided a shifting coalition, with de Gaulle as the President, and it is to their credit that they began the rebuilding of the French economy, and a restoration of the war-damaged areas, especially in the matter of factories, roads, bridges, and so on, and despite the grave shortage of coal and transport.

Naturally, a good deal of nationalization was part of the government programme, just as it was in Britain with the postwar Labour administration in power. Civil aviation, electricity, coal, even the Renault car factories, all came under state control. Some war criminals were tried, including Pétain and Laval, but their trials were handled badly, and revenge rather than justice seemed to be the main theme in the courts. De Gaulle found that it was almost impossible for him to control the coalition ministers, and he resigned in January 1946. Preparations went on for the new constitution, and, as a result, the Fourth Republic officially came into existence in October 1946. It had been hoped that the new constitution would give French politics rather more stability than they had known before 1939, and the President now had the power to dissolve the Parliament. But the Assembly found that it could still remain in being while forcing a ministry to resign, and so, eventually, there was little change, and foreign powers still found that ministerial changes overnight were typical of the French system. The immediate post-war period was marked by the peace treaties of 1946, made by the representatives of the Soviet Union, the United States and Britain—Molotov, Byrnes and Bevin. Bidault, the French Foreign Secretary, was also called in, and the final arrangements included the cession to France of Briga and Tenda, near Nice; the French occupation of the Saar and the Rhineland Palatinate as one of the four occupying powers in Germany; and the payment of indemnities. The French occupation continued until, in 1949, the zones occupied by the western powers amalgamated to form the German Federal Republic, with its capital at Bonn. France also became a permanent member of the Security Council of the United Nations.

Another factor of considerable importance in the years after 1945 was inflation. This was a serious drawback to French recovery, and the efforts of Mendès-France, the Economics Minister, came to nothing because he was not allowed to take measures to stabilize the currency and to prevent the operation of the "black market", which had become so important during the German occupation. The shifting coalitions continued in office until May of 1947, when the so-called Third Force, opposed to the communists on the one hand and the right-wing Gaullists on the other, came into power. The communists had already shown themselves to be eager to prevent the Assembly from making parliamentary democracy work smoothly, and had used their power in the unions and the C.G.T. to foment strikes during the bad winters of 1946, 1947 and 1948. Their power grew so much that, in 1947, the unions which did not come under their influence left the C.G.T. to join Jouhaux's *Force Ouvrière*. De Gaulle's sympathizers, equally dissatisfied by the pattern of French politics, formed the *Rassemblement du Peuple Français* in 1947, which, despite de Gaulle's talk of non-party national unity, soon came to be one of the chief right-wing parties. The communists were well aware that they still had the largest single party in France, but that their power might decline if economic recovery were hastened—and this seemed likely with the promise of "Marshall Aid" from the United States, which was to do so much to help French recovery and to slow down the financial inflation. It was for this reason that they fomented strikes, and

I

that Ramadier expelled them from the coalition government and sent them into permanent opposition.

The "cold war" began in 1947, between the western states supported by the United States, and the Soviet-dominated eastern European *bloc*. One of its causes was Soviet suspicion of the motives of the capitalist powers, and especially of America; another was Soviet suspicion of the intentions of the statesmen who controlled the atomic bomb, which had brought the Japanese War to an end so decisively in 1945. The decision to drop an "iron curtain" across Europe dated from the announcement that the Americans would make "Marshall Aid" available, and the Soviet decision to have no part in the plan. Against this background, the modernization of French industry was growing, while the socialists and the Catholic M.R.P. were debating the financial grants to Catholic schools, which would not have occurred before the war, but which the Vichy government had introduced. The matter was complicated by the fact that the increase in the numbers of children of school age made the state schools unable to deal with the problem of providing a universal education. There was much bitter discussion before a decision to grant state aid to Catholic schools was taken in 1951. The Monnet Plan, to modernize industry, and especially transport, agriculture, coal and steel, was enabled to make good progress once American aid had begun to flow, and productivity increased greatly, except in farming, where efficiency was difficult to introduce into a system which was still based upon the small peasant proprietor, still politically important enough to demand the protection of subsidies and tariff walls. In common with other western states, France was also introducing measures for social security, including insurance and family allowances. The trade unions were playing a significant part in this "welfare state" development. The Fourth Republic was, at least, learning some lessons from the past. She was realizing that her security, in an insecure world, depended upon her productivity and her willingness to join in such international organizations as the Organization for European Economic Co-operation. Led by Bidault and

Schuman, members of the M.R.P. and largely responsible between them for foreign affairs in the period up to 1954, France made a treaty with Britain (1947), and went on to engage herself with Britain and the Benelux countries (Belgium, the Netherlands and Luxemburg) in the Brussels Treaty of 1948, which bound the contracting parties to joint military action, whenever necessary.

These were years of crisis. The North Atlantic Treaty Organization (N.A.T.O.) was created in 1949, when, at the time of the Berlin air-lift, when the Soviet Union refused to let land routes to Berlin from western Germany remain open, the Brussels Treaty powers came into a greater alliance with the United States, Canada, Italy, Portugal, Denmark and Norway. To answer the crisis, and to try to persuade the eastern powers to keep the peace, other international organizations were set up. It appeared that the United Nations was encountering too many difficulties for the western powers to have much confidence in its ability to prevent war. A Council of Europe was proposed in 1949, with the long-term idea of creating a federal European state. It began to meet in Strasbourg in 1950. Alongside it, and linked with it, was the Schuman Plan, from which there was to emerge the idea of a Coal and Steel Community, a "common market" in these products for France, Western Germany, Italy and the Benelux states. The French statesman, Monnet, was largely responsible for the successful development of this plan, which was regarded with pleasure by the federal United States. Another French idea was Pleven's European Defence Community, which was to remove the threat of German military power by placing the German army under international control. Unfortunately, the growth of the German military forces, at a time when the French military commitments in Africa and the Far East were swallowing most of her available resources, meant that the French government began to distrust the idea, and eventually the E.D.C. Treaty was not ratified by the French government.

During these years of the "cold war", France was engaged in a colonial crisis which was eventually to bring the Fourth Republic down. The period from 1945 to 1962 was to see the disintegration of the French colonial empire. The mandated territories of the Lebanon and Syria had achieved their independence in 1944. The French colonies elsewhere, which had always been economically important to France but which had been subservient to her, wanted their independence, too. In January 1944 de Gaulle had announced at a conference at Brazzaville that all colonial subjects should be French citizens in a *Union Française* after the war. But the idea had come too late, especially in North Africa and in Indo-China. The latter had suffered Japanese conquest during the war, and, after hostilities ended, the French discovered a League for the Independence of Vietnam, led by Ho Chi-Minh, a communist nationalist who was claiming to be President in opposition to the French puppet-ruler, Bao Dai. The League, called Viet-Minh, was given help by the Chinese communists, from 1949 onwards, when fighting had already been in progress for three years. The French power was insufficient to hold back the communist threat, and, as help was not available from the United States and Britain, a conference was called to settle peace terms at Geneva in 1954. During the negotiations, news came through of the defeat of the French at Dien Bien Phu, and, with no cards left to play, the French agreed to the division of Vietnam, along the 17th parallel, by which a communist state of Viet-Minh was to be established to the north, and an American-supported state, ruled by Bao Dai, was to exist to the south. Bao Dai was deposed in 1955. Cambodia and Laos were also lost to France, so that the French adventure in the Far East, which had begun in 1863, had come to an end, with a vast loss in men, money and prestige.

A different situation existed in North Africa, but this again was to end in French withdrawal. Here the enemy was Moslem nationalism, and the fact that there was a long-standing tradition, dating back to Lyautey before the 1914 war, of insubordination on the part of the white settlers in Morocco, who frequently ignored the orders and advice sent from Paris. This explains the deposition of the Sultan by the settlers, in flagrant disobedience to the Treaty of 1912. There was terrorism on both sides, both in Morocco and in Tunisia, where the forces of independence were led by Bourguiba. With the end of hostilities in Indo-China, Mendès-France, the chief minister, determined to withdraw from Tunisia as well. The war effort was too costly for France. Bourguiba took over power in an independent Tunisian state in March of 1956. The Sultan of Morocco was reinstated, and his state was also granted independence in the same month. French pride was hurt—but there remained Algeria. This state was not a colony in the true sense, but a part of metropolitan France; or, at least, this was the French argument. It was indisputable that the million white settlers had created much prosperity there. The French were determined to hang on to their power in this part of North Africa. Nevertheless, the Moslem Algerians wanted their independence, and an expensive guerilla war broke out which continued from 1954 onwards. After four years, it seemed certain that France must let Algeria go—but this was too much for many French settlers. The year 1958 saw a *coup d'état* in Algeria, led by the right-wing commander of the French paratroops, General Massu. A Committee of Public Safety was set up, and there was a strong likelihood of civil war in France. The politicians of the Fourth Republic, seeing that a strong government alone could settle the difficulty, turned to de Gaulle. He had been in retirement from active participation in the government since 1946, and now, invited by President Coty and the Assembly, he took office as chief minister with emergency dictatorial powers for six months.

By a referendum of September 1958 it was decided to give France a new constitution; the Fifth Republic was in being. By the new constitution, the President was to rule, aided by a chief minister and a council of ministers. Parliament was to consist of a National Assembly, elected by universal franchise, for a period of five years; there was also to be a Senate, the members of which were elected by a college of electors, and one-third of which was to be re-elected every three years. De Gaulle was made President, and set about the problem of bringing France into the world of the 1960's. France became a founder member of the European Economic Community, and also set up a French community, which included various former colonies, now independent, and other areas which retained a direct link with France. The members of the Community included Guiana, Réunion, Martinique, Guadeloupe, Madagascar, the Congo, Sénégal, Gabon, Chad, and the Central African Republic. The year 1958 was one of destiny for the French colonies in northern and western Africa. De Gaulle, a right winger, naturally incurred the displeasure of many Frenchmen for his policies—but they showed an awareness and a realism that brought him gratitude and popularity with the majority. In 1962 he decided that the constitution needed amending, so that future presidents should be elected directly by the nation, and, his government having been defeated by a vote of no confidence, and having resigned, a new referendum was held. This resulted in another victory for de Gaulle, and his presidency continued. Algeria was granted independence in 1962, and, despite the strange result of the trial of Salan, for his active opposition to the government in North Africa, the President continued to build up his own power with that of France. With Pompidou as chief minister and Couve de Murville at the Foreign Ministry, he has gone his own independent way, ignoring attempts at assassination, vetoing Britain's attempt to enter the Common Market, ordering the French to continue nuclear bomb tests, and building up a friendship with the German Federal Republic of a kind that Frenchmen twenty years ago would have thought impossible. January 1963 saw, not only the signature of a pact of friendship with Germany, but also the refusal to permit British entry into the Common Market on the grounds that Britain was too insular and maritime, and calling from the British Prime Minister, Mr. Macmillan, the comment that de Gaulle was trying to dominate Europe. If the criticism is true, then de Gaulle, at least, is not the first Frenchman to try. Meantime, French domestic affairs, overseen by de Gaulle's vast majority in the Assembly in his *Union pour la Nouvelle République—Union Démocratique du Travail*, with its 233

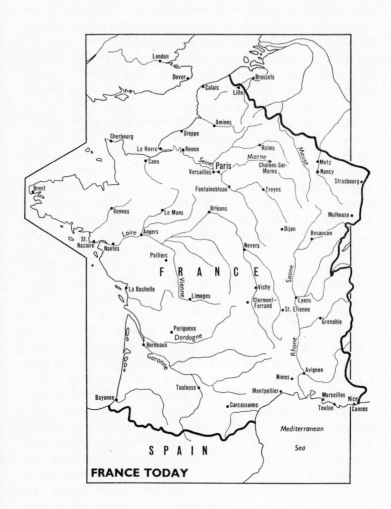

MAP 8

members, as against the 66 socialists (S.F.I.O.), 41 communists and 38 M.R.P. members, continued to be concerned with the creation of a modernized and industrial France, no longer dominated by the outdated demands of small business men and peasants. Whatever the news from France, whether it concerns de Gaulle's state visit to Mexico, or his illness from a prostate gland operation (April 1964), it is clear that today, France is de Gaulle, and de Gaulle is France.

The last half-century has made its contribution to the civilization of literature. In poetry, beginning with the surrealism of Dada at the time of the 1914–18 war, all kinds of developments came with André Breton, Prévert, Michaux, Aragon, Eluard, Supervielle, Jouve and his disciple, Emmanuel. Between them, they produced a good deal of interesting poetry, but it is doubtful if any one of them was a great poet. The novelists have been far more sure of creating important work. Beginning with Proust's long study of a society in decay, from 1880 to 1920, *A la récherche du temps perdu*, many writers have added their contribution in this particular literary field. Among them were Colette (1873–1954) whose *Claudine* books made a deserved reputation. Barbusse (1874–1954) attempted a description of the first war and its fighting, but his work seems destined not to last. Nor, perhaps, will the work of the novelists of the 1920's—Morand and Carco. However, the chronicle novels of Duhamel, and the writing of Romains and Bernanos, the latter a Catholic and a violent opponent of the attitudes of Anatole France, may well survive. So will the novels of François Mauriac, set in the area around Bordeaux, and those of Montherlant, who was so much inspired by the culture and life of Spain. In more recent years, one must acknowledge the ability of Malraux, the former communist and resistance fighter who turned to de Gaulle as the saviour of France; to Saint-Exupéry, who was killed while serving as a pilot in the 1939 war; and, since them, to Camus, whose pessimistic *La Peste*, published in 1947, was a considerable creation.

The theatre has had its triumphs, too. Possibly the most original dramatist of the century was Claudel (1868–1955), who began as a symbolist and went on to write all sorts of important plays, some with considerable satire and a concern with the destiny of the individual. New writers after 1918 included Copeau, Romains, and the four great figures of the twentieth-century drama—Giraudoux (1888–1944), the author of *Amphitryon 38* (1929) and *Electre* (1937); Cocteau, whose *L'Aigle à deux têtes* created such a stir in 1946; Anouilh, who wrote *Eurydice, Antigone* and *Médée*, besides some pleasing comedies; and Sartre, the existentialist, whose *Les Mouches* (1943) began to make a reputation that was enhanced by *Huis Clos* in the following year. Sartre's name, however, may yet depend upon his novel, *Les Chemins de la liberté*, which he began to publish in 1945. Better known in England than either Sartre or his disciple, Simone de Beauvoir, are the much lesser figures of the biographer, André Maurois, and of Simenon, the Belgian creator of the greatest French detective of fiction, Maigret. To all of them, the civilized world of the twentieth century owes a considerable debt, as the world always has, to France, her writers, her culture and her ambitions.

## RECOMMENDED READING

*Europe since Napoleon.* D. THOMSON. Longmans, Green. 1957.

*France: Change and Tradition.* S. HOFFMANN and others. Gollancz, 1963. (Harvard Centre for International Affairs.)

*Short History of France to 1958.* Ed. J. HAMPDEN JACKSON. Cambridge, 1959.

*The Development of Modern France.* D. W. BROGAN. Hamish Hamilton, 1940.

# Index